P9-DDP-941

ELIZABETH I AND TUDOR ENGLAND

Stephen White-Thomson

Illustrations by Gerry Wood

The Bookwright Press
New York · 1985

LIFE AND TIMES

Julius Caesar and the Romans
Alfred the Great and the Saxons
Canute and the Vikings
William the Conqueror and the Normans
Elizabeth I and Tudor England
Richard the Lionheart and the Crusaders
Columbus and the Age of Exploration

Further titles are in preparation

FRANKLIN PIERCE COLLEGE
LIBRARY
RINDGE, NH 03461

CURR
DA
355
.W43
1985

First published in the United States in 1985 by
The Bookwright Press, 387 Park Avenue South
New York, NY 10016

First published in 1984 by
Wayland (Publishers) Ltd,
49 Lansdowne Place, Hove
East Sussex BN3 1HF, England

© Copyright 1984 Wayland (Publishers) Ltd

All rights reserved

ISBN 0-531-18008-5
Library of Congress Catalog Card Number: 84-73570

Printed by G. Canale & C.S.p.A., Turin, Italy

Contents

1 **THE STORY OF ELIZABETH**
Early life   4
The young queen   6
The later years   8

2 **HOW ENGLAND WAS GOVERNED**
Queen and Parliament   10
Local government   12

3 **INTERNAL THREATS**
Mary Queen of Scots   14
The Earl of Essex   16

4 **THREATS FROM ABROAD**
Piracy and the power of Spain   19
The Spanish Armada   20

5 **RELIGION**
The Reformation   22
Elizabeth's answer   24
Witchcraft   26

6 **EVERYDAY LIFE**
'Life at court   28
Life in London   30
At ease in the country   32
Merchants and traders   35
The poor in the country   36
The poor in the towns   38
Education   40
Poverty and the Poor Law   43
Crime and punishment   44
Health and medicine   46
Arts and theater   48

7 **VOYAGES OF DISCOVERY**
Exploration and settlement   51
Drake's voyage round the world   53

8 **THE ELIZABETHAN AGE**   55

Table of dates   56
New words   57
Further information   58
Index   59

1 THE STORY OF ELIZABETH

Early life

A portrait of the red-headed Elizabeth as the young queen.

Tudor is the surname of an English royal family, founded by a Welshman, Owen Tudor. Altogether, there were five Tudor monarchs. Here are their names, with the dates of their reigns in brackets: Henry VII (1485-1509); Henry VIII (1509-1547); Edward VI (1547-1553); Mary (1553-1558); and Elizabeth I (1558-1603).

Henry VIII had three children: Edward, Mary and Elizabeth. All of them wore the English crown. It was not always certain that Elizabeth would become queen, but the early deaths of her half-brother and half-sister left her the throne, a position that she occupied for forty-five years, until her death in 1603 at the ripe old age of 69.

Elizabeth was lucky to have survived long enough to become queen. Her early life was spent under the shadow of the ax. When her mother, Anne Boleyn, was executed, Elizabeth too fell out of favor. She had to use all her native wit and intelligence to keep her head above water — and on her shoulders.

During the reigns of Elizabeth's father and brother, a change in the religion of England took place. This was called the Reformation (see page 22), and meant that England became a Protestant country and rejected the religion of the pope — Catholicism. When Queen Mary came to the throne however, she was determined to restore the Catholic religion. Unwittingly, Elizabeth became the center of Protestant plots to overthrow the Catholic queen. There is no evidence that she supported any of these plots. Nevertheless, when Sir Thomas Wyatt rebelled against Queen Mary, Elizabeth was accused of being involved and was imprisoned in the Tower of London. There she spent her time studying. For her daily

4

exercise she walked along the battlement walls and looked down on the courtyard where her mother had been beheaded.

All these experiences shaped her character. Elizabeth's difficult childhood endowed her with cunning. This, combined with great intelligence, made her one of the most successful monarchs ever to sit on the English throne.

Princess Elizabeth walks along the battlement walls of the Tower of London where she was imprisoned.

A medallion to commemorate Elizabeth's coronation.

The young queen

The English people shed few tears when Mary died in 1558. They welcomed Elizabeth to the throne because she was a Protestant and had a reputation for courage. Some people were afraid that a woman would be unable to cope with the many problems that faced England at this difficult time. Apart from a tricky period in the 1590s, she proved most doubters wrong.

Elizabeth's coronation was a magnificent spectacle. The new queen was tall and slim, with a shock of fiery red hair. She had the bearing of a queen and was able to win popular support by governing with a mixture of firmness and flexibility.

There was one thing that puzzled Elizabeth's subjects. Why did she refuse to marry? She could have married anyone — and yet she never did. People were terrified that she would die without leaving a son and heir. Many bloody wars had been fought in the past because it had not been clear who should succeed to the throne. People wanted to avoid this happening again.

Elizabeth would not hear of marriage. She kept a number of suitors dangling on a string. At one time it looked likely that she would marry her favorite, Robert Dudley, the Earl of Leicester, but this never happened.

She had definite reasons for not marrying. She wanted to govern without interference from a husband, and said "I will have but one mistress and no master!" She also saw that marriage might spoil the special relationship that she had with the English people. She claimed that she was married to the kingdom of England and all her subjects were her children.

Right *Londoners crowd the streets to cheer their queen on her way to her coronation.*

The later years

As the years slipped by, Elizabeth's good looks faded and her temper grew shorter, but she lost little of her dignity and authority. "I know I have the body of a weak and feeble woman," she told her troops at Tilbury who were preparing to fight the Spanish Armada, "but I have the heart and stomach of a king."

On another occasion she hinted at the secret of her success. "Though God has raised me high, yet I count the glory of my crown that I have reigned with your loves."

Not everyone agreed with her, and the last years of her reign saw some troubled times. Taxes were high, beggars were on the increase, Spain was a constant threat, and one of her favorites rebelled against her. Yet even her critics admitted that Elizabeth was a great woman.

A story goes that a certain John Stubbs had published a complaint against the queen. He had his right hand cut off for his impertinence. After the dreadful punishment was over, he raised his hat with his left hand and cried, "God save the Queen!"

Her reign was a time of great contrasts — of adventure and discovery, success at war, splendor at court, great theater and poetry. For thousands of ordinary people, however, life was hard. Elizabeth tried to care for all her subjects, but many went hungry, lived in hovels and cound not find work. It was a glorious time for England, but not for all English people, as we shall see.

Above *The south bank of the Thames River showing the Bear Garden and the Globe theater.*

Left *Queen Elizabeth gives her famous speech to the troops at Tilbury as they prepare to fight the Spanish.*

2 HOW ENGLAND WAS GOVERNED

Queen and Parliament

Queen Elizabeth addressing her most important citizens in Parliament.

When it was known that the queen was dying, Robert Cecil, her principal minister, urged her to go to bed and rest with the words: "Madame, you must go to bed!" "Little man! Little Man!" she retorted, "Must! Must is not (a word) allowed to be used to Princes!"

This episode shows that the queen believed that she was the boss. She alone was in charge of the affairs of her country. Although she might listen to advice, she was not forced to act upon it.

Elizabeth sat at the top of a pyramid of power. Below her was the Privy Council, a small group of advisers that met regularly with her to discuss the affairs of the realm. It included Robert Cecil's father William (Lord Burghley) and Sir Francis Walsingham who both served the queen loyally all their lives. After consulting the Privy Council, Elizabeth would decide what had to be done.

Occasionally she would call Parliament to let its members — the most wealthy and influential men in the kingdom — know what she was intending to do. The idea was growing that the monarch needed help and guidance to make sure that she acted in the interests of all English people. Elizabeth did not always have an easy time with Parliament. They could be argumentative, but they were always loyal. Parliament even imprisoned one of its

Right *Queen Elizabeth liked to show herself to her people as often as possible. Here she is being carried through the crowds who are desperate to catch a glimpse of their queen.*

members — Peter Wentworth — for being critical of the queen.

The key to her success was that most English people agreed with Elizabeth about what was best for their country.

Local government

Above *A Justice of the Peace checks the quality of beer in a country inn.*

It is no use making a law unless there are officials all over the country who see that it is obeyed. To achieve this the Tudors created a system of local government. This meant that there were officials throughout England whose job it was to try to make sure that the queen's laws were actually enforced.

Communications were bad. There were no national newspapers, no radio and no television. In those parts of the country farthest from the influence of the capital, London, there were councils, which had to keep the law and order in their areas. The "Council of the North" was in charge of the country north of the Trent River. The "Council of the Marches" cared for the troublesome border country between England and Wales.

Away from those areas, the country was divided up into counties. In charge of each county was a lord-lieutenant,

A pewter tankard used during Elizabeth's reign.

chosen by the queen. He had a team of men working for him. At the local level, the most important of these officials were the Justices of the Peace (J.P.s) who were the "eyes and ears of the Crown."

Sir Nathaniel Bacon was one such J.P. He lived in Norfolk and came from a well-to-do family. His work as a J.P. was varied and time-consuming. He had to deal with the punishment of criminals, witches and rogues. He had to check inns to make sure that the beer was good. He collected taxes, supervised the Poor Law (see page 42), and made sure that his area contributed enough men, money and equipment in times of war.

The system seemed to work efficiently and continued to do so as long as the outlying counties had faith in their monarch. Elizabeth had such command over the loyalty of her subjects that this trust was seldom in doubt.

13

3 THREATS AT HOME

Mary Queen of Scots

Mary, Queen of Scots.

It would be wrong to pretend that there was no opposition to Elizabeth within England itself. The biggest threat to the queen came from her cousin, Mary, Queen of Scots, and from Mary's Catholic supporters.

Mary had an extraordinary life. It started with great promise and ended in tragedy. She became Queen of Scotland when she was less than a week old, and, on her marriage to Francis II, Queen of France as well when she was still a teenager. Added to this, many people believed that she — and not Elizabeth — was the rightful Queen of England.

Things started to go wrong when she returned to Scotland and became involved in murder and intrigue. Her second husband, the unpleasant Lord Darnley, was murdered on the orders of the Earl of Bothwell who became Mary's third husband only three months after Darnley's brutal murder. As it was obvious that Mary had something to do with the killing, the Scottish people rebelled against her. She fought and lost the Battle of

Left *Catholics plot to overthrow Elizabeth and put Mary on the throne.*

Langdale, and fled to England to seek Elizabeth's protection.

Mary's presence in England was awkward for Elizabeth. Mary immediately became the focus of Catholic plots to overthrow Elizabeth. Anti-Catholic feeling was strong but for almost nineteen years, Elizabeth ignored the advice of her councilors that Mary was dangerous and should be put to death.

Finally she became convinced by evidence from her spies that Mary was actively plotting with Catholics to overthrow her. Even so, it was with great reluctance that she ordered Mary's execution. Her command was carried out in the Great Hall of Fotheringay Castle on the 8th of February, 1587.

Mary, Queen of Scots goes bravely to her death.

The Earl of Essex

Robert Devereux, the Earl of Essex.

Robert Devereux, the second Earl of Essex, was a handsome, proud and ambitious man. He soon became a favorite of the ageing queen because of his good looks and charm.

At court, Elizabeth was in a position to give favors. Those courtiers who received her favors could become rich and powerful men. This system of patronage, as it was called, was a way of buying support. It had worked well for most of the reign.

Unfortunately, after Lord Burghley's death in 1598, two rival groups emerged. One was led by Robert Cecil, Burghley's son, the other by the dashing and headstrong Earl of Essex. There was not room for both of them at court. Although Elizabeth loved Essex, she was not prepared to give important posts to his supporters. He could be very rude to her and once Elizabeth boxed his ears in public.

In 1599, Elizabeth decided to send him to crush a rebellion in Ireland, to get him out of the way. After six months of useless fighting, Essex returned to England without being asked to do so. He knew that the longer he was away from the court, the more powerful his enemy, Cecil, would become. The queen was furious that he had disobeyed orders. He was arrested. His days of greatness were numbered.

In a foolish attempt to take revenge for his fall from power, he planned an uprising to "save the queen from her wicked advisers." In February 1600, he rode through London with 200 armed men, a group of misfits who had a grudge against Cecil. The Londoners ignored him and the rebellion fizzled out. Essex was convicted of high treason and executed on February 25, 1601. For months afterwards, the queen wept for the death of her wayward favorite.

An Elizabethan soldier.

Below *Poorly-armed Irish soldiers prepare to attack a column of English troops led by the Earl of Essex.*

4 THREATS FROM ABROAD

Piracy and the power of Spain

"It is easier to find flocks of white crows than one English-man who loves a foreigner," a historian once wrote. Englishmen disliked all foreigners, but especially the Spanish. Spain in those days was the wealthiest and most

powerful country in the world. England was jealous of her riches, and there were many other reasons why the two countries became such bitter enemies.

Spain was the pioneer of exploration in the New World across the Atlantic Ocean, and had carved out a great empire in South and Central America. No one was allowed to trade with her colonies, which infuriated the English merchants and seamen. A band of English sea dogs decided to take the law into their own hands.

Sir John Hawkins, a young sea captain, started an illegal trade in slaves. He bought them in Africa, and sailed across to Central America where he sold them to the Spanish landowners at a huge profit. On his third expedition, he was trapped in the Mexican port of San Juan de Ulua. The Spaniards swore to let him and his men go free, but broke their promise. They opened fire, and only two ships escaped. Aboard one of them was Francis Drake, a fiery young adventurer.

Drake swore to pay the Spaniards back for their treachery. For the next twenty years (1567-1587), he waged a private war against Spain. He plundered Spanish settlements in America, and captured Spanish ships which were overflowing with treasure.

King Philip II of Spain was infuriated by these acts of piracy. He was sure that Drake's ships were gifts from Elizabeth, the "heretic" queen. He determined to teach her a lesson that neither she nor her people would ever forget. Plans went rapidly ahead to invade England and return it to the "true faith" — Catholicism.

An Elizabethan sailor.

Left *A battle rages in the Mexican port of San Juan de Ulua between the Spaniards and a force of English sea dogs led by Sir John Hawkins.*

The Spanish Armada

In 1588, Drake was enjoying a quiet game of bowls in Plymouth when a frantic sea captain interrupted him with the news that the Spanish Armada had been sighted in the English Channel. He made the famous reply "We have time to finish the game, and beat the Spaniards too!"

The Spanish plan was to send their Armada of 130 ships to defeat the English fleet at sea. It would then link up with a massive army waiting in the Netherlands, and escort it over to England where Spain assumed her troops would be victorious.

The plan misfired for a number of reasons. The English were better sailors. Their ships, slightly smaller, could sail faster, and they had heavier firepower. The Spanish fleet was an army afloat. They were unable to get close enough to the English ships to board them and so benefit from their greater size. The English also had better leaders. Lord Howard of Effingham and Sir Francis Drake were excellent commanders. The Spanish leader was the Duke of Medina Sidonia. He was seasick as soon as his flagship put to sea. He was no match for his English rivals.

The skills of the English fleet were shown as they chased the Armada down the Channel, sinking or capturing any galleon that came adrift from the pack. Yet the Armada still remained intact. Almost in desperation the English sent fire ships into the massed Spanish fleet as they lay at anchor off Calais. Panic ensued, the Armada split up and fled north. They met terrible storms. Many were shipwrecked on the west coast of Ireland. Weeks later, the survivors — less than half the original fleet — limped home. The Spanish army in the Netherlands was never used. The Armada had failed.

Right *A Spanish galleon explodes after suffering a direct hit during the fierce fighting in the English Channel.*

Above *A medal struck in 1588 to celebrate England's victory over the Spanish Armada.*

20

5 RELIGION

The Reformation

Above *Thomas Cranmer, Archbishop of Canterbury.*

The Tudor period up to Elizabeth's accession was a time of great religious turmoil. The Catholic Church claimed to be the "One True Church." At its head was the pope, the "Vicar of Christ," who lived in Rome. In Europe a man called Martin Luther (1483-1546) challenged the pope's authority. He disagreed with many things the Catholic Church said and found that he had many supporters. This break with the pope was called the Reformation. The new faith was called Protestantism.

In Henry VIII's reign, these ideas filtered across the Channel to England. He used them because they suited his selfish purposes. He wanted to annul his marriage to Catherine of Aragon because she had not produced a son and heir to the throne. The pope refused, so Henry took matters into his own hands. He proclaimed himself — and not the pope — the head of the English Church. The marriage was dissolved.

Henry VIII also needed money, so he ordered that the monasteries be destroyed. Many of them were fabulously wealthy. Their riches went to the Crown. Few people objected — some remained loyal to the pope, but most English people were happy to break with Rome.

In Edward VI's reign, anti-Catholic feeling continued and the Protestant Church grew in strength. Queen Mary was a devout Catholic and she tried to reverse this process. She ordered that 300 Protestants be burned at the stake, including Archbishop Cranmer; she renewed links with the pope; and she married King Philip II of Spain, a Catholic. She soon found that she was swimming against the tide, and died a desperately unhappy woman.

Far Right *Cranmer is burned at the stake in the reign of Mary Tudor.*

Elizabeth's answer

When Elizabeth came to the throne, the Protestants breathed a great sigh of relief. Elizabeth wanted to please them. She also wanted to keep the Catholics happy. Her chief concern was to make sure that her subjects were loyal to her. She knew that if they were content, they would be less likely to rebel. So she tried to steer a middle course between the extreme Protestantism of Edward VI's reign, and Mary's rigid Catholicism.

Sometimes it is hard for us to imagine what all the fuss was about. As long as you believed in God, what did it matter whether you called yourself a Catholic or a Protestant?

Protestants asked themselves important questions. How could they make sure that they would go to Heaven and not burn in the fires of hell forever? Is there any human being who can really speak for God? Who should be the

Queen Mary I

Above *A Puritan prayer meeting.*

head of the Church? Is it right that the Church should have so much money? Should priests be allowed to marry? They came up with very different answers from the ones the Catholic Church had given for centuries.

Both sides believed that they were right. If they were right, then the other side must be wrong and must be punished until they changed their minds and saw the truth.

The answers Elizabeth gave to these questions allowed Catholics a certain amount of freedom. They also pleased most Protestants — but not all. There was a group of people who believed that Elizabeth had not gone nearly far enough to stamp out all traces of Catholicism. This group was growing in power and importance. They were called the Puritans. They were to play an important part in the history of the next hundred years.

Above *A Puritan prayer meeting.*

A witch in a ducking-stool about to be submerged in a river.

Witchcraft

Religion played a big part in everyone's life, from the richest person to the poorest. No one doubted that God existed. The church (along with the manor house and the village) was the center of people's lives. A law said that everyone over six had to go to church on Sundays. If they did not, they had to pay a fine.

It was a difficult law to enforce and priests moaned that people preferred to go to markets and fairs on Sundays. The churches were cold and damp and the services long and often dismal, so perhaps you couldn't blame them.

This did not stop them from believing in God. They also believed in the devil just as much. They feared that if they did not lead good lives they would burn forever in the fires of hell. They were very superstitious too. If anything went wrong with their lives and they could not explain it, they searched for a scapegoat.

Witches were blamed for ruined harvests and other accidents. Shakespeare wrote about some witches in his play *Macbeth*. They are typical of what people believed witches to look like. They were usually haggard old women casting evil spells over a bubbling cauldron:

"*. . . For a charm of powerful trouble,*
Like a hell-broth, boil and bubble."

In Europe, thousands of "witches" were tortured and killed by the Inquisition. In England, only a few "witches" were killed, but many were pilloried or put in ducking stools. It was a long time before people realized that there were no such things as witches.

Right *Hag-like witches cast a spell to call up demons to carry out their evil wishes.*

6 EVERYDAY LIFE

Life at court

The queen's court was one of the most magnificent in all Europe. It was the place where young men and women gathered to "pay court" to their queen, hoping to impress her. Wherever Elizabeth stayed — in Whitehall Palace, Greenwich Palace, or in other stately homes throughout the country — a troupe of courtiers, ladies-in-waiting and hangers-on would follow.

For most of the day, the queen would work quietly in the Privy Chamber on affairs of State. In the evenings or on weekends, Elizabeth held audiences when courtiers could speak to her and suggest ideas which they hoped would meet with royal approval. A favorable word from the queen could make you rich and famous.

A miniature painting by Nicholas Hilliard of an Elizabethan courtier.

Right *Queen Elizabeth dances the "Galliard" with one of her courtiers.*

There were other ways to impress the queen. The Elizabethan court was the scene of lively entertainments — music, dancing, and the clowning of Richard Tarleton, the court jester. The young courtiers spent a fortune on their clothes. They strutted around in their jewel-studded doublets and breeches like splendid peacocks, trying to catch the eye of the queen. Only a few succeeded in winning her favor.

In the summer months, the queen and her court traveled around the country on magnificent royal "progresses." Wherever she went, crowds lined the roads, cheering their queen.

Many courtiers found the court a "glittering misery." They paid out a lot of money — and got nowhere. However, it served the queen well. It meant that she could reward loyalty and impress visiting royalty with the splendor of her Majesty.

Life in London

A view of London and the Thames River.

In a rage, Queen Mary I had once threatened to take her court away from London. The unspoken answer of Londoners had been, "Fine. Take your court, but leave us the River Thames." The Thames was the main artery of the kingdom, its lifeline with Europe and the outside world. It brought trade and wealth into England. On its banks, like a leech sucking up its riches, prospered the city of London.

Already, London was the third biggest city in the western world — after Naples and Constantinople. It was the political, judicial and financial center of the land. Some 200,000 people lived there and the number was growing all the time.

London was a city of contrasts. It was an exciting but risky place. A city of whirlwind activity — for those lucky enough to have a job. It was beautiful in parts — and squalid in others. It was a city filled with palaces, rich merchants' houses, the shops and halls of the Master Guilds — and hovels too. The queen lived near London. Her poorest citizens lived within its walls.

London had wonderful things to look at — London Bridge spanning the river; and horrific things to see — the heads of executed men decaying on Traitor's Gate. It was a place of opportunity — and disease. What you could not escape from was the stench of the open drains and rotting garbage. Or the deafening sounds that echoed down the narrow streets — the crashing of cartwheels on the cobbles, the clanging bells of the numerous churches, the shouts of hawkers selling their wares, or the watermen calling you to take their boat up or down the river.

31

At ease in the country

By the time of Elizabeth's death, there were almost five million people in England. Nine out of every ten lived in the country. Although only a few of them were rich, this minority owned most of the land in England. They built themselves magnificent houses. Some, such as Longleat and Montacute House, still stand today.

These country houses — made from timber or stone — were designed to be comfortable dwelling-places. The peace of Elizabeth's reign meant that great landlords no longer had to wall themselves up in drafty fortresses. They could concentrate on comfort and fine living. Their houses had large glass windows to let the sunlight in, and were topped with a maze of chimneys to allow the smoke to escape from the large fireplaces.

Montacute House in Somerset, built in 1600.

These mansions were often far away from towns and could only be reached along very bad roads. The people who lived in them had to be self-sufficient — to provide the things they needed for themselves.

While the master of the house was away — either at court or looking after his farm — his wife was in charge of keeping a well-run house. She and her staff of butlers, cooks and maids had to make candles, brew beer, collect firewood, and provide food. This last task alone kept her very busy. When a lord and his lady once entertained the queen and her court, they got through three oxen and 140 geese for breakfast!

Despite a full day, there was always time for fun. The rich pursued the age-old sports of hunting and falconry, and showed an interest in some new games, such as "real tennis." In the evenings, they entertained their guests with music and dancing.

A nobleman discusses building plans for his house with the architect.

Merchants and traders

If it had been possible to fly over England in Elizabeth's day, you would have noticed that much of the country was covered by forest. Dotted around were villages, surrounded by strips of cultivated land and joined by twisting cart tracks. Occasionally, you would have spotted small towns, usually close to the sea.

London was by far the biggest city, but even though it was spreading beyond its medieval walls, it was an easy walk from anywhere in the city into the countryside. No other English town had more than 20,000 inhabitants. Towns like Norwich, Exeter and York had grown up because they were well placed for commerce and industry.

People were rich in the country if they owned land. In towns, money was to be made in business. During Elizabeth's reign England became one of the top trading nations and her merchants became very wealthy. They were often to be seen in their fine clothes down by the docks, welcoming a valuable cargo of wine, silk and spices from abroad. Their profits came from buying these goods cheaply and selling them at a higher price. Such men belonged to one of the important craft or trade associations — the Drapers and the Goldsmiths for example — which had great influence within the towns.

A wealthy London merchant.

If they were successful, these men built fashionable town houses and lived very well. Like their country counterparts, they too had time for fun. In London they could watch one of Shakespeare's plays at the Globe, gamble on the cockfights in Drury Lane, practice their archery in Moorfields, or enjoy the latest craze, smoking tobacco. Although they owed their riches to what towns could offer, most of these men had one ambition — to buy land and build a house in the country.

Opposite *A bustling scene in London's busy docks.*

The poor in the country

Life for the poor was not so enjoyable. Most of them lived in one-room, mud-floored dwellings that they shared with their animals, and worked on the land as agricultural laborers. A handful owned a few fields, but mostly they rented their land from a big landowner or smaller farmer. Some worked on the noble's estate itself.

They sweated away from dawn to dusk, often seven days a week, on the grinding routine of plowing, harrowing, sowing, reaping and harvesting the crops. They worked to provide enough food to survive.

Elizabethan writers believed that there was something romantic about the lives of these hardy laborers, particularly the shepherd and the blacksmith. In fact, they had a tougher time during Elizabeth's reign than before. The population was growing, which led to worse poverty because there were more mouths to feed. Also, rich

A boy's leather jerkin.

farmers started to enclose their fields and rear sheep on them where before people had been growing crops and vegetables. The result was unemployment and hunger among the poorest people.

On rare occasions there was something to break up the dull and back-breaking pattern of life. There were Christian festivals to celebrate, and rituals, like the crowning of the "Lord of Misrule," who was the person presiding over Christmas revels in a nobleman's house. Actors, minstrels and jugglers traveled around the country performing to enthusiastic audiences.

The main "sport" was poaching, to add some meat to their diet. Occasionally, the men played a violent game similar to soccer, or sat on river banks and fished for their supper. The greatest escape was the ale house where they often drank themselves into a stupor to forget the drudgery of their working lives.

Farm workers burn the hedgerows that landowners put up to enclose their fields.

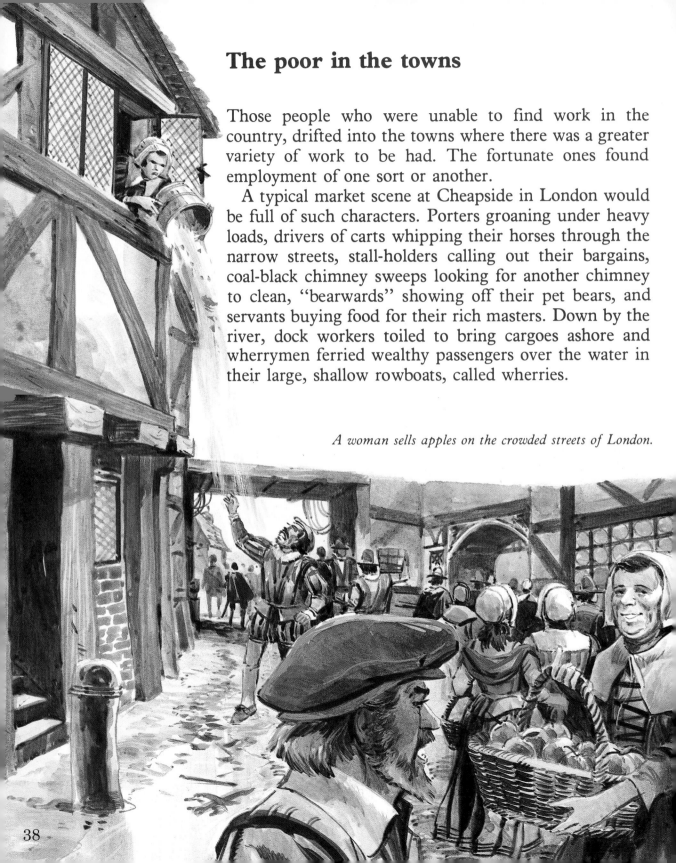

The poor in the towns

Those people who were unable to find work in the country, drifted into the towns where there was a greater variety of work to be had. The fortunate ones found employment of one sort or another.

A typical market scene at Cheapside in London would be full of such characters. Porters groaning under heavy loads, drivers of carts whipping their horses through the narrow streets, stall-holders calling out their bargains, coal-black chimney sweeps looking for another chimney to clean, "bearwards" showing off their pet bears, and servants buying food for their rich masters. Down by the river, dock workers toiled to bring cargoes ashore and wherrymen ferried wealthy passengers over the water in their large, shallow rowboats, called wherries.

A woman sells apples on the crowded streets of London.

The very lucky ones managed to become apprentices in one of the Master Trades. At the end of a long seven-year apprenticeship, they became craftsmen and could set up their own business in printing, or shoe-making, for example. The apprentices had a reputation for being riotous. A law was passed in 1588 to try and make them wear less outrageous clothes and behave better. It did not have much effect!

For entertainment, the poor people in the towns watched the bloodthirsty sports of cockfighting and bear-baiting or, as in 1581, went to Fleet Street to see human "wonders of the world" — a huge giant and a tiny dwarf — on display.

There were some people who were too poor even to enjoy these spectacles. Their dream of living in a town had become a nightmare. Unable to find work, they turned to crime as the only way to make ends meet. They lived in squalid, rat-infested slums and must have had miserable lives. They had no share in the glories of Elizabeth's reign.

Two rubbish collectors try to keep the streets clean.

Education

It is sometimes said that your schooldays are the best days of your life. Although you may not agree, one thing is certain — education today is far more lively and varied than it was for Tudor children. Their workload was hard, the hours long and the discipline tough.

Their schoolday began at 6 a.m. in the summer, and 7 a.m. in the winter. Apart from a break for lunch and fifteen minutes off for breakfast, it was all work and no play until they finished at 5:30 p.m. This grueling program started when you were only five or six years old and could last for ten years with only short vacations to break up the routine.

In the poorly-lit and heavily-timbered classrooms, children were fed a diet of Latin, more Latin, Greek, English grammar and religious knowledge. Using goose quill pens which spattered ink everywhere, they were required to write out chunks of *Aesop's Fables* or Caesar's *Gallic Wars* — and then learn them by heart.

A child practices reading to his teacher.

The idea was that information should be drummed into you. If you failed to take it in, the teacher thrashed you with a birch rod. They always had a bundle of switches close at hand — and used them freely. Not everyone went to school. Girls and children from poor families often went without education, and so had little chance of improving themselves.

If all this sounds grim, things were in fact getting better. During Elizabeth's reign, many still famous schools were founded; printed school textbooks were far more widely used; and the system did produce some remarkable and cultured people (see page 48).

A Tudor classroom scene showing the consequences of bad work.

Poverty and the Poor Law

"Hark! Hark! The dogs do bark. The beggars are coming to town." So chanted the townspeople as hordes of vagabonds invaded their towns, their bodies covered with sores and dressed in rags. The vagabonds were poor people — without money, a home or a future. Their numbers were increasing all the time.

During Elizabeth's reign, prices of food and goods rocketed, but pay did not. There was also high unemployment with thousands thrown out of work by the policy of "enclosure" of fields (see page 37). Many tramped the roads searching for a living — and were forced to beg to keep themselves alive.

Below A band of hungry vagabonds causes havoc in a peaceful market town.

What did Elizabeth do about the poor and the home-less? The monasteries had looked after the poor and now they were gone. Her answer was to pass some laws intended to help the poor.

The most famous of these Poor Laws went into effect in 1601. It was harsh toward those who were poor but also physically fit. They could be whipped, branded or even executed if they kept on begging. Toward those too weak to work, the law was more caring. The rich people of each parish were forced to pay some money which was used to build shelters for the poor.

A rich man gives money to a beggar.

Unfortunately, most Tudors believed that poverty was a punishment from God. Others thought that beggars were just lazy. They were not willing to help, and therefore many people stayed poor and hungry. Without the Poor Laws, they would have been even worse off.

Crime and punishment

The Tudors had a simple and harsh attitude towards crime. If you were caught committing a serious crime, you might hang for it, or spend a lifetime in prison. But, despite brutal punishments, crime was common.

In towns, you had to watch out — there was a "coney-catcher" about! This would be a man or woman who tried to get you to part with your money either by tricking you into giving it to them, or by stealing it. Many wealthy visitors to the crowded market-places would discover their money had been stolen by a pickpocket or a "cutpurse." Sometimes the thieves worked in gangs, like those in Dickens' *Oliver Twist*, 300 years later.

There were other types of criminals too. On moonlit nights, highwaymen held up travelers by deserted roadsides; horse-thieves raided stables on lonely country estates; "anglers" stole richly-embroidered clothes from clotheslines using a long pole; and "moonmen" asked farmers for shelter — and then stole their poultry in the middle of the night. Of the more serious crimes, murder seemed to be more a habit of the rich and powerful people in the country, and so they often got away with it.

One of the reasons that criminals took so many risks was that they seldom were caught. There was no organized police force and no effective methods of detection. Law enforcement was the job of the parish constable. He

Left *A cut-purse wearing a large cloak to hide the bag of money that he has cut from the belt of a wealthy man.*

and his dog wandered around the streets keeping an eye open for trouble-makers and calling out the hour: "Twelve of the clock, look well to your locks." If trouble did break out, what could one man do on his own?

Criminals often got away with their crimes, but not always. An Essex woman, Agnes Osier, stole two sheets and sixty shillings and was hanged for it. Then, as now, crime was not worth the penalty.

Above *Petty criminals were punished by being put in stocks like these.*

Below *An able-bodied vagabond is tied to a stake waiting to be branded with a red-hot iron.*

Health and medicine

In Tudor times there were no free clinics, no preventive medicine, no anesthetics and no vaccines. People had only the vaguest idea of how the body worked and so most bodies went unmended.

The general state of health was very poor. Most children died before the age of five. Only one in ten reached old age — 40 years old. Queen Elizabeth lived to be 69, which was very old in those days. She nearly fell victim to smallpox when she was only 29. Although she survived, she bore the ugly scars of the disease to her grave.

Lack of hygiene helped spread disease. Poor sanitation created a breeding ground for germs. The Tudors had no

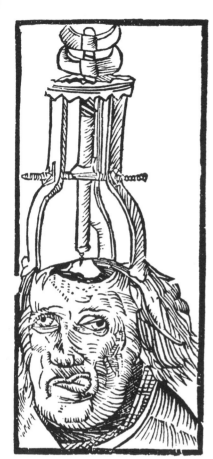

Above *A trepanning operation to raise a crushed skull.*

Right *A man grits his teeth as his leg is amputated without anesthetic.*

barriers against these germs, and once their bodies were infected they could do little to make themselves healthy once more.

Most people prayed that the illness would leave them — but their prayers were seldom answered. The popular practice of blood-letting was of no use. Some tried horrific rituals. For example, victims of epilepsy drank water from the skull of a murdered person — and died just the same.

Others used herbal remedies, but these rarely worked. Limbs that had gangrene were brutally amputated with a saw and without anesthetic. Teeth were extracted with no injection to relieve the pain.

There were few skillful doctors, surgeons or dentists. Some individuals tried hard to improve medical knowledge and practice, but progress was slow. Death from disease was always just around the corner and Tudor people always lived in its shadow.

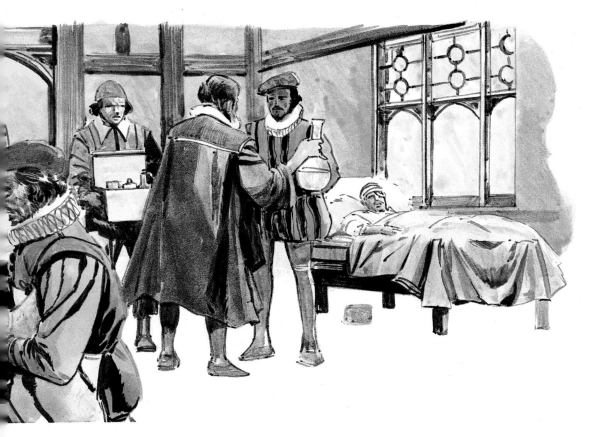

Above *William Shakespeare, the famous playwright.*

Above *The Globe theater.*

Arts and the theater

Elizabeth's reign saw a phenomenal rise in the popularity of the theater. Tudor people had a great sense of fun and loved to watch plays so they could forget about the harshness of their lives. Traveling players still toured the country as they had done for centuries, but under Elizabeth, three permanent theaters were built in London.

The most famous of these was the Globe. It was here that the plays of William Shakespeare — perhaps the best known Englishman of all time — and Christopher Marlowe, killed in a pub brawl, were first performed.

Today, there is usually a hushed silence in theaters. In those days, audiences could be incredibly rowdy. The "groundlings" — those who paid a penny to get in — crowded around the stage. They jeered and cheered, cracked nutshells under their feet and slurped steaming bowls of soup. If they did not like the villain of the plot, they would hurl rotten vegetables at the unfortunate actor.

However, just as often they could be spellbound by the beautiful costumes, the fine speeches and the gory death scenes when guts from the local butchers were splashed across the stage. Not everyone enjoyed the fun though. Many Puritans in London frowned on the riotous goings-on. They even closed down one of the theaters — a foretaste of things to come.

Other arts flourished too. The period is remembered for the delicate miniature portraits by Nicholas Hilliard; the poetry of Sir Philip Sidney, tragically killed in battle; and the music of Thomas Tallis and William Byrd. Culturally, it was a period of almost unequaled richness and creativity.

Right *A dramatic scene from one of Shakespeare's well-known plays.*

7 VOYAGES OF DISCOVERY

Exploration and settlement

Today, it is the vastness of space that is unexplored and unknown. In those days, earth itself was as much of a mystery. During this period, intrepid explorers set out to solve the puzzle.

Why did sailors and merchants risk their lives on these perilous missions? Sir Walter Raleigh, a daring English explorer, gave us an answer: "to seek new worlds, for gold, for praise, for glory." Apart from curiosity, a more selfish reason was to find fame and fortune.

Spain and Portugal were the pioneers of exploration. Vasco da Gama, Christopher Columbus, Ferdinand Magellan and others sailed from their ports to make exciting discoveries. When the English realized that money was to be made, they organized their own expeditions.

When the Arctic missions of Sir Martin Frobisher and Richard Chancellor failed to find a northern passage to the riches of the East, merchants resorted to the safer

Right *A ship in Elizabeth's navy.*

50

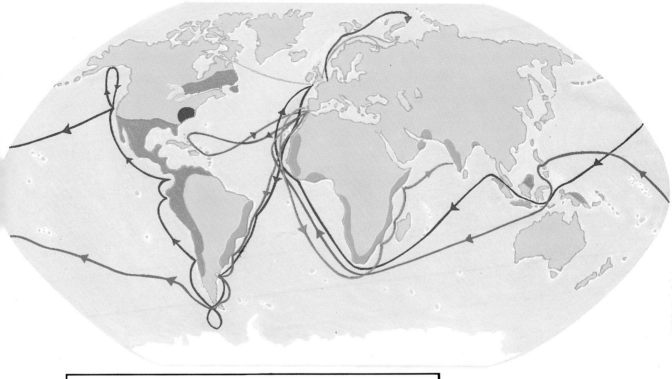

■ British	➤	Columbus 1492	➤	Frobisher 1576
■ Spanish	➤	Vasco de Gama 1497-99	➤	Chancellor 1554
■ Portuguese	➤	Magellan 1519-22	➤	Barents 1594
■ French	➤	Drake 1577-80		

Above *A map of the world showing the major voyages of discovery in the period.*

route around Africa. They founded the East India Company in 1601 which became very profitable.

The idea was growing that once a place had been explored, people should settle down to live there. England experimented with these "colonies" and in 1548, Sir Walter Raleigh set up the colony of Virginia. Unfortunately, due to lack of supplies and hostile Indians, this community failed to take root. Within a few years however, similar colonies would be flourishing.

These voyages fired the public imagination. By the end of the Elizabethan age, the world was a smaller and more familiar place.

Below *An astrolabe used to measure the height of the stars.*

Drake's voyage round the world

Above *An illustration drawn to celebrate Drake's epic voyage round the world.*

Left *Drake's ship, the "Golden Hind," struggles through rough seas.*

The Spaniards called Francis Drake "El Draque," which means the Dragon. They believed that he had magical powers and could see ships over the horizon. He was feared and respected by both friend and foe. Under his leadership, men were prepared to go to the ends of the earth.

In 1577, Drake set out on an expedition to plunder Spanish settlements in South America. He had no idea of where his voyage would take him, or how long it would last. In the giant seas off the southern tip of South America, one of his small fleet sank and the others returned home. By the time that the storm had blown itself out, Drake's ship, the *Golden Hind*, was alone in the Pacific.

Undaunted, Drake sailed up and down the coasts of Chile and Peru stealing treasure from the Spanish. Laden with gold and precious stones, he sailed west across the Pacific. He almost met with disaster when the *Golden Hind* ran aground on a reef in the unexplored seas north of Australia. Luckily, when they had jettisoned some of their cargo, they floated free.

The rest of their epic voyage went without a hitch. They rounded the Cape of Good Hope, at the southern tip of Africa, and returned to Plymouth in September 1580 to a heroes' welcome. They had been away almost three years.

It was an incredible feat of endurance for Drake and all his crew. Sailing in those days was tough and dangerous. The food was usually bad, the water stale, and living quarters cramped. On any long voyage, a large number of the crew died from disease. One can only admire these men as they risked their lives in search of riches and adventure.

Elizabeth

54

8 THE ELIZABETHAN AGE

Queen Elizabeth I died on March 24, 1603. Only a few months earlier, she had been riding ten miles a day. She had decided that her job was done, and life slipped away from her "easily, like a ripe apple from a tree." The whole nation mourned the death of their beloved queen. In a magnificent and somber ceremony, over a thousand people walked behind her coffin to Westminster Abbey. They were watched by crowds of weeping men, women and children. Their "good Queen Bess" was gone, never to return.

Elizabeth had been their queen for almost 45 years. She was not perfect, and is not above criticism. Elizabeth had spent most of the crown's own money so that her successor, James I, found himself poor and therefore weak. The religious differences had been shelved — not solved. Her government perhaps relied too heavily on her own skillful and strong personality for it to work efficiently. Although she cared about all her people, life for the poor remained hard.

Nevertheless, she was a remarkable queen who was widely loved and respected. One foreigner wrote, "It is more to have seen Elizabeth than to have seen England." Elizabeth symbolized England's new-found strength, prosperity and prestige. She had inherited a deeply-divided nation. Using a mixture of charm and firmness, she soothed the differences and brought peace to her people.

Her reign is famous for the defeat of the Armada, Drake's voyages and Shakespeare's plays. It is also a fascinating story of a relationship between a queen and her people, a "marriage" that made England feared and envied throughout Europe.

The great events and figures of the Elizabethan Age showing Lord Burghley, Shakespeare, Mary Tudor, Raleigh, Drake, Marlowe and Elizabeth I herself.

Table of dates

1485 Henry VII, the first of the Tudors becomes king.

1492 Christopher Columbus discovers America.

1509 Henry VII dies. His son, Henry VIII, succeeds him to the throne.

1533 Henry VIII's marriage to Catherine of Aragon is declared null and void. Henry marries Ann Boleyn. Their daughter, Elizabeth, is born.

1536 Ann Boleyn is beheaded.

1536-39 Dissolution of the Monasteries.

1542 Mary, Queen of Scots, born.

1547 Henry VIII dies. His son, Edward VI, succeeds to the throne.

1553 Expedition of Sir Willoughby and Richard Chancellor to search for a northeast passage to the East.
Edward VI dies. Mary comes to the throne.

1554 Wyatt's rebellion. Elizabeth is sent to the Tower.

1558 Mary dies. Elizabeth becomes queen.

1562 Elizabeth almost dies of smallpox.

1564 William Shakespeare is born.

1566 Lord Darnley, Mary, Queen of Scots' second husband, is murdered.

1567 Spanish treachery at San Juan de Ulua, in the Caribbean.

1576 Peter Wentworth, M.P., is imprisoned by Parliament.
Frobisher's first expedition in search of a northwest passage to the East.

1577-80 Drake's voyage around the world.

1584 Colony of Virginia founded.

1586 Sir Philip Sidney killed at Battle of Zutphen in the Netherlands.

1587 Mary, Queen of Scots, executed at Fotheringay for high treason.

1588 The Spanish Armada sails against England and is defeated.

1593 Christopher Marlowe, leading playwright, is killed in pub brawl.

1598 William Cecil (Lord Burghley), Elizabeth's leading adviser, dies.

1598-99 Globe theater is built.

1601 The Earl of Essex is beheaded after his abortive rebellion in 1600.
East India Company is founded.
The most important Poor Law is passed.

1603 Elizabeth I dies. James VI of Scotland becomes James I of England.

New words

Breeches Short trousers fastened below the knee.

Colony A group of people that leave their own land, and settle in a distant, often unexplored part of the world.

Court The place where the queen is staying, or the people (courtiers) who spent their lives in attendance on the queen.

Doublet A short, fashionable jacket.

Ducking-stool A stool on the end of a long pole that was balanced out over a river. For a punishment, a witch would be placed in the stool and "ducked."

Enclosure The policy of farmers to take over common land, put a hedge around it, and graze sheep on it.

Falconry The sport of using birds of prey to hunt for small animals like rabbits.

Guild An organization to which members of a profession or trade belonged.

Hawker Someone who sells things on the streets or in markets.

Hovel A very poor dwelling-place.

Inflation A state of the economy when prices rise very rapidly.

The Inquisition The ruthless persecution and horrible torture of people who were suspected of not being true Catholics. It was carried out in Europe for centuries.

J.P. Justice of the Peace — a local government official with various duties to perform in the countryside where he lived.

Minstrel A traveling musician or singer.

Poaching Hunting for game on land that does not belong to you.

"A Progress" A trip that Elizabeth used to make from London to visit her friends and see her subjects in the country.

Parliament A gathering of the most important people in the kingdom at Westminster to advise and assist the queen in the running of the country.

Pillory (also called "the stocks") A wooden frame with holes for the head and arms. People who had misbehaved were locked into the frame which stood in a public place. They would then be ridiculed and pelted with mud etc.

Privy Council A group of advisers close to the queen who helped her in the difficult task of governing the country.

Puritans A religious group opposed to Catholicism and the authority of the pope.

Quill The hollow stem of a feather made into a pen and used for writing.

Real tennis A game that the Tudors played which resembled modern tennis.

Reformation A European religious movement in the sixteenth century that abandoned many doctrines of the Catholic Church, and started the Reformed — or Protestant — Churches.

Scapegoat An innocent person who is blamed when something goes wrong.

Sea dogs English sailors who raided Spanish shipping and Spanish land in South America.

Treason Disloyalty to the monarch.

Vagabond A wandering beggar.

Further information

Books

Brown, John R. *Shakespeare and his Theatre.* New York: Lothrop, 1982.

De Mare, Eric. *London's River: The Story of a City.* Bridgeport, CT: Associated Booksellers/Merrimack, 1978.

Fletcher, Anthony. *The Elizabethan Village.* New York: Longman, 1980.

Goodnough, David. *Francis Drake.* Mahweh, NJ: Troll Associates, 1979.

Hodges, C. Walter. *Shakespeare's Theatre.* New York: Putnam, 1980.

Lane, Peter. *Elizabethan England.* North Pomfret, VT: David & Charles, 1981.

Peach, L. Dugarde. *First Queen Elizabeth.* Bedford Hills, NY: Merry Thoughts, 1968.

Reeves, Marjorie. *The Elizabethan Court.* New York: Longman, 1980.

Roll, Winifred. *Mary I: The History of an Unhappy Tudor Queen.* Englewood Cliffs, NJ: Prentice-Hall, 1979.

Trease, Geoffrey. *Seven Queens of England.* New York: Vanguard, 1981.

Zamoyska, Betka. *Queen Elizabeth I.* New York: McGraw-Hill, 1981.

Index

Africa 19, 51, 53
America
  Central 19
  North 19, 51
  South 19, 53
Apprentices 38, 39
Armada, Spanish 8, 20, 55, 56
Atlantic Ocean 19

Boleyn, Anne 4, 56
Burghley, Lord *see* Cecil,
  William

Catherine of Aragon 22, 56
Catholics, *see* Religion
Cecil, Robert 10, 16, 17
Cecil, William 10, 16, 55, 56
Chancellor, Richard 51, 56
Colonies 19, 51, 56, 57
Columbus, Christopher 50, 51,
  56, 57
Court 8, 16, 28, 29, 33, 57
Cranmer, Archbishop of
  Canterbury 22
Crime and punishment
  crime 13, 39, 44, 45
  ducking-stool 26, 57
  pillories 26, 57

Da Gama, Vasco 50, 51
Devereux, Robert (*see* Earl of
  Essex)
Drake, Sir Francis 19, 53, 55,
  56
Dudley, Robert (*see* Earl of
  Leicester)

East India Company 51, 56
Education 40, 41
Edward VI 4, 22, 24, 56
Elizabeth, Queen
  early life 4, 5
  young queen 6
  later years 8, 9

at court 16, 28, 29
in danger 14, 15, 17, 19, 20
death 55
Enclosure 36, 37, 57
Entertainments 29, 33, 37, 39
Essex, Earl of 8, 16, 17, 56

Fotheringay Castle 15, 56
Frobisher, Martin 51, 56

Globe theater 9, 35, 48, 56
Guilds 31, 57

Hawkins, Sir John 19
Henry VII 4, 56
Henry VIII 4, 22, 56, 58
Howard, Lord of
  Effingham 20

Inquisition *see* Religion
Ireland 17, 20

James I, King of England
  55, 56
J.P.s 12, 13, 57

Leicester, Earl of 6
Longleat House 32
London
  the city 7, 12, 17, 30, 34,
    35, 38, 48, 57, 58
  London Bridge 31
  Thames River 9, 30
  Tower of London 4, 5, 56

Magellan, Ferdinand 50, 51
Map of voyages of
  exploration 51
Marlowe, Christopher 48, 55,
  56
Mary Tudor 4, 6, 22, 24, 55
Mary, Queen of Scots 14, 15,
  56
Medicine 46, 47
Medina Sidonia, Duke of 20
Merchants 19, 35, 50
Monasteries *see* Religion

Montacute House 32

Netherlands 20

Pacific Ocean 53
Parliament 10, 57
Philip II, King of Spain
  19, 22
Poor Law 13, 42, 43, 56
Portugal 50, 51
Privy Council 10, 57
"Progresses" 29, 57
Protestants *see* Religion
Puritans *see* Religion

Raleigh, Sir Walter 50, 55
Reformation *see* Religion
Religion
  Catholics 4, 14, 19, 22, 24,
    25, 57
  Inquisition 26, 57
  Monasteries 22, 56
  Protestant 4, 6, 22, 24, 25,
    57
  Puritans 25, 48, 57
  Reformation 4, 22, 57

Sailors 18, 19, 20, 50, 53, 57
Shakespeare, William 26, 35,
  48, 55, 56, 58
Ships 19, 20, 50, 53, 58
Spain 8, 9, 18, 19, 20, 21, 22,
  50, 53, 56, 57

Trade, overseas 19, 30, 35,
  50, 51
Trades 36, 38

Vagabonds 8, 42, 45

Walsingham, Sir Francis 10
Wentworth, Peter 10, 56
Witchcraft 13, 26
Wyatt, Sir Thomas 4, 56

Picture Acknowledgments

The illustrations in this book were supplied by: courtesy of the Ashmolean Museum 20; BBC Hulton Picture Library 41 (top); courtesy of the Trustees of the British Museum 6; John R. Freeman (Photographers) & Co. Ltd. 10, 17, 53; Mansell Collection 13; National Monuments Record 32; National Portrait Gallery 4, 14, 16, 24. The remaining photographs are from the Wayland Picture Library.

P9-DYB-179

La Bermuda

Tropicus Can

Abreoyo

Anguilla
Sombrero
S. Martin
S. Bartholome
Saba
Barbada
Stacio
S. Christoval
Nives
Redonda
Montserrate
Antigua
I. de Aves
Guadalupe
La Disada
Todos Sanctos
Mari galant
S. Domingo
Matalino
S.ta Lucia
Barbados
S. Vincente
Bahia
Vogel Eylant
Granada
Tabago

I. de la Trinidad
I. de los Blanquesales
Winthelberg R.
R. Amanacura

ZVELA.   PARIA.

NVEVA ANDALVZIA

GVAIANA

MERICANA

SCOURGE
of the
SEAS

Buccaneers, Pirates and Privateers

SCOURGE
of the
SEAS

Buccaneers, Pirates and Privateers

ANGUS KONSTAM

First published in Great Britain in 2007 by Osprey Publishing,
Midland House, West Way, Botley, Oxford OX2 0PH, United Kingdom.
443 Park Avenue South, New York, NY 10016, USA.
Email: info@ospreypublishing.com

Previously published as Elite 69: *Buccaneers 1620–1700*, Elite 67: *Pirates 1660–1700*, Elite 74:
Privateers & Pirates 1730–1830 and New Vanguard 70: *The Pirate Ship 1660–1730*, all written
by Angus Konstam.

© 2007 Osprey Publishing Ltd

All rights reserved. Apart from any fair dealing for the purpose of private study, research,
criticism or review, as permitted under the Copyright, Designs and Patents Act, 1988, no part of
this publication may be reproduced, stored in a retrieval system, or transmitted in any form or
by any means, electronic, electrical, chemical, mechanical, optical, photocopying, recording or
otherwise, without the prior written permission of the copyright owner. Enquiries should be
addressed to the Publishers.

Every attempt has been made by the publisher to secure the appropriate permissions for
materials reproduced in this book. If there has been any oversight we will be happy to rectify the
situation and written submission should be made to the Publishers.

A CIP catalogue record for this book is available from the British Library.

ISBN: 978 1 84603 211 0

Page layout by Ken Vail Graphic Design, Cambridge, UK
Index by Alison Worthington
Typeset in Stone Serif, Optima, Gill Sans, Truesdell and Copperplate
Originated by United Graphics Pte Ltd, Singapore
Printed and bound in China through Bookbuilders

07 08 09 10 11   10 9 8 7 6 5 4 3 2 1

For a catalogue of all books published by Osprey please contact:

NORTH AMERICA
Osprey Direct c/o Random House Distribution Center
400 Hahn Road, Westminster, MD 21157, USA
E-mail: info@ospreydirect.com

ALL OTHER REGIONS
Osprey Direct UK, P.O. Box 140, Wellingborough, Northants, NN8 2FA, UK
E-mail: info@ospreydirect.co.uk

www.ospreypublishing.com

Front cover: *An English Ship in Action with Barbary Corsairs, c. 1680*. (© National Maritime
Museum, London. Acquired with the assistance of the National Art Collections Fund.)
Back cover: Sir Henry Morgan. (Stratford Archive)
Title page: © 2005 TopFoto / Fotomas
Endpapers: © National Maritime Museum, London
Contents page: *Marooned*, painting by Howard Pyle. (Stratford Archive)

CONTENTS

Introduction 6

Part I: Buccaneers 1620–1700 14

Part II: Pirates 1660–1730 72

Part III: Privateers and Pirates 1730–1830 162

Glossary 227

Further Reading 230

Index 233

Introduction

When we think of pirates, we usually imagine those who operated in the Caribbean and the American eastern seaboard during the decade on each side of 1700. In fact, pirates were around for a lot longer than that. Julius Caesar was captured by pirates before Pompey swept them from the Roman *Mare Nostrum* (the Mediterranean). Pirates plagued medieval and Renaissance shipping from the Baltic to the Mediterranean, and Barbary Coast pirates operated until well into the 19th century. As European explorers ventured further afield, they encountered new forms of piracy, off Africa, in the Indian Ocean and in the Pacific. Rivalry among European powers as they carved out overseas empires also provided the nucleus for a resurgence of piracy in foreign waters, often sponsored by the European powers themselves. These 'privateers' were pirates in all but name, and their ranks included national heroes, such as Drake, Hawkins and Frobisher.

As the spread of Spanish rivals into the Caribbean, or 'Spanish Main', continued in the 17th century, a more organized form of piracy began. From the 1630s, many of these French, English and Dutch 'interlopers' took to piracy, attacking passing Spanish shipping using small boats. Although not strictly pirates, their actions were piratical in nature but often carried the blessing of their sovereign country. Known as 'buccaneers', their name was derived from a word referring to backwoodsmen on modern Haiti in the mid-17th century. The term later came to be used when speaking of the mainly English and French raiders of the Spanish Main, who acted as semi-legalized pirates, based in Port Royal and Tortuga. A 'freebooter' or 'filibuster' was the name given exclusively to French buccaneers, and came from the small 'flibotes' (fly boats) they sometimes used.

In 1655, the English captured the island of Jamaica, providing a safe harbour for these buccaneers. The scale of the attacks intensified to encompass raids on small Spanish settlements, until by the late 1660s full-blown amphibious operations were being launched against Spanish strongholds in the New World. Buccaneer commanders such as Henry Morgan plundered their way through the Spanish Main, and by the time the buccaneering era drew to a close in 1697, the Spanish American colonies had been devastated, and Spain reduced to the status of a near-penniless minor power.

The end of the buccaneering era gave rise to the period known as 'the golden age of piracy', which encompassed piratical actions in the Americas as well as in

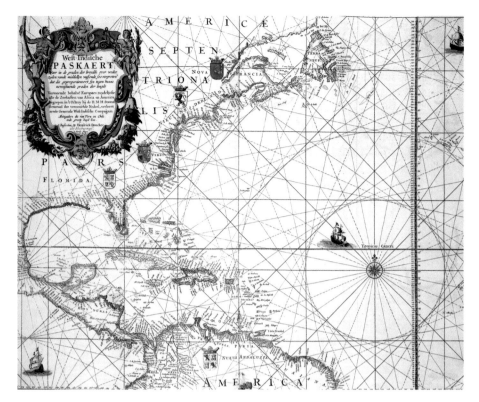

The Spanish Main encompassed the northern coast of South America and the entire Caribbean basin. In this practical Dutch chart dated 1683, the navigational lines crossing the eastern approaches to the North American continent were designed to aid navigators in selecting the most appropriate transatlantic course. The near-barren patch east of the Bahamas represents the doldrums of the Sargasso Sea, where no favourable winds could be found. (Mariners' Museum, Newport News, Virginia)

the Indian Ocean, the South China seas and off the west coast of Africa. The piracy boom was the result of circumstances: the end of a long war between Britain and France meant that ports were full of unemployed sailors and there was a lack of legal employment. The majority of the pirates who have gripped the popular imagination operated during this period, and characters such as Blackbeard, Captain Kidd and Black Bart have become the stuff of legend.

Hollywood and the writers of historical fiction have done much to glamorize piracy, particularly piracy during the so-called 'golden age'. As this book will show, however, instead of a life of glamour, with crews led by aristocratic swashbuckling heroes, the average pirate was a doomed man, lacking the education, abilities and pragmatism to escape his inevitable fate. A pirate's life was usually nasty, brutish and short. The romantic-sounding description of this era as a 'golden age' belied the cruelty, harshness and misery created by pirates, and unlike other golden ages it was never regarded with any form of nostalgia. The phrase itself was never used by those who lived through it, but was subsequently applied by writers seeking to embellish the pirate story with an aura it didn't deserve. Another term often associated with pirates today is 'swashbuckler'. Though this is a Hollywood epithet, it is based on historical roots, being derived from 'sword and buckler', a preferred Spanish weapon combination in the 16th century, when 'swashbuckler' referred to a weapon-armed thug or brigand, the name coming from the sound of a sword striking a buckler. Although the word fell into disuse, it was revived by 19th-century pirate fiction writers, and has remained closely linked with piracy ever since. During the 17th and 18th centuries, it was never used in conjunction with piracy or piratical activities.

This book will also redress the popular conception of pirate ships as large, well-armed sailing vessels. These vessels certainly existed, as both Blackbeard's *Queen Anne's Revenge* and Bartholomew Roberts' last *Royal Fortune* were vessels of this type. They were the exception to the rule though, and for the most part, pirates relied on smaller, less spectacular craft, such as sloops, brigantines and early schooners. During the late 17th century, the buccaneers who harried the Spanish

Edward Teach (Blackbeard) is perhaps the most notorious of all pirates. This painting by Oliver Frey shows a scene from Blackbeard's last fight in November 1718. (Stratford Archive)

in the Caribbean used a similar range of vessels, but they also employed even smaller launches, pinnaces and even canoes. The types of pirate vessels therefore covered the gamut from longboat to major warship. Some were custom-built privateers, designed to legitimately harry enemy shipping, but whose owners began to prey on any vessel they encountered. Others were vessels captured by pirates, then converted for their own use. Still more were ships whose crews had mutinied, and were then used for piracy instead of legitimate commerce.

Lack of strong government in the majority of the American colonies made the seaboard a pirate hunting ground. The benefits of illicit trade between pirates and townspeople were balanced against the disruption of shipping and rising insurance prices. One by one the colonial governors clamped down on piracy in their waters, and judicial pressure was backed by naval force to put an end to the outbreak. By 1730, the era of rampant piracy was all but over.

With the demise of the pirate scourge of the early 18th century, many sea captains took to privateering as a means of making money. A privateer was a man or a ship under contract to a government, allowing him to attack enemy ships during wartime. This contract, called a letter of marque, meant that the government got a share of the profits. (A pirate, by contrast, attacked any ship, regardless of nationality.) It is important to note that the terms 'pirate' and 'privateer' were not necessarily fixed labels. A privateer might turn to piracy (like Captain Kidd), after a major war. Buccaneers such as Henry Morgan were really privateers, but when he attacked Panama in 1671, England and Spain were at peace, and Morgan was acting as a pirate!

In his painting *So the Treasure was Divided*, Howard Pyle shows the democratic nature of pirate life – any plunder was divided fairly amongst the crew. Unfortunately treasure was a rare find, and most plunder consisted of everyday cargo – rum, sugar, tobacco, cloth or slaves. (Stratford Archive)

This form of nationally sponsored piracy reached its peak during the late 18th and early 19th centuries. Although a world-wide phenomenon, privateering proved particularly popular in the waters of the Americas. Rivalry between European powers and the rise of independence movements among the nations of the New World provided ample opportunities for privateering captains.

Privateering had existed as a tool of maritime warfare since the Middle Ages. Letters of marque, which provided an official sanction to those seeking revenge through retaliatory attacks, were issued to ship owners who had suffered loss from vessels of an enemy country as early as the 14th century. This form of legitimized piracy proved extremely popular, and soon letters of marque were issued to almost anyone who applied for them. At minimal cost, a nation could attack the maritime commerce of an enemy without diverting the resources of its national fleet. For small maritime powers such as the United States of America during the American Revolution and the War of 1812, this proved a vital part of its maritime strategy.

The War of the Austrian Succession in 1739 placed Spanish maritime links with its New World colonies at risk from privateering attacks, and France in turn suffered greatly when trade with her island colonies in the West Indies was devastated. This disruption of maritime commerce proved so lucrative for British and American colonial ship owners that the resumption of hostilities between France and Britain in 1759 prompted an even greater wave of privateering. By the end of the Seven Years' War in 1763, privateering was regarded as a vital element of maritime warfare, and eastern seaboard ports such as Halifax, Salem and Newport became thriving privateer bases.

When the American colonies rebelled against Britain in 1775, sea power was regarded as a dominant issue by both sides. Britain maintained the largest merchant fleet in the world during the late 18th century, and the successful conclusion of the war in the colonies required its control over the Atlantic sea lanes. Similarly, the American economy was dependent on maritime trade, given the poor state of internal communications within the 13 colonies. A crippling British blockade of the American coastline could be expected, so many ship owners thought that their only chance for economic survival was to turn to privateering. With no possibility of being able to match British naval strength, the colonies had to rely on European allies to contest British maritime dominance. All America could hope for was to cause sufficient losses in the British merchant fleet to force her merchants to put pressure on the government to end the conflict.

The Privateer Fly, a painting by Francis Holman, 1779. In the stern view she appears heavily manned, as was often so with privateers. Both the flags and armament are consistent with this being a portrait of the Royal Naval cutter *Fly* of 1779. Fast vessels, like cutters and sloops, made the best privateers. (National Maritime Museum, Greenwich, London)

The French Revolutionary War and the Quasi-War between America and France both provided opportunities for privateers, but the failure of the French fleet to effectively challenge British control of sea power meant that by 1802, French prizes were rare. The French invasion of Spain in 1807 made the Spanish allies of the British, reducing privateering opportunities still further. The golden opportunity for ship owners on both sides of the Atlantic came in 1812, when Britain and America found themselves at war once again.

The War of 1812, which lasted until 1815, saw a resurgence of privateering, and by the end of 1812 the actions of hundreds of British, American and Canadian privateers began to take effect on maritime commerce. Ship owners launched purpose-built privateering vessels, and privateering reached its peak during the second year of the war. With over 500 American privateers at sea, the British instituted transatlantic convoys for protection, and by late 1814 a powerful naval blockade of the American coast kept the Americans in port. By the time peace was declared in 1815, British ship owners had lost over 1,000 merchant ships, and the American economy was in ruins. Peace brought a resurgence of maritime commerce, but the threat of privateers was replaced by the spectre of piracy. Privateering was used as a tool by the emerging Latin American nations, who were less able to regulate its use. Many Latin American privateers turned to piracy, and the 1810s and 1820s were marked by a struggle to make the waters of the Caribbean safe for commerce. The eradication of piracy in the Caribbean marked the end of centuries of conflict in American waters, where sea dogs, buccaneers, pirates and privateers had all contributed to the disruption of maritime trade.

Though the anti-piracy campaign ended piratical activity in the Atlantic and Caribbean, for centuries piracy continued to be practised by non-Europeans in the Far East, and piracy is alive and well today. Indonesian waters are still plagued by modern-day pirates, equipped with fast speedboats and assault rifles. Although the methods have changed, the basic nature of violent crime and extortion on the high seas is the same as it was in the time of Caesar.

A note on sources

Sources covering the buccaneering era are sparse, although these can be combined with other documentary evidence to fill the gaps in the story. Several buccaneers and their contemporaries left chronicles of their activities, the most extensive being the work by Dutchman Alexandre Exquemelin (also written Esquemeling), first published in Amsterdam in 1678 and entitled *De Americaensche Zee-Rovers*. An English translation, *The Buccaneers of America*, was published in 1684. This remarkable and vivid account was written by a man who joined the French buccaneers on Tortuga in 1666. A surgeon, he lived among them for 12 years, and the work became a 17th-century best-seller. It is still in print today.

Other accounts by English and French buccaneers and their Spanish victims paint an equally vivid picture, and provide useful information concerning both the driving forces behind buccaneering and the world in which they operated. Some even include gazetteers of the ports of the Spanish Main, with instructions on how best to attack them. A number of modern historians have examined the period in some detail, and the work of Spanish scholars has proved particularly valuable. Other sources include the *Calendar of State Papers (Colonial Series)*, and other similar collections of printed historical documents are readily available either in the Public Record Office in London, the National Maritime Museum in Greenwich, the Library of Congress in Washington, D.C., or the library of the Mariners' Museum in Newport News, Virginia.

Legends in their own time, pirates such as Blackbeard and Bartholomew Roberts now seem larger than life. What we really know of them is surprisingly little and is drawn from the recollections of ex-pirates, former victims, naval officers who encountered them, or the records of courtrooms and confessions. One other source is the book *A General History of the Robberies and Murders of the Most Notorious Pirates* (1724). The author, alleged to be a Captain Charles Johnson, had extensive first-hand knowledge of piracy, and it is suggested by literary critics that Johnson was the nom-de-plume for Daniel Defoe,

THE
HISTORY *and* LIVES

Of all the moſt Notorious

PIRATES,

AND THEIR

CREWS,

From Capt. AVERY, who firſt ſettled at *Madagaſcar*, to Capt. *John Gow*, and *James Williams*, his Lieutenant, &c. who were hang'd at *Execution Dock*, *June* 11. 1725, for Piracy and Murther ; and afterwards hang'd in Chains between *Blackwall* and *Deptford*.
Giving a more full and true Account than any yet Publiſhed, of all their Murthers, Piracies, Maroonings, Places of Refuge, and Ways of Living.

Adorn'd with Twenty Beautiful Cuts, being the Repreſentation of each Pirate.

To which is prefix'd,
An *Abſtract* of the Laws against *Piracy*.

LONDON:
Printed for *Edward Midwinter*, at the *Looking-Glaſs* on *London-Bridge*. 1725. Price 1 s.

The frontispiece of the second edition of Captain Johnson's *History of Pirates* published in 1725, with plates showing blind justice and a sea battle between a pirate ship and a vessel of the Royal Navy. The book was an enlarged version of the original edition, published the previous year. (Stratford Archive)

the author of *Robinson Crusoe*. The book concentrated on pirates operating in the 30 years before its publication. Characters such as Edward Teach ('Blackbeard'), Edward Low and Henry Every were portrayed as ogres, and their actual deeds embellished with bloodcurdling fictional anecdotes. One of the problems is that the line between fact and fiction is extremely blurred. While many elements of his portrayals were based on fact, it is vital to sift through his descriptions, comparing his version with the pirates mentioned in other contemporary accounts.

Where possible, the section on privateering in the Americas has drawn on original material – letters of marque, shipping records from ports such as Salem and Baltimore, reminiscences of privateering captains and newspaper reports written during the last upsurge of piracy. What is apparent is that these records are often incomplete, as folios have been misplaced, returns were never submitted or there was little documentation to begin with. Some of the gaps in the narrative have been filled in by consulting a number of privateering histories, and the most readily available of these are listed in the Further Reading section.

Buccaneers
1620–1700

The Buccaneers and
Their Victims   16

The Buccaneering Art of War   36

Buccaneer Commanders   49

The World of the Buccaneers   61

The End of the Buccaneers   71

Shipping off Port Royal, Jamaica, c. 1760, painting by Richard Payton. Sited on the end of a sandspit spanning most of Kingstown Bay, more than two-thirds of the buccaneering den of Port Royal was destroyed in an earthquake in 1692. (National Maritime Museum, Greenwich, London)

The Buccaneers and Their Victims

In 1650, the Spanish had just emerged from the traumatic Thirty Years' War (1618–48) with the country impoverished and in desperate need of a period of peace. Peace was denied them, however, as war with the French dragged on without intermission until 1659, while Oliver Cromwell turned on Spain in 1654, launching a conflict that would continue intermittently until 1670. Spanish efforts in defending the Catholic faith in Europe drained Spain's coffers, and there was little or nothing left to spend on the defence of her ports in the Spanish Main. Therefore, when the buccaneering era began, Spanish overseas possessions were at their most vulnerable.

During the decade following Christopher Columbus's first voyage (1492), Spain established a firm control over the islands of Cuba and Hispaniola, creating a base for further exploration, settlement and conquest. By 1540, her overseas territories included most of the Caribbean basin and Peru. Under the terms of the Treaty of Tordesillas (1497) arranged by the Papacy, a north–south line was drawn in the Atlantic Ocean. Portugal was granted a monopoly of trade and discovery to the east of the line, giving her control of the trade route to the east around Africa. Spain was awarded everything to the west, which included North and South America except Brazil, which lay in the Portuguese sector. For the next century and a half, the Spanish would fight an increasingly futile battle to maintain this monopoly, particularly in the Caribbean basin, which contained most of Spain's colonial settlements. During the 16th century, interlopers from other European nations raided the region, which by that stage had become known as the Spanish Main. Francis Drake was one of the most notorious, and the Spanish regarded him as a pirate. Justice was harsh in this undeclared war on the Spanish monopoly: an encroaching French settlement in Florida was brutally destroyed in 1565, and its settlers massacred. The rallying cry for both the Spanish and other European adventurers was 'no peace beyond the line'.

By 1655, the Spanish monopoly had been broken. French, Dutch and English settlers had established colonies in many of the islands of the Lesser Antilles, the most prominent being the English colony on Barbados and the French ones on Guadeloupe and Martinique. Even more important was the English conquest of Jamaica in 1655, which gave them a base in the very heart of the Spanish Main. French settlers were also established on the western coast of the Spanish island of

Howard Pyle's *Extorting Tribute from the Citizens* appeared in *Harper's Monthly Magazine* in December 1905, where it was used to illustrate his article 'The Fate of a Treasure-Town'. Many buccaneers tortured their prisoners after capturing a town in an effort to find hidden caches of plunder. (Stratford Archive)

Hispaniola, and within a decade this would develop into the French colony of Saint Domingue. Both this colony and Jamaica would provide the buccaneers with secure bases and supportive colonial administrations. These encroachments, combined with the Spanish lack of preparedness in the Americas for what amounted to a full-scale war, created ideal circumstances for the buccaneers who saw the Spanish empire as a poorly defended treasure house.

Originally, 'Spanish Main' was a term used to refer to the northern coast of South America, the 'mainland' or Terra Firma. By the mid-17th century, its scope had widened to include the entire Caribbean basin, and by 1650 the region was divided into a number of principalities, each commanded by a viceroy or governor. New Spain encompassed Mexico and parts of Central America, with its capital in Mexico City. Lesser governors controlled Panama and Honduras, but were answerable to the viceroy in Mexico. The viceroy of New Granada included what is now Venezuela and Colombia, with a capital at Cartagena. Further to the south, the viceroy of Peru encompassed what was once the Incan empire, the most lucrative part of the Spanish dominions in the Americas. Finally, the islands of the

Map of the Spanish Main, c. 1670. The strategic location of Jamaica in the centre of the Caribbean basin allowed the buccaneers to threaten all parts of the Spanish overseas empire, whose principal ports are shown here. (The Hensley Collection, Ashville, North Carolina)

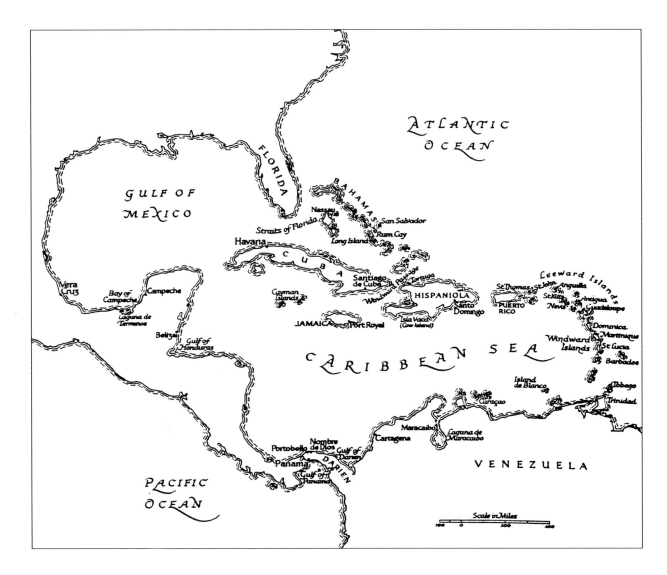

Greater Antilles including Cuba, Hispaniola and Puerto Rico all retained their own governors, although the governor of Cuba, based in Havana, was the most senior.

For the Spanish, one of the most important functions of the Spanish empire was to ensure that a continuous flow of precious metals was produced in her American mines and was safely shipped to Spain. Although legend has surrounded this whole area, 90 per cent of the precious metals shipped to Spain were silver and gold, with the greatest silver mines being in Peru. Silver was also mined in Mexico, while gold and emerald mines were found in Colombia.

The method of shipment centred around a system of secure ports and powerful treasure fleets. First, silver was shipped up the South American coast to Panama, where it was transported onto mules and taken across the isthmus to Porto Bello. Similar shipments were gathered at the ports of Cartagena in Venezuela and Vera Cruz in Mexico. Every year a fleet left Seville in Spain, bound for the New World. It carried settlers, luxury items, weapons and tools, and once it reached the Spanish Main it split into smaller squadrons. One portion sailed to Porto Bello to collect

The port of Cartagena seen from the west, looking into the inner harbour. This print, dating from the mid-17th century, clearly shows the formidable modern fortifications and outlying forts that protected the town. (Stratford Archive)

the year's silver production from Peru, then sailed on to Cartagena. Another squadron made for Vera Cruz, while other ships visited the smaller Spanish ports in the region. All the ships then gathered in the Cuban port of Havana in order that they could sail home in convoy. The same system was used throughout the 17th century, and it proved remarkably successful. Although one fleet was wrecked off the Florida Keys in 1622, and another was captured by the Dutch in 1628, the ships almost always reached Spain safely. For most of the 17th century, the fleets seemed too powerful to attack, and the buccaneers left them well alone.

The weak point of the fleet system lay in the ports. While Cartagena and Havana were considered too strong for the buccaneers to attack, others remained poorly defended. Porto Bello, Panama and Vera Cruz were all vital parts of the Spanish treasure-gathering operation, but they all succumbed to buccaneer attacks. Although both Vera Cruz and Panama boasted impressive fortifications, they were poorly maintained, and supplies of both men and matériel were minimal as Spain required all her resources to fight her enemies in Europe. While powerful colonial governors ensured that their own capitals were well defended, the smaller ports of the Spanish Main had to make do as best they could. Local militias were raised, although for much of the period they lacked the equipment and training to defend their towns against buccaneer attacks.

It was only in the 1670s that the Spanish crown diverted resources to improve the region's defence. Regular Spanish troops were sent to the Americas, and money was spent on the training and re-equipping of the militias. Fortifications that had been easily overcome by the buccaneers were strengthened, and yet more money was spent on local naval patrols by the Armada de Barlavento, tasked with protecting Spanish shipping within the Caribbean basin. Although the Spanish Main was still subjected to attacks from French buccaneers and others, the Spanish were at least capable of putting up a more spirited defence. Spanish attacks on Saint Domingue during the 1690s also showed that they had learned from their enemies, and were capable of employing the aggressive defensive strategy that had been used so successfully against them 30 years before.

THE RISE OF THE BUCCANEERS

While the first Spanish settlements in the New World were established in the Antilles, by the 17th century the emphasis had changed to the development of the more lucrative territories of the mainland of Central and South America. While Spain still maintained colonies in the Greater Antilles, most of the islands in the

The island of Hispaniola. The Spanish policy of concentrating in settlements on the south coast left the rest of the island open to the *boucanniers* and non-Spanish settlers. (Stratford Archive)

chain comprising the Lesser Antilles remained uninhabited by Europeans. Consequently, 'interlopers', or non-Spanish settlers, moved in and established settlements where tobacco crops were grown for illegal sale to Spanish colonial towns. The Spanish authorities undertook several punitive expeditions to drive out these settlers, particularly when there was evidence that they provided bases for English and Dutch 'sea-dogs' to raid Spanish ports.

One of the most devastating of these expeditions was conducted in 1629, when a Spanish force attacked the colonies on Nevis and St Kitts and deported the settlers, but the Spanish action proved to be too little, too late. More settlers reoccupied the islands and even settled on the large Spanish island of Hispaniola. While the Spanish presence on the island was restricted to colonies concentrated on its southern side, the hinterland was unoccupied. This soon provided a haven for English, Dutch and predominantly French settlers, who regarded the very vastness of the island as a safe haven. The pattern was repeated on several of the smaller islands of the Antilles, where cattle and pigs roamed wild and could be hunted down for food and as a source of income. These hunters cured the meat they caught by smoking it in a fire that used a smoking platform known as a *boucan*, a word derived from a native Arawak source. The hunters became known as *boucanniers*, which evolved into 'buccaneer'.

The largest concentration of buccaneers was in the western portion of Hispaniola, far from the centres of Spanish authority. These men established

Depicted here are early buccaneers (c. 1630) in Hispaniola dressed in home-made hunting clothes, who were said to resemble 'the butcher's vilest servants who have been eight days in the slaughterhouse without washing themselves'. In the background is a Spanish patrol, which was almost exclusively mounted and relied on local Arawak scouts as guides. (Angus McBride © Osprey Publishing Ltd)

coastal trading settlements and dealt with smugglers and other passing ships, exchanging smoked meat for weapons, powder, shot or other essentials, including wine. They were constantly under threat of attack by the Spanish, either in the form of coastal patrols or during one of the many Spanish raids into the hinterland. Many of the men had been dispossessed, evicted from their settlements by the Spanish, and they maintained a strong enmity for their old enemy. This was fuelled by religious differences, as the majority of these early buccaneers were Protestants, and the Spanish viewed them as heretics. A near-contemporary described the life of the early buccaneers: 'In general they were without habitation or fixed abode, but rendezvoused where the animals were to be found.' When a ship appeared, they would take their meat to the shore and establish a temporary marketplace. Theirs was an almost exclusively male frontier society, rough men living in primitive conditions.

As a refuge from frequent Spanish sweeps through Hispaniola, the buccaneers established themselves on the island of Tortuga, off the north-west coast. By the late 1620s or early 1630s, this had evolved into a permanent base, and the buccaneers had discovered another, even more lucrative source of income.

The body of water that lay between the westernmost part of Hispaniola and the eastern part of Cuba was known as the Windward Passage. During the early 17th century it was a major coastal shipping lane, linking the ports of northern Cuba and the colony of St Augustine in Florida with the ports of the Caribbean. It was also used by the smaller elements of the treasure fleets heading for their

A mid-17th-century French map showing the island of Tortuga and the nearby mainland of the island of Hispaniola. The bay that formed the harbour of Cayenne is clearly seen in the centre of Tortuga. (Stratford Archive)

rendezvous in Havana, and by the early 1630s it had become a haven for buccaneers. From harbours such as Cayenne on Tortuga, buccaneers preyed on the Spanish ships using canoes (piraguas) or even light pinnaces purchased from smugglers and traders. An early French exponent of this was Pierre le Grand, who with 28 men and a small pinnace, captured a small Spanish galleon. The tactics used by these early buccaneers are discussed later, but stealth and surprise were key elements in buccaneer attacks.

Both the start of attacks on Spanish shipping and the establishment of a base on Tortuga marked a transition for the buccaneers. While before they were predominantly hunters, from the 1630s they began to evolve into pirates, although by restricting their attacks to Spanish shipping they posed no threat to their native countries. Although buccaneers continued to hunt, as they did on islands throughout the Antilles, the association of the name 'buccaneer' developed, until by the 1650s it was used exclusively to refer to maritime raiders. As their numbers grew and they acquired larger and more powerful ships, buccaneering settlements attracted recruits: runaway indentured servants or slaves, deserting seamen or simple adventurers. These bands began to call themselves the 'brethren of the coast', a romantic title for a violent collection of men.

For much of the 17th century, France, England and Holland were at war with Spain, and the establishment of colonial administrations in several of the islands of the Lesser Antilles provided an opportunity for the buccaneers to give their piratical activities a veneer of legitimacy. Colonial governors were authorized to issue 'letters of marque' (also known as 'letters of reprisal') during time of war, granting the recipient the status of a privateer. While a pirate existed beyond the law, privateers operated on behalf of a particular nationality. For example, if France was at war with Spain, letters of marque could be issued to ship captains, and they would then seek out and attack Spanish shipping. In return for a share of the profits from the prizes captured and a secure port, the sponsoring government created a tool with which to disrupt enemy trade. In the Caribbean, where non-Spanish warships were rarely available, privateering became a vital aspect of warfare. From the 1640s, buccaneering crews were granted French or Dutch letters of marque by the governors of St Martin (for Holland) and St Christopher/St Kitts (for France). This employment of buccaneers as auxiliaries became part of national policy during the decades following 1650.

In 1655, an English expedition captured the island of Jamaica from the Spanish. Almost immediately, the newly appointed English governor looked to the

buccaneers for defence. While most of the French buccaneering groups remained concentrated on Tortuga or the western portion of Hispaniola (Saint Domingue), most of the English buccaneers moved to Jamaica. Although many of the Dutch, English and French colonies on the Lesser Antilles harboured buccaneering crews, by 1660 the buccaneers were concentrated in two centres, and were divided along national lines. By 1660, the buccaneers were firmly established as a force in the Caribbean, and the heyday of the buccaneering era had begun.

The English capture of Jamaica, 1655. The English soldiers' lack of uniformity betrays the lack of discipline in the army of the West Indies. Religious differences fuelled the troops' antagonism for the Spanish inhabitants, and while some plundered what they could, others desecrated the capital's churches. (Angus McBride © Osprey Publishing Ltd)

THE BRETHREN OF THE COAST

Between 1660 and 1690, long after the buccaneers had become maritime raiders, many of the characteristics of their community could be traced back to their roots as hunters. While historians are divided over the origin of the phrase 'brethren of the coast', and some attribute it to an appellation created after the buccaneering

This mural painted by Frank Schoonover shows late 17th-century buccaneers and local guests enjoying an impromptu 'banyan' or beach party. According to William Dampier, the English buccaneer Captain Swan enjoyed banyans of this sort in the Philippines. (Stratford Archive)

era, it serves to indicate the unique sense of brotherhood that dominated the society the buccaneers had created for themselves. French writers referred to the 'frères de la côte' or even the 'people of the coast' when speaking of the inhabitants of Saint Domingue, whether buccaneers or colonists. Others suggest that the term was used as early as the mid-17th century, although the phrase was never used by the contemporary writer Exquemelin. Its inclusion here is principally to imply the social system under which the buccaneers operated.

COMPOSITION OF BUCCANEER BANDS

The historian David Cordingly described buccaneers as 'several generations of fortune hunters who roamed the Caribbean looking for plunder. They included soldiers and seamen, deserters and runaway slaves, cut-throats and criminals, religious refugees, and a considerable number of out-and-out pirates.' This amply sums up the polyglot nature of buccaneer crews, who were often men who grouped themselves together for one particular expedition, and returned to the melting pot of their home port when the expedition ended. The links established between the *boucanniers* of the early 17th century and smugglers or coastal traders were strong enough to force the huntsmen to turn their backs on the land. Both groups were interlopers in the Spanish Main whose survival was dependent on avoiding Spanish authority. These early colonial mariners established trading links between the 'interloping' colonies, and sold the cash crops they produced to the remoter fringes of the Spanish overseas empire. The buccaneers who first took to attacking passing Spanish ships were therefore a combination of hunters (who, incidentally, would have been skilled marksmen) and mariners who knew the local waters and were skilled at avoiding detection.

The influx of refugees to these buccaneering communities altered this balance. Every time the Spanish attacked a colony of interlopers in the Lesser Antilles, many of the colonists evaded capture until the Spanish went away. These dispossessed farmers and settlers gravitated towards the buccaneering communities who provided a safe haven, however transitory. The same maritime traders who served the buccaneers provided the conduit along which these people reached the buccaneering settlements. French, Dutch and English colonies continued to develop in the Antilles as more settlers replaced those driven out by the Spanish. This trend intensified during the 1630s as Spanish attacks became increasingly infrequent because of the country's involvement in the Thirty Years' War. The cash crops produced in the island colonies were labour-intensive, and indentured servants were increasingly used to provide a cheap source of labour. Although they obtained their freedom after a tenure of several years, many ran away, and once more the buccaneering communities provided a safe haven. The same protection was sometimes offered to run-away slaves who were increasingly being introduced to the region to work on sugar plantations, although many buccaneers simply sold these unfortunate people back into slavery.

Following the establishment of colonial authority in Jamaica and Saint Domingue, two fresh but vital groups were added to the pool from which buccaneering crews were composed. When the Commonwealth was replaced by the Restoration government in England in 1660, the soldiers who garrisoned Jamaica were paid off. For the buccaneers based in Port Royal, this created a pool of hundreds of skilled soldiers who were ideally suited to the techniques of amphibious raids instituted by men such as the naval captain Christopher Myngs. Similarly, following the end of the Thirty Years' War in 1648, ex-soldiers sailed to the Caribbean in search of employment, and many naturally gravitated towards the buccaneers. From the 1660s, dozens of sea captains and crews arrived in the Caribbean from Europe, drawn by the profusion of letters of marque and the opportunities for plunder. Buccaneer crews were therefore drawn from various

A 19th-century depiction of an early buccaneer produced by Alexandre Debelle for P. Christian's *Histoire des Pirates* (1889). Surprisingly, blunderbusses of this type were found on several contemporary shipwrecks, so were clearly popular maritime weapons. (Stratford Archive)

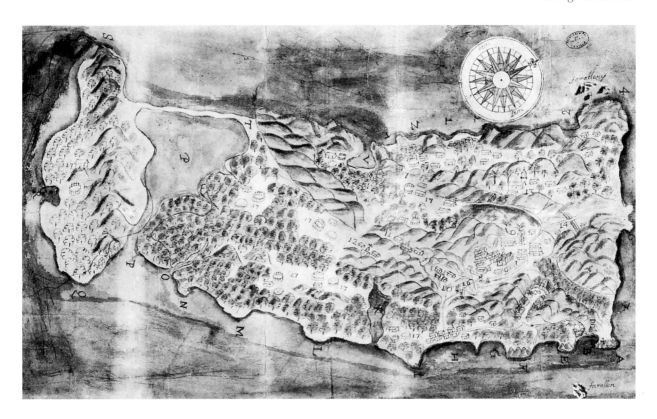

sources and were often composed of men of various nationalities, despite the tendency of the French and English to operate independently. What united them were the twin driving forces of a desire for plunder and a hatred of the Spanish.

BUCCANEER DRESS

A number of contemporary descriptions survive that refer to the dress of the early *boucanniers* of Hispaniola and other Caribbean islands. The appearance of these hunters is reconstructed in the illustration on page 22, although no visual image can portray the smell that must have accompanied these men. Stalking prey and dismembering the carcass was followed by days of smoking the meat, and according to a French clergyman, the Abbé Jean Baptiste Du Tetre, they often slept beside their smoking fires in order to keep the mosquitoes at bay. In an era when personal hygiene was rudimentary at best, the *boucanniers* were clearly exceptionally smelly. Du Tetre remarked, 'You would say that these are the butcher's vilest servants who have been eight days in the slaughterhouse without washing themselves.'

By the time the hunters had become seagoing raiders in the middle of the 17th century, their appearance would have changed. Home-made hunting shirts

The island of Margarita off the eastern end of the Spanish Main was an important Spanish stronghold, as it guarded the windward approach to this vital Spanish coastline. Naturally the island was extremely well defended. Spanish map dated 1661. Original in the Archivo de Indias, Seville. (Stratford Archive)

The Buccaneer Was a Picturesque Fellow. Painting by Howard Pyle. Like all of his pirate paintings, Pyle captured the romance of the pirate in his early 20th-century illustrations – mainly for children's books. The buccaneers who accompanied Sir Henry Morgan might well have looked like this well-armed example. (Stratford Archive)

and breeches were replaced by clothes typical of seamen of the period, and except for a surfeit of weapons, the appearance of a buccaneer would have been the same as that of the smugglers and coastal traders who frequented the region. Contemporary depictions in works such as sketches by the two Van de Veldes and others show how European seamen dressed. The appearance of European seamen in the Caribbean was similar, although allowances were made towards the climate, with light cotton shirts and breeches replacing the heavier materials worn elsewhere. Most commonly, a seaman wore loose, woollen knee-length breeches, a coarse linen shirt and a neckerchief or scarf tied around the neck. Variations included seaman's skirts or wide-bottomed cotton trousers, while a sleeved vest or more commonly a short sailor's jacket would be worn over the shirt. The jackets were woollen or often made from canvas, and contemporary accounts mention that they were soaked in a light solution of pitch or wax in order to make them waterproof. Headgear was almost always worn as protection from the sun, usually in the form of a scarf, a felt slouch hat, a knitted woollen cap or even a straw hat. Footwear was rarely worn at sea.

By the 1660s, buccaneers were more amphibious raiders than privateersmen, and their dress changed accordingly. Many of the discharged soldiers who accompanied Christopher Myngs on his raid on Santiago in 1662 wore their old military uniforms, depicted in the illustration on page 49. This introduced a practical form of military dress, and by the late 1660s, buccaneers bore more of a similarity to contemporary soldiers than sailors. Coats cut in a military style became popular attire, with variations based on a woollen or canvas coat or vest which extended to the calf. The cut changed over the years in line with contemporary military fashion. Following a successful raid, the buccaneers would take clothing as part of their plunder, which further added to their eclectic appearance. Above all, they carried weaponry and the accoutrements of war, and regardless of any other aspect of their appearance, this was the first thing observers noticed about them. Weaponry will be discussed later in this section.

ORGANIZATION AND ALLEGIANCE

Although characterized as a lawless group, buccaneers developed highly structured codes of conduct, based on a system which dated back to the days of the *boucannier* hunters. From their earliest days, buccaneers operated in pairs, living and fighting together. The system developed from the need to protect one another while hunting or while engaged in combat. According to contemporaries, the buccaneers took this pairing even further. If one died, the other would inherit his possessions, and in the buccaneer ports where men outnumbered women, it was even reported that they shared wives or mistresses. This 'buddy system' appears to have died out by the mid-1670s, as there is no mention of its survival after this time. Beyond this, buccaneer organization appears to have been very fluid, but based on a particularly strong sense of egality and pre-arranged terms and conditions.

Buccaneer crews were gathered by individual ship captains, and prominent buccaneers with their own ships had no trouble recruiting suitable crews in the harbour taverns of Jamaica and Tortuga. Exquemelin provides a description of the procedure. After calling a gathering of all those willing to participate, the captain would draw up a written agreement which specified aspects of the operation. This included the division of plunder, compensation for any participant who suffered injury, set wages for non-combatants such as a ship's surgeon or a maritime

Bartolemeo el Portugues (or Bartolomew Portugues) was a small-time buccaneer who was plagued by an almost constant run of bad luck. His story was so pitiful that Exquemelin included it in his book. (Stratford Archive)

The sack of Cartagena, 1697. Depicted here is the return of the buccaneers following the siege of Cartagena by a joint French naval/military and buccaneer force. Cheated of their rightful share of the plunder, the buccaneers are heavily armed and intent on revenge. (Angus McBride © Osprey Publishing Ltd)

artisan, and a non-concealment clause preventing any one seaman from creating his own cache of plunder. All who agreed would sign the document or make their mark, and the crew would join the ship and prepare for sea. Unlucky or unpopular buccaneer captains such as Bartolomeo el Portugues or Rok Brasiliano were reduced to signing on a mere handful of desperate men, as all others avoided contracting with them. Crews could vary from a mere two dozen for a pinnace, to almost 200 for a large three-masted flagship. While the captain provided the ship,

Map of the isthmus and city of Panama, c. 1670. The unusual perspective has the city of Panama and therefore the south at the top of the map. Morgan's buccaneers are shown crossing the isthmus, following the line of the Chagres River (from Exquemelin, 1684). (Stratford Archive)

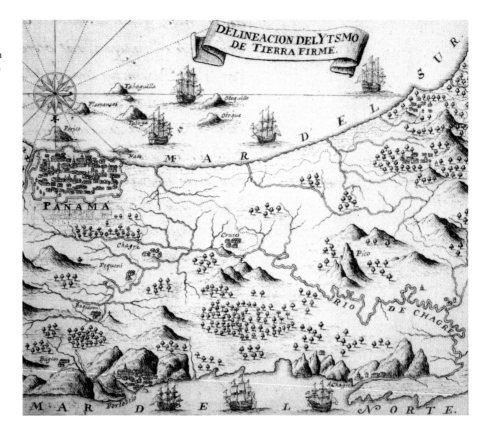

provisions, artillery and powder, it was up to each individual buccaneer to provide his own personal weaponry, such as a musket, bandolier, sword, dagger and pistol.

Large raids were organized by buccaneer commanders such as Henry Morgan who sent word that they were organizing an attack. Individual captains would be called to meet at a pre-arranged rendezvous, such as the Isle-à-Vache off the south-western coast of Saint Domingue, or around the islands off the south-western corner of Cuba. Once a fleet had gathered, the individual captains would be called to a meeting, and another contract would be drawn up governing the entire expedition. Sub-contracts were possible, involving groups of ships, and this was the case during the Anglo-French raid on Cuba in 1668. The target of the raid would be decided upon and all captains present would vote on the choice. In theory, this democratic process was in stark contrast to contemporary military or naval practice, although naval commanders such as Christopher Myngs flourished by combining legitimate national forces with those of the buccaneers. In such cases, Myngs represented the navy and ensured they would share the plunder. A prime example of what happened when this system broke down was after the attack on Cartagena in 1697. As part of the joint naval and buccaneer expedition, the French buccaneers who participated expected a proportionate share of the booty. Instead, the naval idea of shares 'man-for-man' was based on a naval system where ratings gained a fraction of the sum reserved for officers. The buccaneers felt swindled and returned to Cartagena, plundering what they felt was their fair share of whatever was left to take (see illustration page 33).

National allegiance was an increasingly important factor to the buccaneers. By obtaining a letter of marque, buccaneer captains were effectively taking sides on behalf of their sponsor's nationality. While everyone was fighting the Spanish, this was never a problem. Following the Treaty of Madrid in 1670 when Spain and England made peace, the English demanded that buccaneers stop their raiding. Henry Morgan's men attacked Panama flying the English St George's cross alongside individual (and unrecorded) flags of green and red, even though the two countries were not at war. It gave his expedition the appearance of legitimacy, although he still faced charges of piracy on his return to Jamaica. Initially, many English buccaneers obtained French letters of marque, but increasingly France, Holland and England found themselves at war with each other. While buccaneers always fought under their national flags, increasingly they did so against fellow buccaneers.

A detail of the siege of Cartagena, 1697. The buccaneers, led by Ducasse, helped to position and man the French siege guns whose close-range fire forced the city to surrender. Cartagena was the only fortress city on the Spanish Main to undergo a siege during the 17th century. (Stratford Archive)

The Buccaneering Art of War

The buccaneering period introduced a new dimension to warfare in the Americas. In the early 17th century, attacks on the Spanish empire in the New World had been confined to small-scale raids, but from the 1660s, large expeditions were launched into Spanish territory. The forces gathered together by the buccaneer commanders represented the largest European military gatherings seen in America. Although many of the engagements were small by European standards, the scale of warfare would not be repeated until the American Revolution a century later. The buccaneers also evolved their own tactics based on the available weapons and training, and their activities constitute a fascinating and largely unknown chapter in American military history.

BUCCANEER WEAPONS

For much of the buccaneering period, the standard firearm was the matchlock musket. As the weapon measured up to 5ft (1.5m) long, it was cumbersome to carry and operate, and smaller and lighter caliver muskets were sometimes used, although many buccaneers considered them less effective in battle.

Although the Spanish were one of Europe's leading exponents of the development of flintlock ignition systems, few reached her troops in the New World. Officers and dragoons sometimes carried 'miguelet lock' flintlock fusils from the mid-17th century, but flintlocks were only introduced to infantry units at the end of the century. Buccaneers were unconstrained by military contractors and equipped themselves with flintlock guns whenever they were available. Gun dealers in Port Royal performed a roaring trade in the new flintlocks, as bills of export from London gunmakers testify.

Whatever the ignition system, the loading process was the same. A charge was inserted down the barrel followed by a shot and wadding, which was rammed into place. Once the pan was primed, the weapon was ready to fire. Although most Spaniards and some musketeers still relied on bandoliers carrying 'apostles' (individual powder containers) of powder, pre-rolled cartridges containing both powder and shot were also widely used by buccaneers. Cartridges were faster to use in action, but their preparation and use was restricted to the day of battle itself, as the charges were very susceptible to tropical humidity. Bandoliers, with waterproof

A matchlock musketeer following the order, 'Replace your scouring stick', returning his ramrod to its slot in the base of the musket after loading (from *The Exercise of Armes*, 1607). The proficiency of buccaneer musketeers in loading and firing at speed gave them a distinct advantage over the slower and less well-trained Spanish militiamen. (Stratford Archive)

and relatively airtight apostles, were simply more practical in most conditions encountered on the Spanish Main.

Pistols were occasionally carried by buccaneers and by Spanish cavalry, particularly in the later decades of the century. Although some of the earlier wheel-lock weapons were used, most were flintlock pistols. Some English examples certainly reached Port Royal's gunshops, and like English muskets of the time, they used a 'dog-lock' safety latch as part of the flintlock mechanism. Spanish flintlock pistols were also widely available, often the product of Madrid gunmakers

A European soldier of the 1670s preparing a grenade for throwing. From Allain Mallet's *Les Travaux de Mars* (Paris, 1672). Buccaneers frequently used grenades when storming Spanish fortifications. (Stratford Archive)

who supplied the troops of the Spanish overseas empire and therefore by default, the buccaneers, once the weapons were captured.

Unlike firearms, which were fairly standard throughout the period, swords were a matter of personal style and taste. An examination of contemporary or near-contemporary illustrations reveals that the buccaneers carried a wide variety of edged weapons. 'Hangers' were a form of hunting sword adapted for military or naval use, and were the most popular form of blade, although by the end of the buccaneer period they had developed into a weapon resembling the true naval cutlass. Broadswords or other heavy blades were also popular, underlining the buccaneer preference for 'cut' rather than 'thrust' weapons.

Spanish officers still used the rapier, and these Toledo steel weapons were considered to be among the finest edged weapons available. As the century progressed, the rapier was replaced by the small-sword, another narrow-bladed thrusting weapon that became the standard sword of the European officer by the last two decades of the 17th century. Both of these weapons were designed for personal protection and were better suited for duels or for fencing than for use on the battlefield. Spanish infantry were also equipped with either hangers or, by 1690, with a simplified 'munition-quality' version of the small-sword. The heavier swords carried by the buccaneers gave them a distinct advantage in hand-to-hand combat.

Spanish cavalry relied on both heavy cavalry broadswords or heavy thrusting weapons, and at least in the New World rarely seem to have relied on the pistol tactics commonly practised in Europe. This stemmed from the buccaneer's refusal to adopt the pike for defence, and the Spanish believed that a charge home against buccaneer musket formations would be more effective than skirmishing at a distance. Pistols were still widely used by Spanish troops, as were flintlock carbines, although supply was a constant problem for commanders in the Americas, so equipping a militia cavalry or dragoon unit with homogenous weaponry would have been virtually impossible.

Spanish infantry formations retained the pike throughout the period, although the ratio of pikes to muskets fell from one in three in 1650 to one in five by 1690. Despite the fact that the Spanish never needed protection from buccaneer cavalry, their infantry commanders followed Spanish peninsular practices when it came to including pikemen in foot formations. As for the buccaneers, they had no standard tactical doctrine to restrict them, and there were simply not enough Spanish cavalry to make the adoption of the pike worthwhile. By the late 1670s, Spanish infantry in Europe were being issued with plug bayonets designed to fit into the barrels of their muskets. It is probable that this innovation was adopted readily by buccaneers as well as by the Spaniards, so any tactical advantage they provided would be fleeting.

To sum up, while the Spanish were fairly good at equipping their troops with the best weapons available, the buccaneers were free to embrace weapons suited to their style of fighting, not ones designed for a European battlefield. This, combined with their training and better tactical prowess on the battlefield, made them difficult to beat.

TACTICS

Following the establishment of buccaneering centres at Port Royal and Tortuga, large expeditions became possible, with buccaneer groups combining to form striking forces capable of attacking well-defended Spanish towns and cities. In both bases, but particularly in Port Royal, ex-soldiers made up a large pool of skilled recruits and were able to train the less experienced sailors and landsmen. The mid-17th century was a period when warfare was undergoing a transition. The Thirty Years' War was particularly destructive in its devastation of the civilian communities, and rape, plunder and looting were commonplace. This brutality spread to the Caribbean, where the inhabitants of towns captured by buccaneers were often tortured and always plundered. The advantage of employing hardened European ex-soldiers was that they provided training in the latest military tactics, and buccaneer forces made full use of their skills.

Exquemelin describes Henry Morgan's buccaneers advancing 'with drums beating and colours flying', resembling a body of regular troops rather than a band of pirates. These men were trained to fight in ranks in a military fashion, and although they lacked harsh military discipline, they were united in a common goal: the capture and plundering of enemy towns. In a period when the Spanish were hard pressed to provide the garrisons and militia in the New World with sufficient quantities of weapons and powder, the buccaneers had ready access to weapons, and observers recount that they often carried more than one weapon. In 1683, for an attack on Vera Cruz, the Chevalier de Grammont ordered his French buccaneers to bring along as many firearms as they could, and they went into the attack with three or more muskets, pistols or blunderbusses each. This basic firepower was combined with training in the latest volley fire by ranks or even by 'platoons'. The result was a unit which could produce such a volume of fire that Spanish opponents would simply be shot to pieces. Pistols would be fired at close range, then the buccaneers would draw their swords and knives, or even throw grenades. Until the very end of the buccaneering era, no Spanish army had the ability to resist such powerful forces.

During the 1660s and 1670s, the Spanish militia lacked the training they needed to oppose the buccaneers. A string of humiliating Spanish defeats forced the Spanish crown to re-examine its military abilities. After the sack of Panama, Spanish garrisons in the New World were augmented by an increasing number of regular Spanish troops – men who were as well trained as the buccaneers. Similarly, increasing quantities of modern military stores and equipment were being shipped to the Spanish colonies, together with instructors to train the colonial militia. By the 1690s, the Spanish had become a far more powerful force in the region than they had been even 20 years before. Although Cartagena fell to a large French army in 1697, the Spanish troops in the city fought well and almost repulsed the attack. Furthermore, Spanish campaigns in Saint Domingue demonstrated that given the right conditions – superiority in numbers and competent commanders – the Spanish Army could defeat the buccaneers.

Most buccaneer attacks followed a similar pattern. A leader such as Henry Morgan or the Chevalier de Grammont would gather a force together and agree terms over the division of any spoils. An advance party would reconnoitre the target to solicit intelligence. Often the buccaneer band would anchor their ships well away from the target and either march overland or approach it in canoes (piraguas). A favourite time of attack was at dawn, and Sundays or holy festivals also helped to ensure the town would be unprepared to defend itself. The attack would use the element of surprise to achieve its two main objectives. The first was to prevent the civilian population from escaping. Once rounded up they were often held prisoner in a suitably large building, usually a church. The second objective was to overrun the garrison, assaulting any forts if necessary, but by preference, capturing them by stealth and subterfuge. Once they held the town the buccaneers would sack it, and if necessary they would torture their captives to make them reveal where they hid their valuables (see illustrations pages 42 and 55). Often ransom demands would be sent to the regional governor, when the buccaneers would threaten to destroy the city if payment was not forthcoming. After several days, the buccaneers would sail away, taking whatever slaves they captured to sell in the markets of Jamaica or the West Indies. At some agreed rendezvous they would then anchor their ships and divide the plunder, allowing the various buccaneer crews to go their own separate ways. This basic scenario had several variations, including using a city as a base for further attacks into the hinterland, or even using it as a base for a large expedition to another city.

Morgan interrogating prisoners outside Panama, 1671. The buccaneers spent weeks torturing the townspeople, forcing them to reveal where they had hidden their valuables. The real treasure was spirited away by sea, while the buccaneers captured the city, as shown in the background of the engraving (from Exquemelin, 1684). (Stratford Archive)

The effect on the towns and cities of the Spanish Main was catastrophic. One Spanish resident of Cartagena noted that most of the towns in what are now Venezuela and Colombia had been sacked at least twice and burned once, while others such as Maracaibo and Santa Marta were sacked or burned regularly. Some settlements such as Riohacha had simply been abandoned, as their inhabitants left for the relative safety of well-defended cities such as Cartagena or Havana.

BATTLES

Although only the battle of Panama has received acknowledgement as a full-scale battle involving a buccaneer army, several other engagements were also worthy of the title. The basic nature of buccaneer tactics was to conduct hit-and-run raids, and not to engage in a stand-up battle unless it could not be avoided. In some cases, the buccaneers had to fight in order to gain control of the city they were attacking. At Santiago de Cuba in October 1662, Christopher Myngs was forced to fight a Spanish force drawn up in line of battle in front of the city. During Henry Morgan's Panama campaign, he had to defeat a Spanish blocking force at Venta de Cruces in December 1670 before he could reach Panama.

Offensive action by the Spanish was a second cause of battle. A Spanish invasion of Jamaica in 1658 by 550 troops and artillery from Vera Cruz was defeated when Christopher Myngs met them with 500 buccaneers and ex-soldiers from Port Royal (then called Cagway). The Spaniards were decimated by volley fire, then surrendered en masse, and the captured guns were dragged back to Cagway. Henry Morgan easily ambushed and defeated a Spanish force marching to the relief of Porto Bello in 1668. During the Chevalier de Grammont's campaign against Campeche, a Spanish relief force was defeated as it approached the city from the north in August 1685, while a week later a buccaneer column was in turn beaten by the Spanish at Hampolol in the Yucatan Peninsula. This last action marked a change in the status quo, where better-trained and led Spanish

The battle of Panama, 1671, a scene which includes many of the features of the conflict, in no particular order. Of note are the stampeding cattle in the centre, and a buccaneer musket body repulsing Spanish cavalry in the right corner (from Exquemelin, 1684). (Stratford Archive)

forces were able to defeat buccaneers in open battle. This Spanish victory was repeated in 1691 during a Spanish invasion of the French-held island of Saint Domingue (formerly Hispaniola). The French tried to block the Spanish advance along the north coast of the island at Sabane de Limonade. The resulting battle, fought on 21 January 1691, saw the blocking force of heavily outnumbered buccaneers defeated and the survivors put to the sword. In the summer of 1694, Jamaica was invaded by French buccaneers led by Jean-Baptiste Ducasse. The local English garrison at the landing site was no match for the buccaneers, so a British-backed force of buccaneers was formed in Port Royal. Before they could march on their French counterparts, Ducasse withdrew back to Saint Domingue. Most of these actions involved forces of 500 to 1,500 men per side, and in the European scheme of things would hardly rate as a skirmish. In the Americas, 1,500 men constituted an army.

The battle of Panama (28 January 1671) is a perfect example of the buccaneering art of war in action. Henry Morgan commanded a buccaneer army of around 1,200 men, a force imbued with a confidence of victory that stemmed partly from Morgan's charisma and the rest from belief in their own abilities.

In the battle off Maracaibo Bar (1669), the English buccaneer Henry Morgan attacked a blockading Spanish fleet by sending a fireship against the enemy flagship. He then sailed through the blockading line in the resulting confusion. (Stratford Archive)

During the brief campaign, Morgan used surprise, mobility and superiority in morale to cross the isthmus without any serious opposition from Spanish militia. At Guayabal and again at Venta de Cruces, blocking forces melted away when probed by the buccaneer vanguard. This gave the buccaneers an advantage in morale by the time they reached the city of Panama, where the Spanish formed a line of battle at Mata Asnillos, a mile in front of the city. The 1,200 militia infantry were drawn up in six ranks, while their flanks were protected by militia cavalry, 200 horsemen on each side. Although it was not mentioned if artillery pieces were present, they would have been deployed in front of the infantry.

Morgan began his final advance, 'red and green banners clearly visible to the Spaniards', and he deployed into a three-deep line, his force split into three divisions. The left flank was commanded by the Dutch buccaneer Laurens Prins, who advanced in a wide sweep around the Spanish right flank and occupied a hill overlooking the Spanish line. This stung the Spaniards into committing to an attack, but it also disrupted their secret weapon. The Spanish commander Juan Pérez de Guzmán had collected a herd of cattle and kept them behind his infantry line. His intention was to let them pass through his lines and stampede them into the buccaneers, disrupting them just before the Spanish foot advanced into contact. The advance by Prins scared the cattle drovers, who fled, leaving the cattle to wander through the Spanish lines (see illustration page 53). A simultaneous advance on Morgan's men and on the hill held by Prins ended in disaster. Concentrated volley

The main square of the strategic Spanish treasure port of Panama as it appeared in 1670 – the year Sir Henry Morgan captured and sacked the city. Unfortunately for the buccaneers, much of the city's wealth had been shipped out down the Pacific coast before the buccaneers arrived. Original in the Archivo de Indias, Seville. (Stratford Archive)

fire from the buccaneers felled the Spanish, who lost over 100 militiamen in the first volley alone. Stampeding cattle and a withering fire were enough to break the Spaniards, who fled the field, leaving between 400 and 500 dead and wounded. As Pérez de Guzmán stated, 'hardly did our men see some fall dead and others wounded but they turned their backs and fled'. This was not completely fair, as even veteran infantry, particularly those who suffered 40 per cent casualties in a few minutes, would be inclined to break. As in numerous other actions, superior buccaneer firepower and tactical initiative proved more than a match for the Spanish militiamen who opposed them.

More common than battle was the assault of a Spanish-held fort (*castellano*). Morgan's tactic of using a human shield at Porto Bello was unusual, and usually surprise was the best ally of the buccaneers. If the defenders were forewarned, then the capture of a fort was extremely difficult as the buccaneers lacked siege equipment. When Morgan's lieutenant Joseph Bradley led an assault on Castellano San Lorenzo guarding Panama's Chagres River in January 1671, the Spanish knew he was coming. The garrison had been reinforced and repulsed four buccaneer assaults despite a constant barrage from snipers and buccaneer warships. A fifth assault found a weak spot and entered the fort, where the remaining defenders were overwhelmed and massacred. This was an exception to the norm, where a quick surprise assault would normally suffice to capture the crumbling and undermanned Spanish defences guarding the ports of the Spanish Main.

FIGHTING AT SEA

The first buccaneers took to the sea as a sideline, augmenting the money they made as hunters on Hispaniola by attacking passing Spanish shipping. The tactics used were noted by Exquemelin and others, the earliest being in reference to the French buccaneer Pierre le Grand. These early buccaneers used small pinnaces or even piraguas, exploiting their small size to avoid detection. If spotted, it was hoped the Spaniards would think the buccaneer craft was a harmless fishing boat. Once within range, marksmen would fire at the helmsman or anyone seen above deck, preventing the Spaniards from handling their ship or raising more sails to get away. If more than one craft was involved, one would sail to the stern of the Spanish ship and immobilize its rudder. They then swarmed aboard.

By the 1650s, buccaneers were seamen rather than hunters with canoes, and their method of attack altered. Larger ships, such as sloops and brigantines, were available in Port Royal, most vessels being captured Spanish ships. The buccaneers

OPPOSITE Henry Morgan at Porto Bello, 1668. With Porto Bello under his control, Morgan's next task was to capture the main fortress of Santiago. He forced prisoners – most of whom were priests and nuns – to advance ahead of his storming party, acting as a human shield. Here the Spanish gun crew are debating whether to open fire. (Angus McBride © Osprey Publishing Ltd)

The Spanish port of Santo Domingo on Hispaniola (now the capital of the Dominican Republic) was no stranger to attack. This chart, which was probably produced by Baptista Boazoi of Leiden in 1588, shows Sir Francis Drake's successful attack on the settlement in January 1586. (National Maritime Museum, Greenwich, London)

who cruised in these were able to venture throughout the Caribbean basin, and Spanish coastal shipping provided their main target. Typically, the buccaneers would overhaul a Spanish vessel, then fire on it using small arms rather than artillery to prevent damage to the hull or sails. Their tactics were identical to those used by the pirates of the early 18th century (see pages 79–83). If a quarry refused to surrender, a volley of small-arms fire preceded a boarding action. As the buccaneers usually outnumbered their opponents and were better armed, the result was rarely in doubt.

Although the emphasis changed from naval attacks to raids on Spanish settlements during the 1660s, Spanish shipping was still attacked wherever it was encountered. It simply made more sense to capture a port and all the ships at anchor rather than to hunt down individual Spanish ships. It must be noted that the buccaneers were never strong enough to attack the annual treasure fleets which sailed between Spain and the New World, or if they were, the fleet was deliberately delayed until the buccaneer threat dissipated. The few treasure galleons captured by the buccaneers were all taken at anchor.

Buccaneer Commanders

This sample of the major buccaneering leaders of the period illustrates the range of activities the buccaneers were engaged in and the scope of their raids on the Spanish Main, tracing the development of buccaneering from the conquest of Jamaica in 1655 to the sacking of Cartagena in 1697. For those seeking more information, the Further Reading section lists a number of excellent sources.

CHRISTOPHER MYNGS (1620–66)

In February 1658, the 52-gun Cromwellian warship *Marston Moor* dropped anchor off Port Royal, and her captain Christopher Myngs became commander of the squadron charged with the defence of Jamaica. He had been there before, having served as deputy to the previous commander for 18 months from January 1656. He already had some experience of raids on Spanish settlements, and he used this

Christopher Myngs' assault on Santiago de Cuba, 1662. When Myngs and his force of 1,300 buccaneers reached San Juan Hill, they found the outnumbered Spanish garrison drawn up in front of the city. The Spanish were quickly routed, and the city fell to the buccaneers. (Angus McBride © Osprey Publishing Ltd)

to form a new strategy for the defence of Jamaica. For nine years, from 1656 to 1665, Myngs would pioneer the use of buccaneers to thwart an invasion by leading pre-emptive raids on Spanish ports that could be used to launch an attack on Jamaica.

In 1658, he repulsed a small Spanish invasion with a combination of Commonwealth troops and buccaneers. He then sailed to the northern coast of South America, where for the next two years he attacked Spanish ports from Cumaná to Santa Marta, capturing a substantial haul of booty and sending the Spanish into a panic. These raids demonstrated that buccaneers were vital to his strategy of an aggressive defence, and the role of the buccaneer in the defence of Jamaica was established. Myngs led these raids in his frigate *Marston Moor* accompanied by two or three smaller buccaneer vessels, and ostensibly he operated under the authority of the Commonwealth government. His biggest haul came in mid-1659, when he captured Coro, a small port in modern Venezuela. A large cargo of Spanish silver was captured in the harbour, the plunder valued at over a quarter of a million English pounds. Contrary to orders, Myngs split the haul with his buccaneers and crew before the treasure was brought back to Jamaica. The governor of Jamaica accused Myngs of embezzlement, describing him as 'unhinged and out of tune'. Myngs was ordered home in the *Marston Moor* to stand trial. Fortunately for him, the restoration of the monarchy paralysed the government and the case was dropped. Myngs gained the support of Charles II, and he returned to Jamaica in command of the 40-gun royal warship *Centurion* in August 1662.

Although England and Spain were not at war, the new governor, Lord Windsor, encouraged attacks on the Spanish as part of a secret national policy. He paid off the remnants of the Commonwealth Army in Jamaica, creating a pool of skilled ex-soldiers just when Myngs needed them most. Within two months, Myngs led a buccaneer attack on Santiago de Cuba, defeating the garrison in a brief pitched battle. After destroying the city's formidable fortifications, he returned to Port Royal accompanied by a string of prize ships filled with plunder. This was the first instance of a full-scale buccaneer raid, and it set the scene for scores of similar amphibious operations over the next 30 years.

During the winter, Myngs announced he would lead another expedition, and hundreds of men flocked to Port Royal, including Dutch and French buccaneers. In February 1663, Myngs set sail for the Mexican coast with 12 ships and 1,400 buccaneers. The buccaneers attacked Campeche, but Myngs was seriously wounded during the assault. After plundering the town, the buccaneers withdrew to Port Royal with a fleet of prize ships, and Myngs returned to England to convalesce. A change of policy by the new governor, Sir Thomas Modyford, meant that further raids were forbidden. In 1665, Myngs was promoted to vice-admiral, and was knighted following the 'Four Days' Battle' against the Dutch in June 1666. Two months later he was dead, killed by a cannon ball during another engagement with the Dutch.

HENRY MORGAN (c. 1635–88)

Although his early life is obscure, Morgan, a Welshman, arrived in Jamaica in the wake of the Cromwellian invasion in 1655. From 1658 until 1672, he was one of the most formidable buccaneers in the Caribbean. He accompanied Myngs on some of his expeditions, and in 1662 was named as the commander of a privateering vessel. In 1664, he sailed with a group of other buccaneer captains harassing Spanish shipping and towns along the coast of the Yucatan Peninsula and even marched inland to

Henry Morgan standing before the city of Panama in 1671. The well-dressed buccaneer commander is carrying a flintlock musket, indicating how readily the buccaneers embraced the weapon, which was technically far superior to the matchlock musket. (Stratford Archive)

sack the regional capital of Villahermosa. The same surprise attack overland was repeated the following year when Morgan and others crossed Central America to attack the town of Grenada (near the modern Nicaraguan capital of Managua). Morgan made enough money to buy a plantation when he returned to Jamaica, and married his cousin. He also became friends with the governor, Sir Thomas Modyford.

In January 1668, Modyford ordered Morgan to attack the Spanish in Cuba, so armed with a privateering letter of marque, he gathered ten ships and 500 men, half of them French. Havana was too well defended, so the expedition landed in western Cuba and marched inland to attack Puerto Principe. The Spaniards were forewarned, and after defeating the local militia and capturing the town, Morgan's men had little plunder to show for their efforts. The French contingent sailed home in disgust, but Morgan proposed to continue his raid, this time in the isthmus of Panama.

Morgan had intelligence that the defences of the treasure port of Porto Bello were not as formidable as they appeared, so he led his men in an attack on the city in July 1668. Anchoring some distance away, he advanced by canoe, then on foot, until he reached the southern side of Porto Bello. He seized one of the three forts and the town itself in a lightning assault, then used a human shield of prisoners to cover his men when he attacked the second fort (see illustration page 46). The garrison was butchered, and by the time he advanced on the third fort the following morning, the Spanish had had enough and surrendered. The buccaneers looted the town and held it for ransom for a month. After his relief force was defeated by Morgan's men, the governor of Panama paid the asking price and the buccaneers returned to Port Royal laden with plunder.

In October, a second joint expedition with the Tortuga buccaneers got off to a bad start when HMS *Oxford*, the warship lent by Governor Modyford, blew up at its moorings. Cartagena was abandoned as a target, and instead Morgan entered Lake Maracaibo in Venezuela. The buccaneers held the region throughout the winter, looting far inland and defeating a Spanish naval squadron sent to capture them. Morgan spent a year adding to his growing estates, but in late 1670 he proposed an attack on Panama, undertaken with the approval of the governor.

In December 1670, he sailed for the isthmus of Panama with a large fleet and 1,200 men. An advance force captured the fortress of San Lorenzo guarding the Chagres River, allowing the buccaneers to cross most of the isthmus by canoe. In early January, they defeated a Spanish army drawn up to defend Panama and they captured the city. Forewarned, many Spaniards had fled with their valuables, but

the buccaneers tortured those remaining to make them reveal where they had hidden their possessions. By February, the buccaneers had given up, destroyed the city and returned to their ships with a poor haul of plunder. This was Morgan's last great raid, as a change of policy prevented further attacks on the Spanish.

Spain and England had been at peace when Morgan attacked Panama, and within a year the governor was recalled to London to answer charges levelled by the Spanish ambassador. The new governor had Morgan arrested in April 1672 and sent to England, but the buccaneer had powerful friends. He was never imprisoned, and instead managed to have the new governor removed from office. Morgan himself was knighted and appointed as the new deputy governor.

Morgan served as a colonial official for eight years from 1674 to 1682, during which time he strengthened the defences of the island but never returned to buccaneering. A wealthy landowner, he spent his last years plagued by disease brought on by excessive drinking, but remained an influential figure and was accorded full military honours when he died. More than anyone else, Morgan has been regarded as the archetypal buccaneer, the terror of the Spanish Main and the defender of Jamaica. It is also hardly surprising that he has a rum named after him.

Henry Morgan at Panama, 1671. The Spanish commander planned to stampede cattle in the buccaneers' ranks, but the drovers ran away when the firing started; the cattle ran amok among the Spaniards. Morgan and his men decimated the Spanish. The disciplined nature of the buccaneers' line can be seen here. (Angus McBride © Osprey Publishing Ltd)

JEAN DAVID NAU, 'L'OLONNAIS' (c. 1635–68)

'The man from Olonne', the Frenchman Jean Nau, arrived in the Caribbean in the 1650s as an indentured servant, but by 1660 he had joined the buccaneers in Saint Domingue (now Haiti), the French-run western portion of Hispaniola. His buccaneering career lasted seven years, beginning in 1662 when he participated in several attacks on Spanish shipping and was given a prize vessel by the French buccaneer governor of Tortuga. He cruised off Cuba and the Yucatan Peninsula, and at some stage he was shipwrecked off Campeche. The buccaneers were massacred by the local militia as they came ashore, but L'Olonnais escaped by feigning death. In an attack on a town in Cuba, he held the town to ransom, then captured and killed the crew of a ship sent to its relief. One man was spared to tell the governor of Havana that L'Olonnais was responsible. By 1667, England and Holland were at war, and the French buccaneers sought to exploit the conflict as France had allied itself with the Dutch. During the spring of 1667, L'Olonnais planned an expedition to cruise the Caribbean looking for a suitable English target to attack.

Nau's growing reputation ensured that men signed on for his next expedition, and he sailed from Tortuga with over 600 men in eight ships. While cruising in the Antilles, news reached him that France was now at war with Spain, giving him an even better opportunity to profit from Europe's conflicts. In July, the buccaneers set sail for Lake Maracaibo in modern Venezuela. The large lagoon was defended by a small fortification with 16 guns, which Nau and his men stormed from the landward side and captured. The lagoon was now at the mercy of the buccaneers. The first town they attacked was Maracaibo, a prosperous settlement which had been abandoned as the buccaneers approached. For the next two weeks, L'Olonnais and his men searched the woods for the inhabitants, then brought them back and tortured them until they revealed where they had hidden their treasure. The buccaneers then crossed the lake and landed near Gibraltar, on its eastern shore. The garrison outnumbered the buccaneers, but L'Olonnais defeated them in a brutal engagement that left 70 buccaneers killed or wounded. They plundered the town and its environs for a month, extorting a ransom that was paid to prevent them burning the town. A return visit to Maracaibo boosted profits and produced another ransom, then the buccaneers returned to Saint Domingue and Tortuga.

In late 1667, L'Olonnais organized another expedition and 700 buccaneers joined him. His six ships cruised off Cuba before sailing for Honduras. The flotilla was becalmed in the Gulf of Honduras, and spent weeks foraging along the coast before reaching the small port of Puerto Cabellos. L'Olonnais captured the town without much problem, but when he marched inland to attack the settlement of San Pedro his men were ambushed. He tortured Spanish prisoners until they revealed a back route to the town, free of further ambushes. The buccaneers reached the town and captured it, but there was little plunder to be had. Within months of their return to Puerto Cabellos, L'Olonnais was reduced to one ship, as his colleagues gave up and sailed home. In the spring of 1668, Nau sailed to Nicaragua's Mosquito Coast, where his ship ran aground. While some of his crew

L'Olonnais at Maracaibo, 1667. Perhaps the most sadistic of all the buccaneers, L'Olonnais earned his reputation from the excessive cruelty he showed to Spanish prisoners. Upon attacking Maracaibo, L'Olonnais hacked several prisoners to death, then tortured the rest to reveal where they had hidden their possessions. (Angus McBride © Osprey Publishing Ltd)

L'Olonnais torturing Spanish prisoners during his march through the jungle of Honduras in 1667. One is shown having his tongue pulled out, one of the French buccaneer's less horrific forms of cruelty. On another occasion he reputedly cut out and ate the heart of a victim. (Stratford Archive)

built boats, L'Olonnais probed south, only to run into a Spanish patrol. The buccaneers were defeated, and the dwindling band sailed south to the Gulf of Darien. While attempting to find food in an Indian village, they were attacked and slaughtered. According to Exquemelin, L'Olonnais was eaten by cannibals.

MICHEL DE GRAMMONT 'LE CHEVALIER' (c. 1650–86)

De Grammont arrived in the Caribbean during the mid-1670s, a Parisian serving in the French Navy. Presumably he was paid off, as by 1675 he was a buccaneer captain with his own vessel, yet he clearly remained on the right side of the authorities as he was given letters of marque.

This situation changed when he illegally captured a Dutch vessel and chose to remain in Saint Domingue to avoid the repercussions. War between France and Holland relieved any legal threat to de Grammont, who participated in an expedition against the Dutch island of Curaçao in 1678. The joint buccaneer and French naval force was commanded by the Comte d'Estrées, who ran most of his fleet aground on the Islas de Aves as he approached Curaçao from the east. The fleet withdrew to Saint Domingue, but the buccaneer contingent elected to stay and raid the Spanish coast of Venezuela, after looting what they could from the French wrecks. The charismatic de Grammont was duly elected their leader, and he decided to repeat L'Olonnais's achievement and enter the Lake of Maracaibo.

The French buccaneer Michel de Grammont (known as the 'Chevalier') operated against both the Spanish and the Dutch in the 1670s and 80s. He led several large-scale and highly successful raids against cities such as Maracaibo, Caracas and Vera Cruz, which made him the French equivalent of Sir Henry Morgan. (Stratford Archive)

In June 1678, he captured the San Carlos bar fortification guarding the entrance to the lake by landing guns from his ships and forming a siege battery. The Spaniards were battered into submission, and de Grammont's six ships, 13 pinnaces and 700 men were loose inside the lagoon. His main ships remained at the mouth of the lagoon to guard the entrance, while he led the rest to Maracaibo. The long-suffering town was looted, followed by Gibraltar on the south-east side of the lagoon, the same towns that had suffered from the attentions of L'Olonnais. He then marched inland, and in September he captured the town of Trujillo, even though it was defended by 350 militia and a gun battery. His victory was assured when he circled the town undetected and stormed it from behind. He also used captured Spanish horses to mount his men, creating fast-moving raiding parties. The French buccaneers returned to Petit Goâve in December, laden with booty.

In May 1680, he led a second expedition to Venezuela, capturing La Guaira, the harbour port of Caracas, with 600 men. Although de Grammont's men held the town and its two forts, the prompt arrival of 2,000 Spanish reinforcements from Caracas penned them inside the port. Several Spanish assaults were repulsed, and de Grammont was seriously wounded in the fighting. The buccaneers evacuated the port, taking several prominent hostages with them for ransom, and returned to Petit Goâve almost empty-handed.

Buccaneers threatening to shoot a Spanish captive unless he reveals where he has hidden his valuables. Spanish colonists became adept at rapidly hiding their possessions and fleeing when a buccaneer force approached. (Stratford Archive)

By May 1683, de Grammont was ready to go buccaneering again, and allied his men with the Dutch-born French buccaneer leader Laurens de Graaf for an attack on Vera Cruz. The assembly of over 1,300 buccaneers was probably the largest since the days of Henry Morgan. The buccaneers reconnoitred the city and decided a land attack was the most promising, as the landward defences had been neglected. A dawn assault through the streets overwhelmed the garrison of 300 regulars and 400 militiamen, and the city was captured. The buccaneers sailed away after a week of looting and torture, taking hundreds of prisoners with them to ransom. As they left, they ran into the annual treasure fleet, but avoided combat and returned to Saint Domingue to divide the spoils. In the summer of 1685, de Grammont and de Graaf joined forces again to attack Campeche, in Mexico. They held the city for three months despite Spanish relief attempts, and as a ransom was not paid, they burned it when they left in September 1685.

In the following year, de Grammont raised a new band and cruised off the Yucatan Peninsula looking for a suitable target. He was planning a raid on Spanish Florida when a hurricane scattered his squadron in August 1686. When the tempest passed, de Grammont's flagship was nowhere to be seen, and he was presumed lost at sea.

LAURENS CORNELIS BOUDEWIJN DE GRAAF (c. 1651–1702)

As a teenager, de Graaf spent three years serving as a sailor in the Spanish Navy before deserting in the West Indies. By the mid-1670s, he had reached Hispaniola, where he joined the buccaneers and pirates who operated in Samana Bay in the north-east of the island, beginning a career that lasted 19 years, from 1676 to 1695. Although technically under Spanish control during the late 17th century, the region was a lawless area beyond the reach of the colonial authorities. Jacques Pouançay, the governor of Saint Domingue, recorded de Graaf's rise to power, saying he captured a small bark, then a ship, then a bigger one and so on until he commanded the 28-gun privateering vessel *Tigre*, a ship he captured from the Spanish Navy in late 1679. By this time, de Graaf was the acknowledged leader of the Samana Bay buccaneers, who raided shipping throughout the waters of Hispaniola and the Leeward Islands. In July 1682, he captured the *Francesca* in the Mona Passage off Puerto Rico, a 30-gun warship that was carrying the annual pay for the Havana garrison. This achievement brought de Graaf instant notoriety, and he was asked to join an expedition raised by another Dutch buccaneer, Nikolaas van Hoorn.

Together with the French buccaneer de Grammont, de Graaf and van Hoorn attacked the Mexican port of Vera Cruz in May 1683 in one of the largest attacks on the Spanish Main in a decade. The two Dutchmen fell out over the treatment of captives, and de Graaf wounded his countryman in a duel. Van Hoorn died of his wounds, leaving de Graaf and de Grammont as undisputed buccaneer leaders. In December 1683, he was cruising off Cartagena when he was attacked by three Spanish warships. De Graaf and his men captured them and sent a note to the city governor, thanking them for their Christmas presents! He renamed the captured 40-gun *San Francisco* the *Fortune* (and later *Neptune*), making it his latest flagship.

In January 1684, he learned of a new war between France and Spain. He immediately sailed to Petit Goâve and was awarded with a French letter of marque. De Graaf remained in the port until winter, then joined a buccaneer force gathering off the Colombian coast. The buccaneers could not agree on whom to attack, so in April 1685 de Graaf called his own rendezvous on the Cuban Isla de Pinos. Together with de Grammont, de Graaf proposed an attack on Campeche. Unlike the attack on Vera Cruz two years before, the Spaniards had advance warning of the assault, and although the city was captured on 6 July and held for three months, the inhabitants had time to remove most of their valuables. In the bitter struggle for the city, de Graaf landed guns from his ships to lay siege to strongholds in the city, including the cathedral and the main city fortress. As the governor of Yucatan refused to pay a ransom to the buccaneers, they destroyed the town when they left. On the return voyage to Saint Domingue, the buccaneer fleet became separated, and de Graaf's ship was caught by a Spanish naval squadron. De Graaf in the *Neptune* spent a day exchanging broadsides with two large Spanish ships before escaping under cover of dark. He repaired his ship on a remote spot on the southern coast of Cuba and returned to Saint Domingue. The next year he led 500 men in an attack on the Yucatan Peninsula, capturing Tihosuco and threatening the regional capital of Valladolid before withdrawing. This was his last major raid, as the French crown put pressure on the buccaneers to stop their indiscriminate attacks on Spanish settlements. Although de Graaf participated in Ducasse's attack on Jamaica in 1694, he spent most of the next decade serving the French governor of Saint Domingue as a military commander. He was present at the disastrous battle of Sabane de Limonade in 1691, and in 1694 and 1695 he fought against English buccaneer attacks and a full-scale Anglo-Spanish invasion. After the invasion he retired, although he took part in the expedition that settled Louisiana in 1699.

The World of the Buccaneers

BUCCANEER PORTS

Although buccaneers used several remote islands or bays as temporary bases or rendezvous, only two places could be considered safe home ports. The second half of the 17th century was still a period when the Spanish dominated the Caribbean basin, and other European nations had only begun to establish footholds in the Spanish Main. The English used the islands of Barbados and Jamaica, although both were struggling colonies under threat of attack from the Spanish. The French position was more precarious. French buccaneers in the west of Hispaniola established their base on the offshore island of Tortuga, then in the 1650s they founded several small settlements along the western coast of Hispaniola itself. The French government declared that the settlements formed part of Saint Domingue and sent a royal governor, but the Spanish were less enthusiastic. As the French colony shared the same island with the Spanish, they were constantly threatened by Spanish attack. Similarly, although the Spanish ostensibly controlled the chain of islands which made up the Lesser Antilles, in practical terms most of these had been

Long before the buccaneers began attacking Spanish ships and cities, the Dutch had been harrying the Spanish in the New World. This engraving shows a Dutch attack against Spanish ships off Cuba during the early 17th century. (Stratford Archive)

abandoned and were settled by French, English and Dutch colonists. Constant warfare between all four European powers in the Caribbean meant that these vulnerable outposts changed ownership regularly. The first of the great buccaneering bases was established during the 1630s on the island of Tortuga, located off the north-western corner of Hispaniola (now modern Haiti and the Dominican Republic). 'Île de La Tortue' or Turtle Island was less than 12 miles long and six wide at its broadest point, and took its name from its shape, which resembled the back of a giant turtle. The name gradually evolved to become 'Tortuga'.

The island's first European settlers were *boucanniers* who used the island as a safe haven from the Spanish, and by the 1620s a settlement called Cayenne had been established on the island's southern side. It included a marketplace where beef and hides were traded for supplies from passing ships. Smugglers also started using the island as a haven, and by 1630 the buccaneers based there began to attack passing Spanish ships. The island elected an English governor, but most of the settlers were wiped out by a Spanish attack in 1634. The Dutch took over the island as a privateering base and lived alongside the mainly French *boucanniers*,

By the 1650s, the French occupied Tortuga and used it as a privateering base to harry Spanish shipping. Consequently, the Spanish attacked and stormed the island in January 1654, but failed to evict the defenders of the island's La Roca fortress. Original in the Archivo de Indias, Seville. (Stratford Archive)

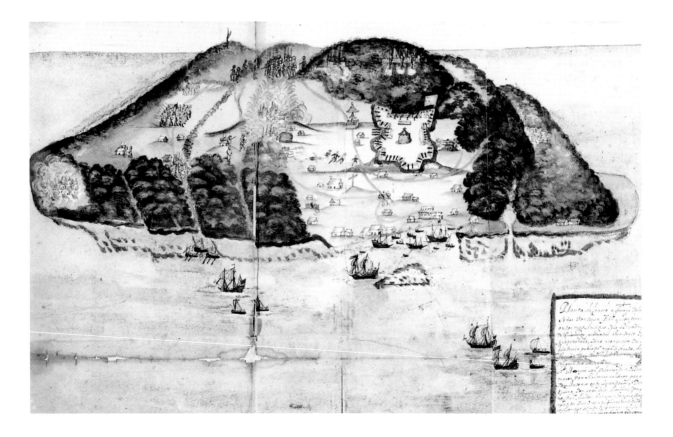

many of whom turned to piracy instead of hunting. A second Spanish attack devastated the poorly defended island in 1638. The French contingent applied to the governor of Saint Christopher for help, and in 1642 he sent a new governor, Jean le Vasseur. A skilled engineer, le Vasseur built a stone fortress overlooking the harbour with over 40 guns, and he encouraged the buccaneers to use the island as a base by providing them with letters of marque. Exasperated by this thorn in their side, the Spanish launched a third expedition against the island in February 1654. Equipped with a siege battery, 700 Spanish troops captured the fort and its buccaneer garrison, who were sent to France under parole. Hoping that the Spanish had abandoned the island, three buccaneer ships returned in August, but found that the Spaniards had already installed a garrison. The Spanish troops were withdrawn a year later when an English invasion of Hispaniola threatened the capital of Santo Domingo. The buccaneers reoccupied Tortuga in 1655 and continued to use it as a base until 1665, when it became part of the new French colony of Saint Domingue. Bertrand d'Ogeron was appointed the island's French governor, and like his predecessors he encouraged buccaneering as a form of defence for the island. Buccaneers such as Jean 'L'Olonnais' Nau used the island as a base during the 1660s, but by 1670 its popularity was on the wane, replaced by the Saint Domingue colony of Petit Goâve, although some buccaneers continued to use it as a base for another decade.

When the English Commonwealth expedition to capture Hispaniola failed, its commanders looked around for a less well-defended alternative. In May 1655, they landed at Cagway on Jamaica, a bay close to the Spanish capital of Santiago de la Vega. The Spanish defenders were brushed aside, and the capital capitulated the same day. The rest of the island fell within a few weeks, giving England a useful base in the heart of the Spanish Main. Cagway was on the south side of the island and formed a large and deep natural harbour protected from the sea by a spit of land. The English quickly established a fortification on Cagway spit, and by 1660 the settlement that grew around it was given the name 'Port Royal'. Governor d'Oyley feared a Spanish counter-invasion, so in 1658 he adopted a policy that encouraged English buccaneers to base themselves in Jamaica by offering them a safe haven and letters of marque. Cagway (or Port Royal) was well located for raids on the Spanish Main, and it soon grew into a bustling port, providing a market for stolen cargoes and plundered valuables. By the mid-1660s, dozens of buccaneer ships were based in Port Royal, their crews augmented by discharged veteran soldiers. Even after an uneasy peace was declared between England and Spain, Lord Windsor, the governor

Morgan's buccaneers in Port Royal, 1668. Although it formed the capital of the English colony of Jamaica, Port Royal was virtually abandoned to the buccaneers. A visiting clergyman reported that 'since the majority of its population consists of pirates, cut-throats, whores and some of the vilest persons in the whole of the world, I felt my permanence there was of no use'. (Angus McBride © Osprey Publishing Ltd)

of Jamaica installed after the 1660 Restoration, continued to promote Port Royal as a buccaneer base and encouraged attacks on the Spanish as an aggressive form of defence for the colony. Christopher Myngs used Port Royal as a base for his attack on Santiago de Cuba in 1662, and although Lord Windsor's replacement, Sir Thomas Modyford, publicly denounced attacks on the Spanish, he privately encouraged them. During his tenure as governor, Port Royal thrived, playing host to buccaneers such as Henry Morgan, John Morris and David Martien.

Buccaneering in Jamaica reached a peak in the 1660s, when profits from Morgan's raids made Port Royal a boom-town of over 6,000 people, and buccaneering had become the island's principal source of revenue. Some successful commanders such as Morgan purchased plantations on the profits of raids against the Spanish Main, and investors and merchants thrived on the plunder brought into the town. Port Royal was a lawless place, with one in every five buildings containing 'brothels, gaming houses, taverns and grog shops'; it was, according to one righteous visitor, the 'Sodom of the New World'. A clergyman claimed, 'its population consists of pirates, cut-throats, whores and some of the vilest persons in the whole of the world'. By the 1680s, the boom had passed, and laws prohibiting buccaneering and piracy were introduced and

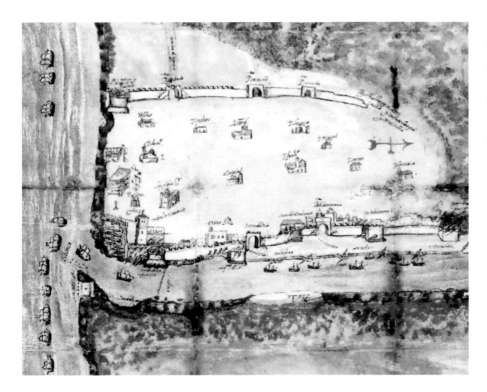

The city of Santo Domingo on the southern coast of Hispaniola had once been an important settlement, but by the 17th century its wealth had gone. Although its governor tried to drive the early buccaneers from Hispaniola, he succeeded only in encouraging them to take to the seas. (Stratford Archive)

enforced. In 1692, Port Royal was struck by a devastating earthquake, and much of the port collapsed into the sea, a disaster from which it never recovered. Some saw the calamity as divine justice for 'that wicked and rebellious place, Port Royal'.

The development of the French colony of Saint Domingue provided the French buccaneers with their own reasonably secure base. While the French governor of the colony and most of the military garrison and colonial administrators were based in the small port of Petit Goâve, the administration spent much of its time and energy developing the northern portion of the colony, and the southern settlement was left to its own devices. This suited the buccaneers, and by 1660 they had established their own armed base in the settlement's sheltered harbour. Sited at the south-eastern corner of the Gulf of Logane, the port was protected by a fort, garrisoned by both buccaneers and local militia and armed with guns captured from Spanish ships or towns. The French governor of Saint Domingue during the late 1670s and early 1680s, Jacques Pouançay, actively encouraged the buccaneers with a stream of privateering commissions and letters of marque in return for help in the defence of the colony. The same policy was also initially adopted by his successor, Pierre-Paul Tarin de Cussy, when he took over control of the colony in 1685. This encouragement ended when the French crown demanded that de Cussy call a halt to the attacks of French buccaneers on Spanish settlements, although the buccaneers still helped him defend the colony. Many buccaneers drifted away, and the settlement staggered on pursuing its legal, although unprofitable, course until a fresh war with Spain allowed the buccaneers to legitimately attack the Spanish once again. Buccaneers assisted de Cussy in resisting a Spanish invasion in 1691, and hundreds of them died with the governor when the Spanish defeated the small French force in battle. The replacement governor, Jean-Baptiste Ducasse, had once served as town governor of Petit Goâve and was a former buccaneer, but even he was unable to prevent the settlement's steady decline as a buccaneering centre. When Ducasse led the Saint Domingue buccaneers in the raid on Cartagena in 1697, it marked the end of a chapter for the port. Peace with Spain brought an end to buccaneering, and the remaining buccaneers either took up legal trading or quit the colony and became pirates. In its heyday during the 1680s, Petit Goâve played host to dozens of buccaneering ships and hundreds of buccaneers. By 1700, it had become a sleepy French colonial backwater.

BUCCANEER PLUNDER

From the first raids on the Spanish colonies in America during the 16th century, the Spanish Main was regarded as a veritable treasure house by other European

This unusual chart shows the Spanish treasure-fleet anchorage of Portobelo (originally Porto Bello) as it looked in 1688 – 20 years after Sir Henry Morgan sacked the port. The bay is still dominated by two large forts – one on either side of the anchorage. Original in the Archivo de Indias, Seville. (Stratford Archive)

powers. Although the flow of silver and gold from the New World to Spain was drying up during the late 17th century, the treasure produced by the mines in Peru and Mexico provided a tempting target for the buccaneers. Silver production at Potosi, the richest silver mine in the world, reached its peak in 1600 at nine million pesos a year. By 1700, this had dropped to a mere two million pesos a year, and the decline was repeated in silver mines throughout Central and South America. The silver that actually reached Spain was less still, as money was absorbed for the defence of the treasure fleet and the ports of the Spanish Main, by corruption and increasingly by the rising cost of mining and production.

To the buccaneers, there was still enough silver to go around. By 1660, much of this silver was shipped in coin form, almost exclusively in pesos. Where the denomination of silver was measured in reals, a peso was an eight-real piece and contained exactly one ounce of silver. These eight-real coins (or pesos) became the 'pieces-of-eight' of pirate literature. To give some indication of value, the average seaman's wage in 1660 was just six pesos a month, while a Spanish naval captain earned 24 pesos. Measured in these terms, the hauls made by the buccaneers during the late 17th century were truly phenomenal, and had a catastrophic inflationary effect on the fragile Spanish economy.

De Graaf's capture of a single warship carrying military pay in 1682 produced 120,000 pesos, to be shared among his crew of 100 men. Morgan's raid on Porto Bello in 1668 netted twice that amount, but the money was shared among just under 500 buccaneers. His raid into Lake Maracaibo the following year produced a similar quantity of silver, and although the sack of Panama produced disappointing results, the haul was probably equally substantial, except that it had to be shared among 1,200 men. As the buccaneers looted personal possessions as well as money, ports such as Port Royal and Petit Goâve became trading centres for luxury goods, and plundered valuables were sold on to traders who shipped them to Europe or even sold them back to the Spanish. By 1680, the English colony of Jamaica was bringing in an income of 750,000 pesos a year through buccaneering raids and her plantations, and Spanish currency was so common on the streets of Port Royal that the authorities acknowledged the peso as legal tender. The last great raid against Cartagena in 1697 brought an end to almost 50 years of plundering on the Spanish Main, but for the Spanish the end came too late. By 1700, a combination of inflation and the devastation wrought by buccaneering raids had plunged the Spanish empire into an economic decline from which it never recovered.

The buccaneering stronghold of Tortuga was first occupied by the Dutch in the early 17th century. This chart of the island dated 1628 depicts an abortive Spanish attack on the island's fortress. The Spanish returned ten years later and drove the buccaneers from the island. Original in the Archivo de Indias, Seville. (Stratford Archive)

BUCCANEERING SHIPS

The earliest buccaneers took to piracy using piraguas or small fishing boats and pinnaces, operating close to the shore of Hispaniola. Although the buccaneers used larger vessels from the 1640s, these small craft were still used extensively throughout the period during raids on Spanish ports. They performed a role similar to modern landing craft, transporting the buccaneers from a secluded anchorage where they would hide their larger ships to a landing site close to the port they wanted to attack. Canoes often formed part of the plans of Henry Morgan, who used them during attacks on Tabasco (1665), Granada (1665), Porto Bello (1668) and the advance on Panama (1670–71). During the first of these, Morgan's men returned from their attack on the provincial capital of Villahermosa to find that the Spanish Navy had captured their ships while they were away raiding. After driving off the local militia, Morgan and his men escaped in two small coastal trading pinnaces.

Unlike a piragua, which could only hold six to ten men, the pinnace was a more substantial vessel of between ten and 60 tons (discussed in more detail on pages 124–125). It was fitted with oars, although it also carried a single mast and a jib sheet and mainsail. Pinnaces were used as tenders for larger ships, and buccaneer vessels often towed a pinnace behind them, allowing them to operate closer inshore than the draught of the larger boat allowed. These were ideal buccaneering craft for raids, as they could carry up to 60 men. Most ships also carried longboats, which

were smaller versions of pinnaces, capable of holding 40 men, and were also oar powered and fitted with a detachable mast if required. A buccaneering ship on its way to conduct a raid would therefore give the appearance of some kind of 17th-century amphibious landing ship, her decks crammed with longboats and canoes, with possibly more longboats and a pinnace being towed behind her. In several raids undertaken close to a home port, pinnaces accompanied the main vessels of the expedition under their own sail. For example, de Grammont and de Graaf's attack on Vera Cruz (1683) was undertaken with a fleet of five buccaneering ships accompanied by eight lesser craft (presumably pinnaces).

Each buccaneer captain had his own ship, and crews signed on for particular ventures. Similarly, entire ships and crews signed on with buccaneer commanders to undertake a major raid. Men such as de Grammont and de Graaf maintained a following, often acting as the leader for buccaneering captains and their crews of a particular nationality or from a particular port. The way these captains acquired their ships is exemplified by de Graaf's method of improving the ships he commanded: 'From a small bark he took a small ship; from this a bigger one, until at last there came into his power one of 24 to 28 guns.' The buccaneer continued the process by capturing even larger Spanish warships of 30, then 40, guns. This process could be taken to extremes. During the last cruise of L'Olonnais in 1668, he acquired the prestigious prize of a small Spanish galleon, although it was such a 'heavy sailer' that

The Spanish thought their rich settlements on the Pacific coast of South America were safe from attack. However, in 1682 the English buccaneer Bartholomew Sharpe penetrated into the 'Great South Sea' and so opened the way for subsequent expeditions. This chart by William Hack dates from 1685. (Stratford Archive)

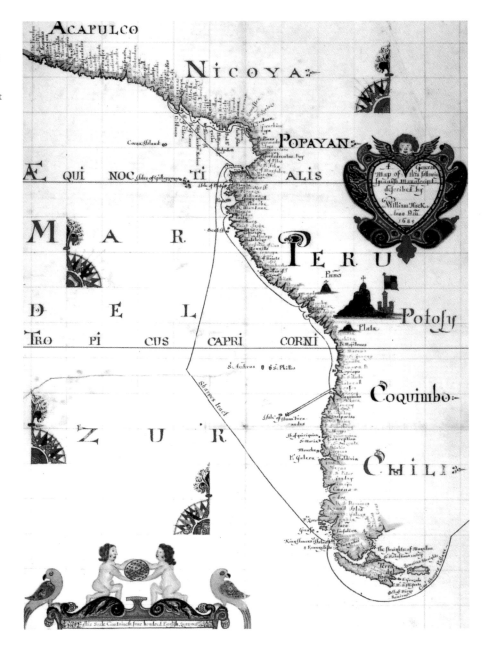

it was difficult to operate in the light winds and treacherous waters found off the Honduran coast, and it ran aground. Like the pirates of the early 18th century, while some sought prestigious flagships, others preferred smaller vessels which combined speed with manoeuvrability. A buccaneer fleet would therefore contain an assortment of vessels, ranging from small pinnaces to medium-sized warships, although barks and small two-masted vessels would predominate.

The End of the Buccaneers

Several factors contributed to the end of the buccaneering era. The English, French and Dutch had all been at war with the Spanish for much of the 17th century, but for the English this ended in 1670. Local governors such as Sir Thomas Modyford of Jamaica found it impossible to lend their support to buccaneering raids, either officially or otherwise. Henry Morgan's attack on Panama in 1670–71 marked a transition, as it occurred after the 1670 Treaty of Madrid brought peace with Spain, and both Modyford and Morgan eventually faced charges levelled in order to placate the Spanish. By the time Morgan returned to Jamaica in 1674, England was at peace with the French and Dutch, and the constant stream of letters of marque had dried up. Clearly, if English buccaneers wanted to continue their actions, they would have to sign on with foreign commanders. Anti-piracy laws were introduced to Jamaica in 1681, making it virtually impossible to use Port Royal as a base. English buccaneers such as John Coxton and Edmond Cooke raided the Pacific coast of the Spanish empire, attacking coastal ports in Peru during the 1680s, but they sailed under French colours. After 1670, the buccaneering torch had been passed to the French.

Based in Saint Domingue, French buccaneers continued their raids on the Spanish Main, assisted by France's belligerent posture towards Spain. Since 1635, the two countries had been at war almost continually, with only four periods of relative peace from 1659 to 1667; 1668 to 1674; 1679 to 1683; and again from 1684 to 1689. Relative peace in Europe meant open hostility in the Caribbean, and the 1670s and 1680s saw a period when French buccaneers conducted some of their largest raids: Maracaibo (1678), Vera Cruz (1683) and Campeche (1685), irrespective of whether the two countries were at war. A succession of French governors in Saint Domingue regarded the buccaneers as the best form of defence for the colony and an excellent source of revenue. The end came with the Peace of Ryswick in 1697. The buccaneers felt betrayed by the French government following their treatment during the attack on Cartagena in 1697, and no more large-scale buccaneer raids were ever attempted. Instead, former buccaneers turned to legal activities or piracy. When the War of the Spanish Succession (1701–14) broke out, many former buccaneers became privateers, but operated independently. The great buccaneering fleets became a thing of the past.

Pirates
1660–1730

The Pirate Crew   74

Pirate Warfare   79

Pirate Dens   84

Pirate Plunder   87

Pirate Captains and Characters   88

The Pirate Ship   107

Pirate Codes   146

Pirate Flags   151

Pirate Justice   157

Which Shall be Captain? This painting by Howard Pyle appeared in *Harper's Monthly Magazine* in January 1911. Given the democratic code enjoyed by pirates, leadership contests of this sort were surprisingly uncommon and were usually settled by straightforward elections. (Stratford Archive)

The Pirate Crew

The largest source of information on the composition of pirate crews comes from court records, although a survey of seamen and a number of personal memoirs and letters also provide valuable information. A study of 700 men indicted for piracy during the early 17th century reveals that almost three-quarters were seamen. Another analysis of early 18th-century pirates shows the overwhelming majority had previously served on board merchant vessels, warships or privateers. They were therefore almost always experienced seamen and came from a variety of seafaring nations, although most were either English or from the American colonies. The historian David Cordingly published a study indicating that of the known pirates active in the Caribbean between 1715 and 1725, 35 per cent were English, 25 per cent colonial Americans, 20 per cent from the West Indian colonies (mainly Jamaica and Barbados), ten per cent were Scottish and eight per cent were Welsh. The remaining two per cent were from other seafaring countries, such as Sweden, Holland, France or Spain. As seamen, the majority came from port cities, such as London, Bristol, Leith, Swansea and the West Country in the British Isles, or Boston, New York or Charleston in the American

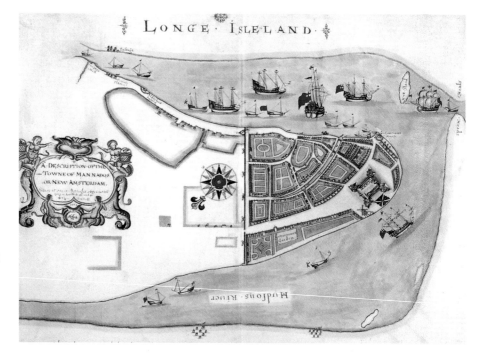

This English version of an earlier Dutch map shows the city of New Amsterdam soon after the English took control of it, when they renamed it New York in 1664. A range of shipping can be seen at anchor, including warships, coastal trading sloops and pinnaces and a few larger merchant vessels. Studies show that the majority of pirates were seamen who came from port cities such as New York. (Stratford Archive)

In the western side of the Caribbean the prevailing winds meant that ships from Jamaica, Honduras or the Spanish Main usually had to round the western corner of Cuba and then sail through the Florida Straits before returning to Europe. This made the area another prime hunting ground for pirates. Detail from a mid-17th-century chart. (Stratford Archive)

colonies. The majority of seamen in the early 18th century were young men in their 20s, with an average age for seaman and pirate alike of 27. The stamina, fitness and agility required to work a sailing ship precluded many older men from crewing a vessel.

A large percentage of pirate crews were also black men of African descent. An account of the crew of Bartholomew Roberts in 1721 reported that they were composed of 180 white men and 48 'French Creole' black men. When his crew were captured by the Royal Navy off West Africa, the prisoners comprised 187 white and 75 black men. Many of these black men were escaped slaves from the West Indies plantations, although a number were volunteers from captured slave ships. As the racial composition contradicts that encountered in merchant or

OPPOSITE William Kidd burying his treasure on Long Island. He is wearing the dress of a gentleman captain as befits his social station. His crewmen are dressed in the standard sailor's garb of 'petticoat' breeches and a linen shirt. (Angus McBride © Osprey Publishing Ltd)

naval ships of the early 18th century, it has to be assumed that the majority of these black men were 'landsmen'. This begs the question of what exactly their role was on board a ship crewed by professional seamen. While a number of historians argue that they served on an equal footing with white men, there is a large body of evidence to suggest that they were regarded as servants, used to carry out heavy or menial tasks on board the pirate vessel. As familiarity and experience grew, these black men may have enjoyed a more integrated relationship with the crew. According to trial transcripts, a number of integrated crews existed, where Africans were considered full crew members. These men had the most to lose by capture, knowing that if they were not hanged they would be enslaved. A number of Africans, including escaped plantation slaves as well as new arrivals, did succeed in becoming pirates in their own right. One exaggerated Jamaican newspaper article of 1725 reported bands of African and African-American pirates marauding the Caribbean and eating the hearts of the white men they captured.

MOTIVATION

The majority became pirates when their merchant vessels were captured, and they elected to join the pirate crew. While landsmen would be killed or put ashore, seamen often had no choice but to sign a charter and join the crew. Many of the more successful pirates started their piratical careers in this manner. Another common route was for privateering crews to turn to piracy. The profits of war encouraged men to become privateers, and subsequently, when peace returned, this caused massive unemployment among the maritime communities of Europe, the Caribbean or the Americas. Although execution was the expected punishment and life expectancy was short, piracy was an attractive alternative to dying of starvation or becoming a beggar or thief on land.

The attraction of a pirate's life was financial: the benefit of all that hard work went to the men themselves. A seaman's life was gruelling, and often involved an existence of constant dampness and discomfort, poor conditions and ever-present danger. Drinking water was usually foul and food was often rotten and insufficient. Half of all sailors' deaths were caused by disease, ranging from scurvy to typhus, tuberculosis, dysentery and smallpox. New ports meant exposure to fresh diseases, and ships were the perfect incubators for illness, with men sleeping and working in close quarters. Unlike sailors on naval or merchant vessels, pirates and privateers at least had the promise of huge financial rewards to make up for all the hardship.

DRESS

Pirates were seamen, and their appearance was the same as that of other seamen of the early 18th century. While 'landsmen' of the period wore knee breeches, stockings, sleeved or sleeveless waistcoats and long coats, seamen wore their own distinctive attire. Short jackets ('fearnoughts') were popular, often cut from a heavy blue or grey cloth, and in bad weather heavier canvas coats were sometimes worn. Some illustrations show sailors of the period wearing a form of waistcoat (red or blue), either sleeved or sleeveless. Shirts were either plain linen or checked, frequently in blue and white. Knee breeches were replaced by canvas trousers or 'petticoat breeches', cut a few inches above the ankle, resembling the culottes of the French Revolution. These were reportedly cut from a 'heavy, rough red nap'. Both forms of trousers were sometimes coated in a thin layer of tar as protection against water. Shoes were often discarded altogether on board ship, although a pair would be reserved for visits ashore. If stockings were worn, grey wool was the usual form for seamen of the day. A neck scarf was commonly worn, reflecting a style common with labourers on land during the early 18th century. Headgear consisted of either a knotted scarf, a tricorne hat, a woollen 'Monmouth' cap, or a form of foul-weather hat resembling a 17th-century 'montero' cap. Headgear was of vital importance as protection against the sun in the Caribbean or off the African or Indian coasts.

As well as plundering the cargo of a captured vessel, pirates would also take clothing, retaining what suited them either to wear at sea or as a suit of shore-going finery. There are records of pirates facing execution wearing velvet jackets, breeches of taffeta, silk shirts and stockings, and fine felt tricornes. These were probably taken from captives or made from plundered materials. Even in the austere navy of the time, sailors retained well-kept clothes to wear when in port. It appears from several accounts that many pirates also wore their finery when they were at sea.

Pirate captains frequently adopted the dress worn by successful merchants, giving the wearer the appearance of a gentleman. This meant wearing breeches, a waistcoat and a long outer coat. Both contemporary accounts and later illustrations support the evidence for the adoption of this gentlemanly persona. One pirate captain based on Madagascar was described in 1716 as 'dressed in a short coat, with broad plate buttons, and other things agreeable, but without shoes or stockings'. The leader in piratical elegance was Bartholomew Roberts, who, according to Johnson and contemporary accounts by his crew, 'dressed in a rich crimson damask waistcoat and breeches, a red feather in his hat, a gold chain round his neck, with a diamond cross hanging to it' (see illustration page 105).

Pirate Warfare

A successful pirate attack began with finding the quarry, and then attacking it. A typical pirate sloop with a look-out at the masthead could expect to see a sailing vessel up to 20 miles away, if the conditions were right. Unlike a naval squadron, which could string ships out in a line and thereby search a large swathe of ocean, pirate vessels often operated alone. On the rare occasions when secondary pirate vessels or prize vessels were available, they could be pressed into service to help in the search. At night, or in poor weather conditions, finding another ship was well nigh impossible. Pirates also needed to be able to identify a vessel as quickly as possible once they found it. Warships were to be avoided – in the worst cases they might be part of a larger force located over the horizon, sweeping for enemy ships or pirates.

Pirates usually operated in cruising grounds that lay across major shipping routes. The waters of the Bahamas were popular as they lay close to the narrow

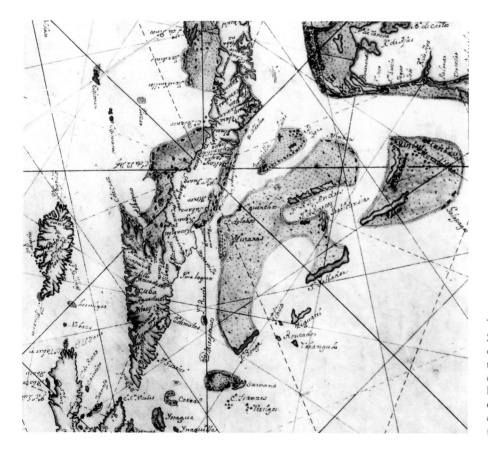

The Bahamas, from a detail of a Spanish chart dated 1747. In the original, west was at the top of the map, with Cuba running down the centre. The pirate base of New Providence (marked 'Providensia' on this chart) is shown in the centre of the Bahamas archipelago. (Stratford Archive)

Florida Straits, and the Bahamian shoals provided a good refuge if pursued. The Windward Passage between Cuba and Hispaniola was another popular cruising area, as were the waters off Madagascar, the West African coast and the seaboard of the American colonies. Pirates often followed seasonal patterns, preferring the Caribbean in winter and the Atlantic seaboard in summer.

Once sighted, the potential armament and crew numbers of the quarry needed to be accurately estimated, along with the vessel's speed, sailing abilities and the quality of her captain. These factors were vital in determining whether the vessel could be overhauled without requiring a long chase. Once sighted and evaluated, the quarry had to be overhauled. This is why the majority of pirate crews preferred small, fast vessels such as sloops and schooners, which often had the edge over a quarry in terms of speed. In order to close within gun range, the pirate vessel also sometimes employed trickery. The use of false flags was fairly common, the hunter trying to lull the hunted into a false sense of security. Another pirate trick was to disguise a vessel by covering the gun ports with a painted canvas screen, or to add impedimenta, like chicken coops, deck cargo or even female passengers in order to get close enough to attack. Similarly, many merchant vessels painted fake gun ports on their sides to make their vessels look like warships and to scare the pirates off.

Once within range, the pirate vessel would usually haul down any false colours, haul up her own, and demand that the quarry surrender by firing a gun. At closer range, this would be accompanied by demands yelled between the ships with the aid of a speaking trumpet. It was well known that any form of resistance could lead to a wholesale slaughter once the pirates captured the defending ship. This meant that intimidation was a major weapon in the pirate arsenal. A victim was then often asked to lower her boats and ferry over a pirate prize crew. A typical assault was recounted by the captain of the merchant ship *Samuel*, attacked by Bartholomew Roberts in 1721. The *Samuel* was overhauled by two ships off the Newfoundland Banks. The larger vessel was a three-masted ship armed with 26 guns. There were about 100 men on board each of the vessels, and only ten on the *Samuel*. Once overhauled, the *Samuel's* captain was ordered to lower a boat and come on board. The pirates then boarded the *Samuel*, took part of her cargo, threw the rest overboard, took the ship's boat and two guns, and press-ganged most of the crew. They were debating whether to burn the prize or not when another sail was spotted, and the pirates gave chase, leaving the *Samuel's* captain and one crewman to sail the ship back to Boston. This was typical of the majority of pirate attacks, where no resistance was offered.

If the quarry tried to defend itself, the pirates were forced to decide how best to overcome the defending vessel. Obviously, the pirates would prefer to capture a victim by boarding rather than by gunfire, which could damage their potential prize. Also, intimidation was a double-edged weapon, as fear of reprisals when captured would increase the ferocity of the defence. The mechanics of attack by gunfire or boarding were straightforward, although effectiveness greatly depended on skill, experience and (at least for the pirates) sobriety.

ATTACK USING GUNFIRE

In the early 18th century, even the smallest merchant vessel carried artillery pieces (guns). To be correct, a cannon referred only to a specific size and type of ordnance. By the late 17th century, cast-iron had replaced bronze as the most common material used to manufacture ordnance, making guns cheaper and easier to produce than before. The wars of the late 17th and early 18th centuries meant that arming a vessel was a necessity. It also meant that most sailors were proficient to some extent in operating guns at sea.

A four-wheeled truck carriage was universally adopted by the late 17th century, which allowed the pieces to be rolled easily back for reloading. The simple but effective elevating system of quoin and stool bed was efficient enough for use at sea. Gun tools such as worm, rammer, sponge and ladle would have been kept beside each gun, ready for action, while powder charges were brought up from the ship's magazine. A 4-pdr, the typical gun size on a small sloop or schooner, could fire a roundshot about 1,000 yards. Larger vessels such as Bartholomew Roberts' *Royal Fortune* carried a more substantial armament. Among her armament she carried four 12-pdrs, 20 8-pdrs and a number of smaller pieces (6-pdrs and 4-pdrs).

By the late 17th century, naval warfare followed a standard pattern. Ships fired broadsides of roundshot at each other, and then boarded the enemy if they still refused to surrender or were badly damaged. If artillery fire was employed, pirates preferred a brief broadside, then tried to exploit the advantage of their superior numbers by boarding 'through the smoke'. In addition to roundshot, which damaged the enemy hull, chain shot (or bar shot) was fired at the enemy's rigging, which cut down the sails and with it, the ability to escape. Grapeshot was fired at close range in order to disable the enemy crew. Knowing what ammunition to load and when was vital to success in warfare at sea. It also helped avoid unnecessary damage to the potential prize.

Henry Every and the crew of the pirate vessel *Fancy* boarding the treasure ship of the Great Moghul of India, the *Gang-i-sawai*, in 1694. One of the most successful pirate prizes ever captured, the *Gang-i-sawai* yielded a fortune in gold, silver, jewels, spices, silks and ornaments. (Angus McBride © Osprey Publishing Ltd)

ATTACK BY BOARDING

Once the ships were alongside each other, the pirates would either fire or throw over grappling hooks to pull the two ships together. This in itself was a skill, as the vessels were likely to damage each other's rigging if they were grappled in the wrong way. The preferred method was to grapple from stern to stern, pulling the ships together at the point that ensured minimal risk to rigging and provided the largest possible area in which to fight. Once the pirates swung aboard, a fierce hand-to-hand fight would ensue. Popular weapons were muskets, blunderbusses and pistols, but swords and cutlasses would also be carried, and even pikes, axes and belaying pins. A pirate favourite was the grenade. In an action between two government sloops and a pirate vessel off Jamaica in 1718, the pirates 'threw vast numbers of powder flasks, grenado shells and stinkpots into her which killed and wounded several and made others jump overboard'. *Grenados* (grenades) derived their name from the Spanish *granada* (pomegranate).

Pistols were the most popular firearms simply because they were so compact. Edward Teach ('Blackbeard') is reported to have carried three pairs of pistols, as well as a sword and a knife, and others carried pistols tied with silk cords to prevent them being dropped overboard during the fight. A pistol recovered from the wreck of Samuel Bellamy's pirate ship *Whydah*, wrecked in 1717, was wrapped in its own long, red, silk looped ribbon. Although full-size military muskets were used at sea (especially by ex-privateering vessels), blunderbusses were more popular, firing a blast of scrap-iron and nails into the face of the enemy. When it came to cold steel, the most popular weapon was the cutlass. Manufactured as a cheap but effective cutting weapon, it was related to the earlier English or Scottish broadsword, or later heavy cavalry blades. Although a clumsy weapon in a confined mêlée, it was the maritime sidearm of choice. Naval officers and some merchant captains preferred the more gentlemanly smallsword. A flimsy weapon, it was designed to thrust with the point, and although effective in a confined space, it lacked the robustness of the cutlass. Other edged weapons used in boarding actions were six-foot boarding pikes, ship's axes and hunting swords (hangers). Every seaman also carried a knife and was presumably skilled in using it.

An account of the fight between Lieutenant Maynard of the Royal Navy and Edward Teach ('Blackbeard') illustrates the violent nature of a boarding action:

Maynard and Teach themselves began the fight with their swords, Maynard making a thrust, the point of his sword went against Teach's cartridge box, and bended it to the hilt. Teach broke the guard of it, and wounded Maynard's fingers but did not disable him, whereupon he jumped back and threw away his sword and cut Teach's face pretty much; in the interim both companies engaged in Maynard's sloop, one of Maynard's men being a Highlander, engaged Teach with his broad sword, who gave Teach a cut on the neck, Teach saying well done lad; the Highlander replied, 'If it be not well done, I'll do better.' With that he gave him a second stroke, which cut off his head, laying it flat on his shoulder.

Pirate Dens

At various times throughout the golden age, piratical bases were formed, providing a safe haven to repair ships, divide plunder and hide from pursuers. The requirements were usually that a base needed to be close to shipping routes, difficult to attack and preferably contain a suitable market for the sale of stolen cargoes. The following locations all provided these facilities during the era.

PORT ROYAL

During the latter half of the 17th century, the city of Port Royal, Jamaica, formed the main buccaneering base in the Caribbean. As mentioned previously, in its heyday it was described as a notorious den of vice, full of taverns, brothels, gambling dens and stores of plundered booty. Between 1655 and 1680, the buccaneers of Port Royal plundered hundreds of Spanish ships and raided scores of Spanish towns and cities. Peace brought an end to the buccaneering era, and a devastating earthquake in 1692 destroyed much of the city. By the 1700s, a strong island government and increasing legitimate profits from sugar made it an unsuitable base for pirates. The Royal Navy maintained a naval base at Port Royal, and the city changed from a buccaneering den to become the base for anti-piracy operations in the Caribbean.

NEW PROVIDENCE

Located close to major American and Caribbean trade routes, the island contained a good natural harbour which was difficult for large warships to enter. It was arid and sparsely settled, although it offered fresh water, timber and wild animals. This natural pirate haven was nominally the capital of the British Bahamas, and the small town there was named Nassau in 1695. Until 1717, local governors accepted bribes to leave the growing number of pirates alone. From the 1680s, it had been used as a small-scale privateering and pirate base, but Spanish raids from 1703 to 1706 made the island untenable. Peace with Spain brought the pirates back in 1716, led by Henry Jennings. The next year, over 500 pirates used the island as a base, including Edward Teach, Charles Vane, Jack Rackam and Benjamin Hornigold. The island economy thrived through trade with the pirates, but word of the haven reached the authorities in London. The British government decided to break up the pirate base, and in July 1718 the newly appointed governor, Woodes Rogers, arrived with three warships. Many of the pirates fled, although Vane fired on the governor as he sailed away. Other pirates gave up their piratical careers. When the warships left, Rogers appointed Hornigold as his main pirate hunter, and a mass pirate hanging in December showed the world that the governor meant business. Without piracy, the island returned to being a backwater, and although Woodes Rogers continued to try to develop the Bahamas, New Providence never regained its former economic vibrancy. Rogers died in Nassau in 1732.

THE CAROLINAS

Although never a true pirate haven, the presence of a colonial government willing to turn a blind eye to trade with pirates made the Carolinas on the American mainland a possible successor to New Providence. When Woodes Rogers threw the pirates out of the Bahamas, the inlets and rivers of the Carolinas appeared to provide a suitable safe haven. Proximity to shipping routes and a ready local market for plunder were other important factors. Edward Teach led the way by establishing a base at Ocracoke, near Bath Towne. Subsequent piratical visitors to the area,

LEFT After blockading Charles Town (now Charleston, SC), Blackbeard established a new pirate lair on Ocracoke Island, in the Outer Banks (incorrectly marked 'Raonack' in this detail of a French chart dated 1718). The lack of widespread knowledge about this isolated piece of coastline suited Blackbeard perfectly. (Stratford Archive)

RIGHT During the late 17th and early 18th centuries, the island of Madagascar in the Indian Ocean became a pirate haven. From their bases in the north-eastern corner of the island, pirates preyed on East India Company ships sailing between India and the Cape of Good Hope. This chart dates from the late 17th century. (Stratford Archive)

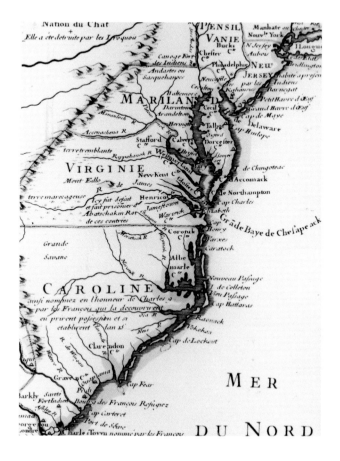

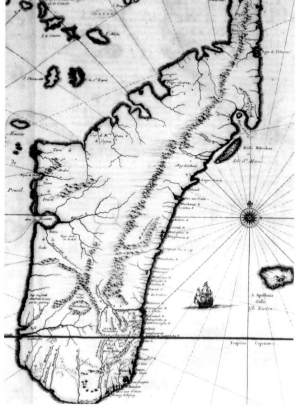

including Stede Bonnet and Charles Vane, led to fears among ship owners that North Carolina would become a nest of pirates. Prompt action by the governors of the neighbouring colonies of Virginia and South Carolina nipped the problem in the bud. Following the death of Edward Teach and the removal of the governor of North Carolina, harsh laws were introduced preventing any trade with known pirates.

MADAGASCAR

Madagascar in the Indian Ocean lay close to the profitable trade routes between India, the Middle East and Europe. From the 1690s, privateers of various nationalities used the island as a base, and by the end of the century it too was known as a pirate haven. With no European power willing to subdue the local population, the island was wide open, and its long coastline provided numerous suitable harbours. The end of the buccaneering era in the Caribbean prompted a growing number of mariners to relocate to the Indian Ocean. Naval expeditions in the 1690s failed to eradicate the pirate settlements, and the ejection of pirates from New Providence led to many establishing a base in Madagascar, including Christopher Condent and Edward England. By the 1720s, a permanent Royal Navy presence in the Indian Ocean made piracy a risky venture. Many former pirates chose to settle on the island rather than to return home.

A group of pirates burying their treasure, a representation of a pirate group operating in the Caribbean in the early 19th century. Of particular interest is the depiction of an African-American crew member. Despite its popularity in pirate fiction, accounts of pirates burying their plunder are extremely rare. (Stratford Archive)

Pirate Plunder

Pirates rarely found ships full of coin chests. In early 18th-century America and the Caribbean, coined money was in short supply, and what was in circulation was rarely standardized. Settlers brought little cash with them, and no mint was established in America until after the War of Independence. Trade between colonists and pirates such as Edward Teach brought much needed currency, and pirates found a ready market for their stolen merchandise. Coins of all nations circulated freely, and each merchant had to be his own exchange broker. Although a fictional character, a pirate in Robert Louis Stevenson's *Treasure Island* owned a notebook with a table for converting French, English and Spanish coinage, so the problem was well known. The problem was that most pirate victims didn't carry much money. Trading vessels in American or Caribbean waters carried cargoes such as sugar or rum from Jamaica, tobacco from the Carolinas, wood from Central America or manufactured goods from Europe. Other common cargoes included furs, ore, cotton or slaves. Ships carrying substantial quantities of money were rare and frequently well protected.

The slave trade was at its height. The triangular trade between Europe, Africa and the Americas was a highly profitable one, and attacks on slave ships could reap large rewards, depending on the leg of the voyage on which the ship was captured. Trade goods such as pewter or iron from England were less profitable prizes than slavers captured off the African coast, which could contain slaves, gold, ivory and spices. Once the slaves were sold, the ship would load up with rum or sugar for her return voyage to Europe.

Every attack on a slave ship yielded a different result. Pirate crews who subscribed to the ideals of a free and democratic society might welcome Africans as equals and teach them to become sailors. Less idealistic pirates used the Africans for labour, treating them as slaves or servants to the other seamen, but usually affording them some share of the booty. Greedier pirates felt no sympathy for their plight, and sold them to the plantations, just as their original shippers had planned. Rum was another welcome cargo. The theme of drinking is interwoven with the pirate image, and frequently the capture of vessels carrying alcohol resulted in unbridled drinking bouts.

Pirate Captains and Characters

This sample of some of the most prominent pirates provides a useful insight into a number of areas, such as motivation, how they held a crew together, weaknesses, favoured tactics and, of course, their ultimate fate. What is instantly apparent is just how short even the most famous pirates' careers were. It also strips away many of the myths and romanticism associated with some of the more notorious characters.

EDWARD TEACH ('BLACKBEARD')

Period of activity: September 1717 to November 1718 (15 months)
Probably the most famous pirate of them all, Blackbeard became a legend following his extravagant biography in Johnson's history. By ignoring Johnson's misleading demonic portrayal of Blackbeard and relying instead on contemporary sources, an accurate portrait can be sketched of this infamous character. A victim in 1717 described him as 'a tall, spare man with a very black beard which he wore very long'. He was apparently broad-shouldered and, according to his nemesis Lieutenant Maynard, he tied his beard up with black ribbons. Johnson's account of him wearing a sling over his shoulders with three brace of pistols is probably accurate, given the limited effectiveness of firearms at sea in the period. A natural authority figure, Blackbeard was obviously intelligent and both socially and politically astute.

Blackbeard's real name is uncertain: Teach, Thatch or even Tache have all been used. The most common and likely version is Edward Teach. He was born in Bristol, but at some stage during his teens he took a passage to the West Indies, and served in Jamaican-based privateers during the War of the Spanish Succession (1701–14). After the war, he found his way to New Providence in the Bahamas. There he encountered the pirate Benjamin Hornigold, who signed Teach on as a crewman. He learned the trade of piracy quickly, and soon set off on his own, after being given a captured slaver by Hornigold, which was renamed the *Queen Anne's Revenge*. He rapidly gained a reputation as bloodthirsty. Based in New Providence, he operated in the West Indies, capturing several vessels. Johnson recorded a sea battle with the frigate HMS *Scarborough*, but there are no official records to support this. With the imminent arrival of Governor Rogers in the Bahamas, a new pirate base had to be found to replace New Providence.

Teach sailed for the Carolinas, arriving at Bath Towne, North Carolina, in January 1718. Establishing a base on nearby Ocracoke Island, he pillaged passing ships and found a ready market for the plundered goods in the nearby town. A bribe ensured a pardon from Governor Eden, providing safety from prosecution. In March, the pirates sailed round Florida and cruised as far as Honduras, capturing Stede Bonnet and his sloop *Revenge* en route. Adding more vessels to his squadron, he plundered several more ships before returning north. His crew numbered over 400 men. In May 1718, Teach blockaded Charleston, South Carolina, plundering eight vessels and capturing, then ransoming, a prominent citizen in return for a chest of medical supplies. It was rumoured that the crew were suffering from a form of venereal disease. He then returned to Bath Towne, but lost the *Queen Anne's Revenge* on a sandbar.

Teach sold his plunder, bought a house and was granted another pardon by Governor Eden. The governor even rigged the local Admiralty courts, who recognized Teach as the owner of the vessels he had captured during his cruise. However, resentment of this legitimized piracy was growing, and ship owners feared that the area would become an established pirate haven. When Charles Vane visited

Edward Teach with a smoking slowmatch tucked under his hat. His ship is depicted as lying off Ocracoke Inlet, North Carolina, while the crew are shown unloading a stolen cargo. Teach found a ready market for plunder in the nearby settlement of Bath Towne. (Stratford Archive)

Edward Teach, from an engraving in an early edition of Johnson's *Pirates*. His reputation as 'the devil incarnate' was probably only partly deserved, and Johnson clearly exaggerated accounts of the pirate's appearance and actions. The figure is shown carrying three brace of pistols, a Teach characteristic which can be corroborated by contemporary descriptions. (Stratford Archive)

Teach in October, these fears increased. Complaints reached the neighbouring colony of Virginia, and the governor, Alexander Spotswood, vowed to flush out the pirate nest. As the waters around Teach's base at Ocracoke were too shallow for large naval vessels, Spotswood hired two sloops out of his own pocket, filling them with Royal Naval crews from HMS *Pearl* and HMS *Lyme*, both anchored in the James River. Lieutenant Maynard of the Royal Navy was placed in command, 'an experienced officer and a gentleman of great bravery and resolution'.

Arriving off Ocracoke Inlet, Maynard attacked at dawn on Friday, 22 November 1718. Many of the pirates were away in Bath Towne, so with 60 men, Maynard's crew outnumbered the pirates by over three to one. Teach had one sloop, the *Adventure*, which unlike the unnamed attacking ships carried nine guns, and tried to escape through the shallows. In their hurry to pursue, the naval sloops ran aground. According to Maynard's account, Teach yelled, 'Rank Damnation to me and my men, whom he stil'd Cowardly Puppies, saying he would neither give nor take Quarter.' The sloops freed themselves with the rising tide and rowed in pursuit. Teach turned and fired a broadside of grapeshot, killing the midshipman in command of the sloop *Ranger*, and killing or wounding several of her crew. Maynard in the *Jane* fired a bow chaser at the *Adventure*, and a shot cut her jib, forcing her aground. Maynard had hidden most of his men below decks, and Teach decided to board the naval sloop. He came alongside, and as he did the naval crew swarmed on deck. A vicious mêlée ensued, and Maynard and Teach fought each other face-to-face. Maynard wounded Teach with a pistol shot, but broke his own sword, giving Teach the upper hand. Maynard was saved by a Scotsman who decapitated the pirate. The mêlée continued until all the pirates were killed or had surrendered.

Maynard sailed to Bath Towne, repaired his ships and sailed back to Williamsburg, dangling Teach's head from the bowsprit of his sloop. In the subsequent trial, 13 pirates were convicted and hanged, while two were acquitted or reprieved.

ANNE BONNY, MARY READE AND JACK RACKAM ('CALICO JACK')

Period of activity: July 1718 to November 1720 (29 months)

'Calico Jack' was typical of the small-time pirates whose small sloops preyed on coastal shipping. Little is known of his origins, but by 1718 he had somehow made his way to New Providence Island. He served with Vane, fleeing the island when Vane escaped from the new governor, Woodes Rogers. By the spring of 1719, he was elected as quartermaster and became Vane's deputy. Soon after, a quarrel broke out among the crew, and Rackam replaced Vane as a pirate captain. Vane was put ashore, and Rackam continued Vane's cruise in two sloops.

According to some accounts, the vessels were both lost when a Jamaican-based patrol sloop captured them while most of the crew were ashore. Rackam returned to New Providence, and in May 1719 he was granted a pardon by Governor Rogers as part of Rogers' general pirate amnesty. It was there that he met Anne Bonny.

Law-abiding life ashore proved unpalatable, and in August 1719 Rackam stole a sloop named the *William* and returned to piracy. His crew included the female pirates Bonny and Mary Reade. Based in Bahamian waters, he cruised between Bermuda and Hispaniola, capturing several ships and a number of profitable cargoes. He then sailed around Cuba, attacking local craft, before reaching the north coast of Jamaica. There

Anne Bonny, the lover of Jack Rackam. She is depicted baring her breasts (to prove her sex), and is shown wearing a seaman's jacket and canvas trousers. Both Bonny and Reade wore men's clothing when at sea. (Stratford Archive)

Nineteenth-century illustration by Alexandre Debelle for P. Christian's *Histoire des Pirates* (1889) shows Mary Reade revealing her sex to a wounded protagonist after a duel.

his luck ran out. While at anchor off the western tip of the island, he was surprised by a sloop belonging to the governor of Jamaica. Most of Rackam's nine male crew were drunk, but according to testimonies, the women roused them into action. The *William* cut her anchor cable and fled, but was overhauled by the Jamaican sloop during the night. The ships exchanged fire, and then Captain Barnet led a boarding party onto the deck of the pirate vessel. Bonny and Reade were the only members of the crew who offered any kind of resistance. Rackam himself was apparently too drunk to defend himself. The women were overcome, and the pirates were taken to Port Royal to stand trial.

The background of the female pirates was recorded by contemporaries during the trial, which caused a sensation throughout Europe and the Americas. The excitement largely stemmed from the revelation that they had lived as men for years, escaping the traditional restrictions imposed on the lives of contemporary women. In other words, they were not only female pirates, but they broke society's strict rules. Their backgrounds were probably embroidered by Johnson,

Mary Reade and Anne Bonny
rousing 'Calico Jack' Rackam and
his drunken crew when the pirates
were surprised by a warship off
the coast of Jamaica, 1720. Anne
Bonny (left) is dressed in a
captured gentleman's waistcoat
and breeches, while Mary Reade
wears the dress of a common
seaman. (Angus McBride
© Osprey Publishing Ltd)

but his account was gleaned from contemporary press reports. Mary Reade's
mother apparently 'bred her daughter dressed as a boy', and after serving as a man
in domestic service, on a warship and also in the British Army, she fell in love and
married a soldier. When he died, she reverted to her 'male' role and took passage
as a seaman on a Caribbean-bound ship. Captured by pirates in 1717, she joined
them and met Rackam's companion, Anne Bonny.

According to contemporary sources, Anne Bonny was raised as a boy to fulfil
the requirements of a will, although she retained her feminine character. When she
left home she married a seaman, who subsequently turned to piracy. Her husband
used New Providence as his base, and there she met Mary Reade, although
accounts contradict each other as to the nature of their first encounter. In any
event, the women became friends, which is not surprising given their similar and
unusual backgrounds. In New Providence she met Rackam, who persuaded her to
abandon her husband. The women were tried separately from their fellow pirates
because of the notoriety of their case. In court, it was reported that 'they were both
very profligate, cursing and swearing much, and very ready and willing to do
anything'. Victims testified that they donned men's clothing when in action, but
otherwise dressed as women. Following the trial, both women were sentenced to
death, but were reprieved when it was discovered that they were both pregnant.
Mary died subsequently in a Jamaican prison in 1721, but Anne's fate is unknown.

Charles Vane became notorious when he defied Woodes Rogers, the new governor of the Bahamas, in the harbour of New Providence in 1718. Subsequently, he was voted out of his captaincy, shipwrecked and then captured by a passing ship. According to Johnson, when hanged he 'showed not the least remorse for the crimes of his past life'. (Stratford Archive)

CHARLES VANE

Period of activity: July 1718 to November 1720 (28 months)

Charles Vane took to piracy in 1716 and served as part of Henry Jennings' crew. A Spanish treasure fleet had been wrecked on the eastern coast of Florida in 1715, and during 1716 Jennings raided the camps of the salvagers, capturing large quantities of silver. Originally based in Jamaica, Jennings found that his illegal attacks made his presence unwelcome. He moved to New Providence in 1717, and when Governor Woodes Rogers took up residence in 1718, he accepted a pardon, settling down to live off his plunder. In this respect, Jennings was one of the more successful pirates. Charles Vane was not so fortunate.

Just before Rogers arrived, Vane made his first independent cruise, capturing a French merchant vessel. When the new governor appeared in August 1718, Vane knew he would either have to give up his plunder or flee New Providence. He set fire to the French vessel, sailing it straight for Rogers' flagship. As the warship carrying Rogers was busy avoiding the fireship, Vane and his pirate crew sailed by in their barquentine, firing at the Royal Naval frigate and jeering. Vane escaped in the confusion, taking his plunder with him. Vessels were sent after him, but Vane eluded them, although they caught a number of other runaway pirates. Subsequently, Vane and his crew bore a grudge against the Bahamas and their governor, and attacked New Providence shipping while passing by in the spring of 1719. Vane then headed for the Carolinas, capturing a sloop which he used as a second ship, and taking a number of prizes. The sloop's crew promptly deserted, the first indications of bad blood between Vane and his men. A number of naval vessels were sent in pursuit by Governor Spotswood of Virginia during late August and early September 1718, but he evaded them. The same ships, however, managed to capture the pirate Stede Bonnet and his crew, who were operating in the same waters.

While operating off the North Carolina coast, Vane met up with Edward Teach and his crew at their Ocracoke base. The two crews celebrated their union by holding a drunken party: a sort of pirate convention. By October, he had set sail again, this time heading north towards New York, taking ships along the way. Operating off Long Island in November, he captured a growing tally of ships before heading back to the Carolinas to sell the cargoes.

When the crews of Edward Teach and Charles Vane met at Ocracoke Inlet, North Carolina, in 1718, they held a week-long celebration and were joined by women and traders from the nearby settlement of Bath Towne. This 19th-century engraving depicts the festivities. (Stratford Archive)

He returned to the Caribbean in early 1719, this time operating in the Windward Passage between Cuba and Hispaniola. His squadron now consisted of two vessels. In March 1719, a quarrel broke out among the crew over an alleged incident of cowardice on Vane's part, and his shipmates elected Jack Rackam as captain instead. Vane was given a small captured sloop and sent on his way with the few remaining crew who remained loyal to him. Starting from scratch again, he succeeded in capturing a couple of small ships before running into a hurricane in the Bay of Honduras. His ship ran aground, leaving Vane and one other survivor stranded on a small island for several months before being rescued by a passing ship. One of the rescuers recognized Vane, and the pirates were locked up, shipped to Port Royal and put on trial. Both Vane and his one surviving crewman were found guilty and hanged in November 1720.

HENRY EVERY ('LONG BEN')

Period of activity: June 1694 to September 1695 (15 months)

Little is known of Every's early life, although in the early 1690s he served aboard a slave ship. Accounts of an early piratical career based in the Bahamas appear unfounded. In 1694, he was serving as the first mate on a privateer named the *Charles*, licensed by the Spanish to operate against the French colony of Martinique. He engineered a mutiny, took over the ship and was elected captain. Renaming the vessel the *Fancy*, the pirates crossed to the African coast, then sailed south, capturing four vessels, including a French pirate vessel returning home with her spoils. Off the Cape of Good Hope, Every wrote an open letter to the English papers, proclaiming his loyalty to England and Holland. It also focused attention on his exploits.

Entering the Indian Ocean, he found the waters around the Red Sea full of pirates, and Every temporarily bonded a group of them into a fleet. Together, they were powerful enough to intercept the well-armed treasure convoys which sailed annually between India and the Middle East. When they saw the approaching pirates, most of the Moghul of India's fleet fled, and nightfall covered their escape. Every was lucky, and when dawn broke he found two ships within range. The smaller one, the *Fateh Mohammed*, was quickly overcome, but the larger, the *Gang-i-sawai*, only surrendered after a tough, two-hour fight. Survivors were killed, having been tortured to reveal hidden caches of treasure, and women passengers raped. The brutality was in keeping with the era, especially given the religious and racial differences between victor and vanquished.

Henry Every shown wielding a cutlass and armed with two brace of pistols. In the background, the engraving depicts the fight between Every's ship, the *Fancy*, and the treasure ship of the Great Moghul, the *Gang-i-sawai*. (Stratford Archive)

Once the smoke had cleared, Every and his crew found they had captured the fleet's main treasure ship, containing over £600,000 of gold, silver and jewels. Each pirate in the fleet received a share estimated at over £1,000, or over 80 years' worth of the average seaman's wages at the time.

The fleet disbanded, and the *Fancy* sailed back to the Caribbean. In New Providence, the governor of the Bahamas offered protection in return for an immense bribe. While many of his crew returned to England – only to be apprehended and hanged – Every sailed for Ireland, then vanished into obscurity.

Known as the 'Arch Pirate', he was the only successful pirate who survived to live off his plunder. Sightings were common over the next few decades, but none proved to be accurate. His success also encouraged others to follow in his footsteps.

STEDE BONNET

Period of activity: March 1717 to November 1718 (20 months)

According to Johnson's history, Stede Bonnet was an ex-army major and Barbados plantation owner who turned to piracy in 1717. Unfortunately, no record of him can be found among the Barbadian archives. Johnson records that he actually purchased his own ship, the sloop *Revenge* of ten guns, crewed it with piratical volunteers and sailed for the Carolinas. Operating off the Atlantic seaboard, he captured and plundered several ships from New York down to the Carolinas, before he wintered in North Carolina, careening his ship and housing his crew ashore. In the spring, he headed south towards the Gulf of Honduras, but en route in March 1718 he ran into Edward Teach with a larger ship and crew. Bonnet surrendered and was taken along as a virtual prisoner. Teach reportedly laughed at the pirate gentleman while he took his ship from him.

By June 1718, he was released with his sloop off the North Carolina coast, and hearing that the newly formed Great Britain was at war with Spain, he approached the pirate-friendly governor of North Carolina for a pardon. He got it, and officially set off towards the Virgin Islands to act as a privateer, with a letter of marque to prey

Stede Bonnet's execution, 1718. The 'gentleman pirate' was expected a degree of leniency, but instead the judge took the opportunity to moralize on social issues, and he was sentenced to death. It was reported that 'His piteous behaviour under sentence very much affected the people of the Province, particularly the women.' (Angus McBride © Osprey Publishing Ltd)

OPPOSITE Captain Kidd shown on the quarterdeck of his ship *Adventure Galley*, in an illustration used in Howard Pyle's *Book of Pirates* (1921). Pyle decided to show Kidd's home port of New York in the background, although the *Adventure Galley* was built in and sailed from London. (Stratford Archive)

on Spanish shipping. He still bore a grudge against Teach and tried to hunt him down, but soon gave up the quest. He then changed the name of his ship to the *Royal James* and adopted an assumed name (Captain Thomas), before reverting to his chosen career of piracy. When lying in the Cape Fear River undergoing repairs, he captured a local ship, and word reached the city authorities at Charleston, South Carolina. A local ship owner, William Rhett, was authorized to attack the pirates with two sloops. In October 1718, the Charleston sloops found the pirate lair and attacked Bonnet, who retreated up the river. Running aground, he was forced to fight. After a five-hour exchange of fire, Bonnet and the surviving crew surrendered. The pirates were taken to Charleston, a city still smarting from its treatment by Teach. While imprisoned in a private house, Bonnet escaped but was quickly recaptured. He was found guilty and hanged in November 1718, along with 30 of his crew. A pirate turned informant and four others were acquitted.

WILLIAM KIDD

Period of activity: May 1697 to April 1700 (35 months)

William Kidd is one of the better-known pirates, more for his fate than his actions. He only made one voyage and took only one significant prize, but it was enough to bring him to trial and cause a major political scandal. His inclusion here is more because of this subsequent fame than because of his deeds.

Before he turned to piracy, the Scottish-born Kidd served in a privateering vessel in the Caribbean. Kidd settled in New York, but in 1695 he sailed to England, hoping to win more extensive privateering contracts. Once there he met Richard, Earl of Bellamont, newly appointed governor of New York and Massachusetts. Bellamont soon talked Kidd into a plan involving semi-legal privateering, to be conducted by Kidd in a specially built vessel, acting on behalf of financial backers. These backers included Bellamont and other influential politicians. They bought Kidd the *Adventure Galley* of 34 guns and presented him with a contract and a letter of marque against the French and against pirates. It was implied the backers would also turn a blind eye to the odd piratical act if it turned a profit. The contract was financially restrictive, meaning Kidd would receive little financial gain for his efforts, and the crew would receive even less. Most of the money was earmarked for the backers. The terms strongly influenced the subsequent actions of Kidd and his crew.

Kidd sailed in May 1696, heading first to New York to sign on a crew of old privateering hands, then crossed the Atlantic to West Africa. He sailed into the

Captain Kidd Burying His Treasure, an illustration used in Howard Pyle's *Book of Pirates* (1921). Kidd was probably the only historical pirate to conform to this particular piratical stereotype: unsure whether he would be arrested, he buried his plunder on Gardiner's Island near New York before entering the port. He was, and the plunder was later dug up and confiscated by the authorities. (Stratford Archive)

Indian Ocean, and in April 1697 signed on more crew in Madagascar and turned to piracy. In August, he attacked East India Company ships but was driven off. Another skirmish with Portuguese warships proved uneventful, and after snapping up a small English prize, Kidd retired to the Laccadive Islands for repairs. By November, he was at sea again, but ran away from a couple of potential victims who seemed too well armed. An argument with the ship's gunner led to Kidd killing the man, and any potential mutiny was quelled. After attacking a handful of small prizes, Kidd came upon the *Queddah Merchant* in January 1698. Capturing her and splitting the booty, Kidd abandoned the rotten *Adventure Galley* and shifted into the prize, which he renamed the *Adventure Prize*. The East India Company forced the government to brand Kidd as a pirate, and any potential pardon was now politically impossible. It also meant his backers could not support him.

A wanted man, Kidd sailed back to the Caribbean, then on to Boston, where he tried to make a deal with Governor Bellamont. He was promptly arrested on Bellamont's orders in April 1700 and shipped to England in chains. Thrown into prison, he was now a political pawn. The opposition tried to make Kidd indict his secret government backers, and Kidd testified in Parliament. The government narrowly avoided a political disaster by 'losing' incriminating documents, and the case was dropped. To the British government, Kidd remained a dangerous liability. In May 1701 after a heavily rigged trial, he was found guilty of murdering his former gunner and of piracy. He was hanged at Execution Dock in Wapping, and his body hung in a cage on the banks of the River Thames as a warning to would-be pirates. Rumours that he buried his loot on Gardiner's Island before entering New York were probably true, although Governor Bellamont recovered most of the plunder soon after Kidd was arrested. He was the only figure to profit from Kidd's pirate career.

BARTHOLOMEW ROBERTS ('BLACK BART')

Period of activity: June 1719 to February 1722 (30 months)

Bartholomew Roberts was born in South Wales and originally called John Roberts. In June 1719, while serving as the mate of a merchant slaver, his ship was captured by another Welshman, the pirate Howell Davis. Davis, in his turn, had chosen a career of piracy when he was captured by Edward England. Roberts joined Davis' crew, and when Davis was killed in a skirmish, Roberts was elected captain. Changing his first name to Bartholomew to cover his tracks, he quickly earned the nickname 'Black Bart'.

After cruising in West African waters, he sailed for Brazil. Coming across a Portuguese convoy, he captured a number of ships, including a warship. Roberts took his growing fleet to the American colonies. Selling ships and cargo in New England, he plundered the fishing grounds of Newfoundland in the summer of 1720, capturing dozens of vessels and destroying numerous others. Trading captured ships for a 26-gun French ship which he renamed *Royal Fortune*, he sailed south along the American coastline, capturing more merchantmen on the way. When he reached the Caribbean in the late summer of 1720, he captured

This somewhat dandified pirate is meant to represent Howell Davis, a Welsh pirate who operated in the Caribbean and off the African coast. He was killed during a skirmish with Portuguese militia on Principe Island in the Gulf of Guinea in 1719. (Stratford Archive)

15 French and English ships and a well-armed Dutch ship carrying 42 guns, in a four-day spree. An attempt at a transatlantic voyage was foiled by poor winds and faulty navigation, so by the autumn the pirates had returned to the West Indies. Attacks on St Kitts and Martinique netted a further haul of ships, and the rampage continued until the spring of 1721. In the process, Roberts managed to capture a

Bartholomew Roberts during his final moments, just before he was killed by the broadside from HMS *Swallow* in 1723. The faces of the men behind him reflect the multi-racial mix of Roberts' crew. Roberts' flag in the background shows the pirate drinking a toast with death. (Angus McBride © Osprey Publishing Ltd)

sworn enemy, the governor of Martinique, who was promptly hanged from the yardarm of his own ship. The 42-gun French warship carrying him was pressed into service and renamed the *Royal Fortune* (as were most of Roberts' large prizes). He eventually returned to the African coast, where he captured several merchant slavers during the summer of 1721. The Royal Africa Company's ship *Onslow* became the last ship renamed *Royal Fortune*. Roberts continued to cruise off Liberia and Nigeria, capturing scores of slave ships. A Royal Naval force was despatched to track down the pirates, and on 10 February 1722, Captain Ogle of HMS *Swallow* caught up with the *Royal Fortune*.

The pirates were at anchor off Cape Lopez, after having captured prizes the day before, and (apparently) having celebrated with a drinking spree. The morning after brought a well-armed naval frigate at action stations as well as a hangover. Roberts had to pass Ogle's ship in order to escape, and steered for the warship, while his crew scrambled to prepare their ship for action. As the ships passed, the *Swallow* fired a broadside of grapeshot at point-blank range. Roberts was killed instantly. His crew threw his body overboard still clad in all its finery, including a splendid jewelled cross, partly to avoid the corpse being captured. The ships continued to exchange broadsides in a running battle. After three hours, the surviving pirates surrendered. Two other ships of the pirate fleet were also captured, along with a haul of 300 tons of gold dust. In what was the largest pirate trial and execution of the era, the survivors were tried and executed at Cape Coast Castle, in West Africa.

Roberts' boldness was his trademark. He led his crew into action wearing a brace of pistols tucked into a silk bandoleer and carrying a sharp cutlass. He attacked ships of all nations, but particularly singled out France and its colonies – he hanged the governor of Martinique, and reportedly tortured and killed French prisoners. A tall, handsome man who loved fine clothes, he was a teetotaller, a rarity among sailors of the period. He was also a gifted leader of men, and held his crews together by the use of prize money, codes of conduct and, above all, constant success. Among the pirates who were hanged was Roberts' lover, John Walden. Although called 'Miss Nanny' behind his back, Walden was a tough character, who was accused during the trial of burning slaves alive. Roberts' career has been upheld as among the most successful and flamboyant of the pirate era. He was one of the most prosperous pirates of all time, following 'the pirate round' from Africa to the Americas and back again, capturing more than 200 ships in the process.

The Pirate Ship

THE DESIGN OF THE IDEAL PIRATE SHIP

All pirate ships tended to share certain qualities, irrespective of the size and origin of the vessel. First of all, ships had to be seaworthy, as they sailed in stormy waters. The popular areas for pirate activity during the period from 1690 to 1730 (known as the golden age of piracy) were the Caribbean Sea, the Atlantic seaboard of North America, the West African coast and the Indian Ocean. The first two areas were particularly susceptible to hurricanes during the hurricane season, which lasts from June to November. August and September are considered the peak hurricane months in the Atlantic and Caribbean. As early as the 17th century, mariners were aware that a hurricane season existed, and that the West African coast was a breeding ground for these storms, which then travelled west across the Atlantic Ocean. They learned to look out for the signs of approaching hurricanes or less dramatic tropical storms. They then had the option of putting to sea in an attempt to ride out the storm, or of securing the ship as best they could in a sheltered bay and hoping for the best. The catastrophic effects of winds of 100mph or more have decimated shipping and coastal communities for centuries. For these pirates, who were denied the shelter of conventional ports, the dangers were increased. Their

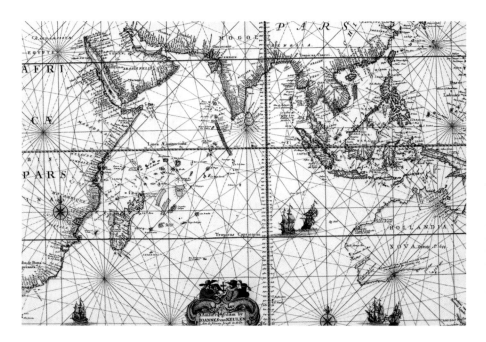

The Indian Ocean became a notorious pirate haunt during the late 17th century, when pirates like Henry Every and William Kidd preyed on British and Indian shipping from the Red Sea down to Madagascar, and on the sea lanes between India and the Cape of Good Hope. Late 17th-century chart. (Stratford Archive)

107

Hurricanes were an ever-present threat in the Caribbean, at least during the hurricane season which lasts from June until November. The destruction of the Spanish treasure fleet of 1715 off the east coast of Florida led to many former privateers and would-be pirates becoming treasure hunters. (Stratford Archive)

ships therefore needed to be seaworthy enough to ride out these hurricanes, with a suite of storm sails, a stout hull, reliable pumps and an experienced crew. For pirates, the only benefit of hurricanes was the damage they inflicted on other shipping. The pirate Henry Jennings started his career by plundering the salvage camps of men recovering treasure from the wrecks of the 1715 Spanish treasure fleet, which was dashed against the east coast of Florida in a hurricane. In the Indian Ocean, the same weather conditions were known as tropical cyclones, while the term typhoon was applied to them in the western Pacific Ocean and the China seas. In the northern Indian Ocean, tropical cyclones strike in May and November, while further south the season runs from December to March. Meteorologists estimate that around the world there are about 85 hurricanes, typhoons and tropical cyclones per year, and we have to assume the same frequency applies to the golden age of piracy. While these storms are dangerous enough to modern shipping, the effects on small sailing craft that lacked any warning from satellites, television or radio could be catastrophic. Added to this seasonal risk was the ever-present danger of mid-Atlantic storms, or passage through notoriously storm-ravaged waters, such as around the Cape of Good Hope.

One remarkable aspect of piracy during this period was the distances these cut-throats were prepared to travel in their ships. Atlantic crossings were frequently made by sloops and other small craft, often no bigger than a modern coastal fishing

An Attack on a Galleon. This painting by Howard Pyle appeared in *Harper's Monthly Magazine* in December 1905, where it was used to illustrate Pyle's own pirate tale, 'The Fate of a Treasure-Town'. (Stratford Archive)

boat. An example is the voyage made by Bartholomew Roberts, who crossed the Atlantic several times and ranged American waters from Brazil to Newfoundland. The stress on a wooden hull making a long ocean passage would have been similar to that imposed on the vessel by a major storm, with the added problem of the collection of marine growth on the hull. Weeds and barnacles adhering to the

The port of Charles Town, as it would have looked in the early 18th century. Shipping tended to crowd into the inner harbour in the Cooper River, where in theory it was protected by the guns of Fort Johnson. During his blockade of the port in 1718, Blackbeard threatened to force his way past the weakly armed fort, but his fleet remained at the outer entrance of the harbour. (Stratford Archive)

underside of a hull could seriously impede the speed of a vessel by as much as three knots. This meant that regular careening (hull cleaning) was vital. Unlike warships or law-abiding merchantmen who could use the shipyard facilities found in the major ports, pirates had to careen their vessels far from prying eyes, in secluded bays or estuaries. For a small brig or sloop, the process could take a week, while for larger ships the task was proportionately longer. During this period the beached vessel was vulnerable to attack, and several pirates lost their ships when they were beached for careening. Another problem affecting seaworthiness was the damage caused to a wooden hull by the *teredo* worm. The waters of the Caribbean contained the highest density of *teredo* worms in the world, meaning that wooden hulls had a short life expectancy in the region. The Spanish, who maintained a number of galleons designed to carry treasure from the Spanish Main to Spain estimated that ten years was the longest a hull could be expected to last if it sailed regularly in Caribbean waters, even if protected. The same timescale would apply to pirate ships. That said, longevity was never much of a problem for pirates, as even the most successful (such as Bartholomew Roberts) never survived more than 2 ½ years as active cut-throats. While larger pirate ships were better suited to making transatlantic voyages, they were harder to careen due to their size. It was far easier to beach and careen a small vessel. Smaller craft with a shallow draught could also navigate the coastal waters (such as the strip of creeks, estuaries, sandbanks and inland waterways) that typify the Atlantic coastline of North America. In 1712, Governor Hunter of New York wrote to his superiors in London, stating, 'This coast has been very much annoyed by a number of small privateers, who by the advantage of their oars and shoal water keep out of the reach of H.M. ships of war.' He requested a flotilla of sloops, capable of harrying any pirate who tried to establish himself in the shallow waters off Long Island or the mouth of the Hudson River.

Another vital prerequisite for a pirate ship was that it had to be fast – as Captain Charles Johnson (1724) put it, 'a light pair of heels being of great use either to take or to escape being taken'. A scientific correlation exists between ship size, hull shape and the amount of sail carried which, taken together, results in speed through the water. In theory, larger ships could carry a greater amount of canvas, and therefore gained more impetus from the wind. Their disadvantage was that their larger hulls displaced more water than smaller vessels, and therefore required greater forward momentum to overcome water resistance. Once momentum was achieved, speed was more dependent on sail power. Smaller vessels such as brigantines had less sail area, but the ratio of sail to displacement was higher than for larger square-rigged ships, giving them a slight advantage. Small, narrow and shallow-draught vessels like sloops and schooners reduced water resistance through improved hull lines, which therefore improved speed. Although the speed correlation was a complex three-cornered equation, certain general rules could be determined. First, for the most part, small

This colourful wind compass or wind chart shows the 32 compass points which were used by mariners until the 19th century, when they were replaced by a compass based on a 360° circle. This version was published in Amsterdam in 1693. (Stratford Archive)

narrow-draught vessels such as pirate sloops were usually faster than larger square-rigged merchantmen. This said, well-designed, large, square-rigged vessels capable of carrying a heavier press of sail (such as naval frigates, 'guineamen' or slave ships) could usually overhaul smaller vessels given time. Certain ships were favoured by pirates due to their reputation of being fast-sailing vessels. For example, many pirates based in the Caribbean favoured the small single-mast sloops built in Jamaica and Bermuda, as they were known to be fast-sailing and sound sea boats.

This scientific correlation was also influenced by less tangible factors. The cleanliness of a ship's hull has already been mentioned. Pirates needed to careen their ships regularly, as they never knew when they might need every available knot of speed from their vessel. Certain ships performed better in certain winds, or sailed better with the wind striking the sails in a particular way. For example, gaff-rigged vessels were capable of sailing closer to the wind than square-rigged vessels, while lateen sails were beneficial when the wind was on the beam or quarter, but were virtually useless with the wind astern. Above all, the skill of the captain and crew were crucial. Skilled seamen could squeeze another knot or so from their ship by keeping a close eye on their sails, the wind and the performance

Buccaneers used fireships regularly – vessels specially converted by filling them with combustibles before sending them towards the enemy. A skeleton crew would steer her towards the enemy, then escape in a small longboat at the last minute. Mid-17th-century Spanish watercolour. Original in the Archivo de Indias, Seville. (Stratford Archive)

of their ship through the water. With all other circumstances being equal, a well-crewed vessel could always outrun or overhaul its opponent. When Royal Naval warships were sent after the pirate Charles Vane's sloop in the Bahamas in 1718, Vane's skill and fast hull allowed him to evade his pursuers. As one naval officer commented, 'Our sloops gave over the chase, finding he [Vane] out-sailed them two foot for their one.'

The final factor that defined the typical pirate ship was its armament. Clearly, the greater the number of guns carried, the greater the displacement of the vessel, and the slower the speed. To the successful pirate, guns were easy to come by, as they could be taken from prize vessels whenever they were needed. Also, pirates preferred not to rely on gunfire to defeat an opponent, as the hull of their victim would be damaged. That said, it is surprising that so many pirates armed their ships as much as they could, or even converted prizes into formidable warships carrying as many guns as a small naval ship-of-the-line. This can be seen as mere bravado, but there is another factor. The more successful a pirate became, the more attention he attracted. Inevitably, warships would be sent to hunt him down. Preparation for a fight with pirate-hunting warships may have been a major influence behind the appearance of heavily armed pirate ships during the early 18th century. Large ships could carry more guns than smaller vessels, and their hulls provided a more stable gun platform. The armament of pirate ships will be examined later, but for the moment, the balance between armament, speed and seaworthiness was approached by different pirates in various ways. While some preferred a small, shallow, fast sloop, armed with fewer than ten guns, other pirates favoured large, imposing warships, capable of carrying a heavy armament and a large press of sail.

THE ORIGINS OF THE PIRATE SHIP

No vessel was ever designed from scratch as a pirate ship. Unlike the navies of the world, or even the owners of privateering ships, pirates could not commission the building of a new ship specifically designed to suit their needs. Pirate ships were created in one of three ways. First, they were created when the crew of a law-abiding vessel mutinied, took over the ship and turned to piracy. Second, and only occasionally, the captain and crew of existing privateering vessels decided to resort to piracy when legitimate targets were no longer available. Third, and most commonly, pirate ships were captured. This occasionally happened in port, such as when 'Calico Jack' Rackham stole the sloop *William* from New Providence in August 1719, aided by Anne Bonny.

The most notorious pirate who gained a ship through mutiny was Henry Every (or Avery), discussed previously on pages 97–98. In 1694, the Bristol-based privateer *Charles* of 30 guns lay at anchor off the northern Spanish port of La Coruña. Her captain had been granted a Spanish letter of marque to attack French shipping in the vicinity of Martinique, and the privateer was preparing to sail for the West Indies. Captain Charles Johnson recorded what happened:

> On one of these ships ... commanded by Captain Gibson, Avery was First Mate, and being a fellow of more cunning than courage, he insinuated himself into the good will of several of the boldest fellows on board ... Having founded their inclinations before he opened himself, and finding them ripe for his design, at length, proposed to them to run away with the ship, telling them what great wealth was to be had upon the coasts of India.

Every struck while the captain was drunk. He had already made sure that all crewmen loyal to the captain were below decks, then the mutineers secured the hatches and cabins:

> When our gentry saw that all was clear, they secured the hatches, so went to work; they did not slip the anchor but weighed it leisurely, and so put to sea without any disorder and confusion, though there were several ships then lying in the bay.

Unlike other nationalities, the Spanish retained the high-sided galleon design well into the 17th century, and small galleons such as these were frequently used as guard ships and patrol vessels during the buccaneering era. Detail from a Spanish chart of 1618. Original in the Archivo de Indias, Seville. (Stratford Archive)

Like many pirates, Jack (or John) Rackam ('Calico Jack') captured his vessel. In August 1719, with the help of Anne Bonny, he stole a sloop named the *William*. (Stratford Archive)

Every renamed the ship the *Fancy*, and sailed towards Madagascar and a waiting fortune in plunder. Off the African coast he released the captain, who was sent ashore in a longboat, accompanied by the crew who remained loyal. Less than a dozen men joined him, leaving Every with over a hundred pirates at his disposal.

The pirate Thomas Anstis conspired with several companions to steal the sloop *Buck* from Providence, Rhode Island in 1718, making the event less of a mutiny than a theft, while most of the crew were ashore. A similar fate befell the captain of the small Royal Africa Company vessel *Gambia Castle*, of 16 guns and 30 men. The

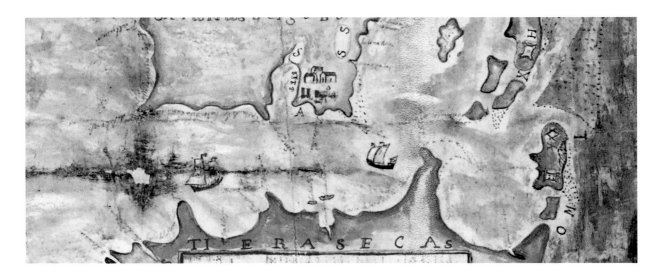

Shipping off Maracaibo Bar, a detail from a map of the Lake of Maracaibo, 1699. A brigantine (left) and a two-mast yacht (a forerunner of a schooner, right) sail the waters where Henry Morgan fought his sea battle in 1669. The setting of the sails on both craft suggests an inshore wind. (Stratford Archive)

ship's First Mate George Lowther colluded with John Massey, a young British Army officer, and together they engineered a mutiny off the West African coast in 1721.

According to Rediker (1987), 48 recorded non-naval mutinies took place on British ships between 1715 and 1737. Of these, as many as one-third (or approximately 16) of the crews turned to piracy. Cordingly (1995) suggests that during the golden age of piracy, no more than 19–20 pirate ships were acquired through seizure by their own crews. Henry Every, Thomas Anstis and George Lowther were obviously the exception rather than the rule.

As for privateer captains turning to piracy, this seems to have been an even more rare occurrence. The most celebrated example of this kind was Captain William Kidd (see pages 100–103), whose ideal pirate vessel was paid for and fitted out by his privateering sponsors back in London. During the buccaneering of the late 17th century, commanders like Sir Henry Morgan blurred the line between privateering and piracy. When there was no convenient war between England and Spain to provide a legitimate excuse for attacking Spanish shipping and coastal settlements, Morgan and his men carried on regardless. The recorded instances of this taking place during the golden age are rare, largely because of numbers. While colonial governors, during the buccaneering era, turned a blind eye to non-licensed attacks on the shipping of rival European powers, the political situation had changed markedly by 1690. Privateers were closely regulated, and illegal attack was regarded as an act of full-blown piracy. As privateering crews were usually large, it was virtually impossible to persuade a majority of the seamen to turn their back on society and turn to piracy.

The most common method of pirate ship acquisition was capture. By working their way up the maritime ladder, longboats could be exchanged for sloops, and brigs for large armed merchantmen. A prime example of how a pirate began his career this way is Captain Worley, a character described by Johnson (1724) without mentioning his first name. In September 1718, Worley and eight fellow seamen rowed out of New York harbour in a longboat, in search of a vessel to capture. They headed south, skirting the New Jersey shore, before entering the Delaware River. Off Newcastle (now a suburb of Wilmington, Delaware), 'they fell upon a shallop belonging to George Grant, who was bringing household goods, plate, etc., from Oppoquenimi to Philadelphia'. They looted the ship but let the cumbersome merchantman go. The account of their plunder continues:

[they] met with a sloop of Philadelphia, belonging to a mulatto whom they called Black Robbin; they quitted their boat for this sloop, taking one of Black Robbin's men along with them … A day or two after, they took another sloop belonging to Hull homeward bound, which was somewhat fitter for their purpose … and enabled them to prosecute their design, in a manner more suitable to their wishes.

Three years later, the London-born seaman Edward Low served on board a British sloop which was anchored off the coast of Honduras, loading a cargo of logwood. Following an argument with her captain, Low and 12 companions seized the ship's boat and deserted. As Johnson (1724) reports, 'The next day they took a small vessel, and go in her, make a black flag, and declare war against all the world.'

Once a pirate captain had his first ship, he could 'trade up' by transferring his men and guns onto a captured prize, if the new ship was more suitable. Clearly, this process was less than ideal and largely random. First, the pirate could only capture a prize which his vessel could catch, and which he could overcome by boarding, gunnery or even intimidation. Piracy was the ultimate crime of opportunity, as on the high seas, the opportunities to identify a target in advance and lie in wait for it were rare. Once a prize was captured, the pirate captain had to decide what to do with the crew, its cargo and the captured ship itself. Unlike the pirates of fiction, the majority of pirates during the early 18th century had to be content with plundering regular merchant ships, which carried mundane cargoes of tobacco, sugar, rum, timber, hides, slaves or other commodities. Often, pirates were denied the opportunity to sell these cargoes, so anything other than rum, spices and, to a lesser extent, slaves were

The pirate Edward Low in a hurricane, with a three-masted ship foundering in the background. Low was active in the Caribbean from December 1721 until he was marooned by his own crew in early 1724.(Stratford Archive)

of limited value. Most captured ships were either set ablaze or simply abandoned, as their hulls were of little use to the pirates. Occasionally, a faster, better constructed or more commodious vessel would be kept and converted into a pirate ship. As an example, the pirate Charles Vane (see pages 95–97) escaped from New Providence in the Bahamas in command of the sloop *Ranger*, a vessel of six guns. In August 1718, when he captured a large, fast slave ship (a brigantine) bound from Guinea, he transferred his guns and men, creating a more powerful pirate ship of 12 guns, which he also called *Ranger*.

While most pirates settled on a particular vessel (usually a sloop or brigantine) and used it for the duration of their piratical careers, others continued the process of trading up, until they acquired vessels which were powerful enough to challenge all but the largest warships sent against them.

During his career, Bartholomew Roberts (see pages 103–106) traded up several times, after gaining command of the pirate ship *Ranger* of 30 guns in July 1719 off the West African coast. When he was on board a prize sloop, the crew of the *Ranger* deserted. Roberts renamed his ten-gun sloop the *Fortune*, and used it to cause mayhem from Africa to Newfoundland, before exchanging it for a 16-gun galley from Bristol. Within weeks, he used this new ship to capture a 26-gun French merchantman, which he renamed the *Royal Fortune*. In the West Indies, he captured a fast 18-gun brigantine, which became the *Good Fortune*. Together, these two ships captured a 42-gun French warship which he also renamed the *Royal Fortune*. This was the ultimate prize in trading up, a formidable warship that could hold its own in any fight. Roberts captured the Royal Africa Company ship *Onslow* and converted her into a pirate ship, again renaming her *Royal Fortune*. This was the vessel that took part in Roberts' last fight against HMS *Swallow* in February 1722. His reason for abandoning his powerful French-built warship in favour of the British armed merchant ship is not recorded, but it is likely that as the French vessel had spent several years on station in the West Indies, her hull was in an advanced state of decay. Edward Teach (Blackbeard; see pages 88–91) followed the same path, trading up until he commanded a fast and commodious 40-gun vessel capable of blockading Charleston. The *Queen Anne's Revenge* ran aground at Beaufort Inlet, North Carolina, and it has been argued that the accident was a deliberate ploy by Teach, who transferred his plunder to one of his

The small sloop *Fancy* served as the private yacht of Colonel Lewis Morris, a militia commander in New York during the early 18th century. It was also typical of the smaller sloops found along the American coastline during the golden age of piracy. Detail from an engraving of New York by William Burgis, dated 1717. (Stratford Archive)

sloops, then left the crew of his flagship stranded off the Carolina shore. It meant fewer men to share the spoils with. Possibly he was prepared to sacrifice his prestigious flagship in return for financial gain, secure in the knowledge that he could always begin the trading up process again whenever he chose.

It was rare that the process continued long enough for a pirate to capture a major warship, or to convert a merchantman into one. Both Bartholomew Roberts and Edward Teach achieved just that.

THE CONVERSION OF A PRIZE

Once pirates captured a ship, the prize had to be converted into a vessel that was ideally suited to the pirates' needs. Unlike the conversion of warships, or even of merchant ships to take different types of cargo, little is known about this process. Few pirates kept records, and the fitting out of captured vessels either took place on the high seas, or in some secluded anchorage, well away from prying eyes.

We do know of the general changes made to prizes, though, as hinted at by survivors of piratical attacks and in the pages of Charles Johnson's *A General History of the Robberies and Murders of the Most Notorious Pirates* (1724). In this work, three passages mention the process of ship conversion. The first is a brief note in 'The Life of Captain England', which states that in early 1719, 'Captain England took a ship called the *Pearl*, Captain Tyzard commander, for which he exchanged his own sloop, fitted her up for the piratical account.' The *Pearl* was later renamed the *Royal James*. The short entry fails to explain what 'fitting her up' for the piratical account involved, although 'The Life of Captain England' provides a little more information. When George Lowther incited the crew of the vessel *Gambia Castle* to mutiny in 1721, his new-found crew set about converting the ship into a pirate vessel: 'They one and all came into the measures, knocked down the cabins, made the ship flush for[e] and aft, prepared black colours, new named her the *Delivery*, having about 50 hands and 16 guns.'

Finally, in 'The Life of Captain Roberts', Johnson records the conversion of the large frigate-built *Onslow*, captured by Bartholomew Roberts in early 1721:

> The pirates kept the *Onslow* for their own use, and gave Captain Gee the French ship, and then fell to making such alterations as might fit her for a sea rover, pulling down her bulkheads, and making her flush, so that she became, in all respects, as complete a ship for their purpose as any they could have found; they continued to give her the name of the *Royal Fortune*, and mounted her with 40 guns.

We now have a reasonable picture of what was involved in 'fitting up' a pirate ship, custom-building her to become the ideal tool for men like Roberts or England. First, the pirates removed any temporary bulkheads set up in the hold, used to keep cargo from moving. This large, open lower deck space could then be pierced to accommodate ordnance. Few merchant vessels of this period carried guns anywhere other than on the upper deck. By piercing the hull for additional ports, the pirates converted the vessel into a warship. Similarly, in line with the egalitarian nature of pirate ships, most internal cabin bulkheads were also removed, with the possible exception of the captain's cabin in the stern, which was seen as a perk of the pirate commander. This knocking-down of the cabins extended to the forecastle as well as the stern, removing partitions used to house ship's stores.

The pirates went even further. Both Roberts and Lowther made their ships flush 'fore and aft'. This involved tearing down the forecastle and lowering any superstructure abaft the mainmast, creating a smooth, flush-decked vessel without any break or step from bow to stern. In the stern on most frigate-built ships or even smaller sloops and brigantines, a roundhouse or cabin occupied a significant portion of deck space, which could otherwise be used to house guns and men. Any impractical decorated rails could also be removed if they were considered likely to get in the way during action. The new deck layout was better suited to the carrying of ordnance or large numbers of boarders when in action, creating an unobstructed

Although this 19th-century illustration is more dramatic than realistic, it does underline the point that pirates didn't often begin their careers with their own ships, but had to seize one by whatever means they could, usually by overpowering her crew while she lay at anchor. (Stratford Archive)

platform for the pirates to fight from. Ordnance was then transferred from the old pirate ship to the new one, and in cases such as the *Onslow/Royal Fortune*, guns were mounted both in the main (lower) deck and on the newly expanded upper deck. On larger ships, the result was the creation of a formidable fighting warship, capable of taking on all but the most powerful opponents. On smaller craft, such as the *Pearl/Royal James* and the *Gambia Castle/Delivery*, the addition of a lower deck armament was probably impossible, but fresh gun ports cut in the upper deck in place of any forecastle or after-deck platforms provided space for additional armament. One further advantage of removing the quarterdeck and roundhouse if present was that this allowed guns to be mounted as bow or stern chasers.

George Lowther, an English pirate active in the Caribbean and Atlantic seaboard between 1721 and 1723. His ship, the *Happy Delivery*, is beached and being careened in the background while the crew live in tents on the shore. During the process, the pirates were defenceless, and Lowther's crew were attacked and captured while careening their ship on the Venezuelan coast in 1723. Lowther escaped but was killed soon after. (Stratford Archive)

Finally, reports of captured pirate vessels indicate that in some cases, the rig of the vessel was altered. If the pirates disliked the rig of a particular vessel, they would change it in an effort to increase speed and, where possible, to provide extra space. This conversion work might involve the replacement of lateen yards with square-rigged ones, the removal of the mizzen mast (the mast aft of the mainmast), and even the stepping of the mainmast aft slightly, to improve the performance of the ship. For example, brigs and snows were both mercantile versions of the brigantine, but with gaff-rigged mainsails. It appears several pirates preferred the more conventional square-rigged brigantine, so they would have converted prizes to suit their requirements. Certainly, the procurement of materials to undertake these conversions was never much of a problem. Johnson describes the haul made by Bartholomew Roberts' men when they captured the *Samuel* of London: 'They carried with them sails, guns, powder and cordage, and 8,000 or 9,000 pounds of the choicest goods.'

The *Royal James* and the *Henry*, Cape Fear River, North Carolina, 27 September 1718. Hearing of Stede Bonnet's presence nearby, the governor of the colony of South Carolina sent Colonel William Rhett to hunt him down. Rhett's sloop *Henry* closed in on Bonnet's *Royal James*, ultimately leading to Bonnet's surrender, trial and hanging. (Tony Bryan © Osprey Publishing Ltd)

SMALL PIRATE VESSELS

We have already noted that the majority of pirates began their careers in small craft. Even if they lacked a proper sailing vessel such as a sloop or a brigantine, this type of ship was their first real stepping stone, allowing the pirates to sail wherever they wanted, and even to undertake transatlantic voyages if need be. For those pirates without a suitable vessel, they had to use whatever craft was available in order to steal something better. Of the smaller craft found in the waters of the Americas during the buccaneering era, the pinnace, the barca longa, the fly-boat and the piragua were the most common. Many of these had been in use in Caribbean waters since the 16th century. The term 'pinnace' had two different meanings. The first (discussed previously on pages 68–69) referred to a small, narrow-beamed, open-topped ship's boat with a single mast, of less than 60 tons' burden. Confusingly, the term 'pinnace' also applied to larger vessels, of 40–80 tons, which were independent vessels in their own right, not the tenders of larger craft. This definition was later expanded to incorporate a three-mast vessel with its own armament, displacing 200 tons or more. Clearly, the terminology meant different things to different people, and these definitions were prone to evolve with time.

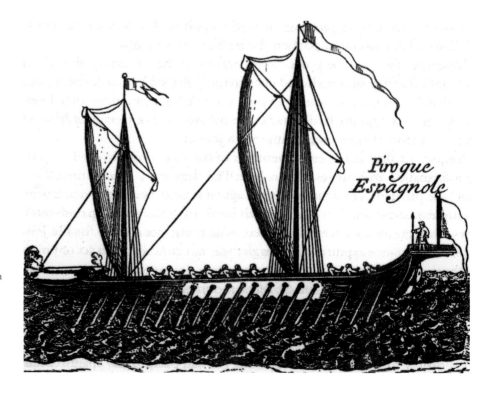

A piragua was a large canoe, more akin to the galleys found in the Renaissance Mediterranean than to any native craft. They could be fitted with ordnance, and served as inshore raiding craft for both pirates and buccaneers in the Caribbean. (Stratford Archive)

The term 'pinnace' originally referred to the oared longboat of a larger ship, fitted with a single mast and rigged with a single lateen or gaff-sail. Typically, these measured less than 35ft (10.7m) in length and served as the tender to large merchantmen or warships. Although maritime historians still disagree on its exact definition, the term 'shallop' most probably also referred to similar tenders, but these craft were usually (but not exclusively) fitted with square sails. The Spanish equivalent of these smaller vessels was the barca longa, a vessel that carried a single square sail, rather like a shallop. The Dutch equivalent was the 'pingue', a term which applied to small trading vessels that plied the waters of the Caribbean during the 17th century, and which could displace as much as 80 tons. All these small craft were used as raiding vessels by buccaneers during the late 17th century, and were often towed behind larger craft, ready for use as assault craft.

The other definition of a pinnace refers to independent vessels of anything from 40 to 200 tons' displacement. These could have any number of masts, but by the buccaneering period, three-mast pinnaces were commonplace. These craft carried a variety of sails, but usually included a combination of square and lateen rigs. The armament of one of these larger pinnaces could range from eight to 20 guns. During the late 17th century, buccaneers such as Sir Henry Morgan used larger pinnaces as the mainstay of their fleets, although these squadrons usually formed around a handful of larger, better-armed, square-rigged sailing ships. A variant was the 'fly-boat', a term originally associated with the Dutch merchant vessel 'fluyt'. By the late 17th century, the term 'fly-boat' had come to signify a small rounded vessel, used as a small coastal trader but equally valuable as a converted warship. A Spanish version of this craft was the balandra. Both were used extensively as coastal patrol craft, scouting vessels, troop carriers and even as small warships or raiders. At the bottom of the maritime ladder in the 17th-century Caribbean was the canoe used by the indigenous peoples of the region. Inevitably, these boats were used by buccaneers and varied in size from craft capable of carrying fewer than four men to the piragua, a large canoe fitted with a mast, ordnance and served by a sizeable crew.

By the last decade of the 17th century, the terms 'pinnace', 'barca longa' and 'fly-boat' had fallen into obscurity. Although there was no sudden change in the appearance of the craft that plied the waters of the Americas, a new series of terms had come into being. Small merchant ships were now classified more by their sail plan and number of masts than by hull shape or purpose.

Before we continue, it is important to define the basic forms of small craft that operated during the golden age of piracy. A sloop was a small vessel with a single mast,

The barca longa was the Spanish version of a pinnace and was widely used as a fishing craft in the waters of the Caribbean during the 17th and early 18th centuries. Buccaneers favoured these craft for coastal raids or night attacks on larger ships. (Stratford Archive)

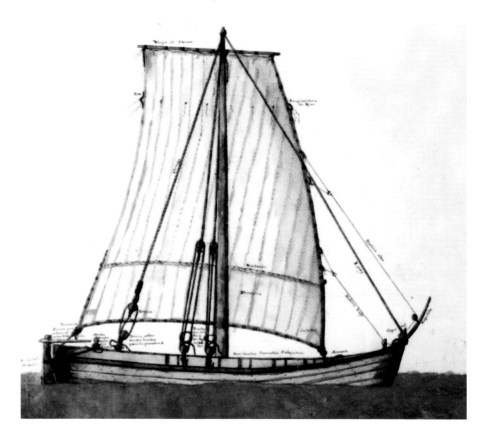

rigged with a fore-and-aft-rigged mainsail and jib foresail. A brigantine was a two-mast vessel with a square-rigged foresail, a fore-and-aft-rigged mainsail and square-rigged topsails on both masts. In addition, she carried jib sheets attached to her bowsprit. A variant of the brigantine was the brig, which carried square-rigged lower sails on both masts and a fore-and-aft sail, which in turn was related to the snow.

An analysis of pirate attacks between 1710 and 1730 in American waters shows that over half of those recorded were conducted by sloops (Cordingly, 1995). The majority of the remainder were carried out by square-rigged ships, such as Bartholomew Roberts' *Royal Fortune*. At the bottom of the list, one attack in eight was made by a brigantine, brig or snow, while a mere handful of attacks were conducted by pirates in open boats such as ships' longboats. However impressive the pirate flagships of Roberts and Teach might have been, they were less successful than sloops. In part, this bald statistical analysis hides some important facts. First, the success of individual pirates such as Bartholomew Roberts, who captured over 200 prizes, clouds the statistics, as vessel for vessel his series of square-rigged flagships were far more effective than a host of smaller

This merchant 'snow' is typical of the long-distance European trading vessels which plied the waters between the Caribbean and Britain during the 18th century. A snow was the largest two-masted vessel of its day, and differed from a brig by having a small trysail mast stepped immediately behind its mainmast. (Stratford Archive)

craft. Also, pirates such as Teach and Roberts operated in squadrons of several vessels, and the smaller sloops in the force would be sent ahead to intercept merchantmen, knowing that the larger pirate flagship was near enough to support them if they encountered any heavy resistance.

That said, it is clear that vessel for vessel, the sloop was the most important type of pirate ship of the period, as almost all pirates began their careers in this type of vessel. To modern sailors, the term 'sloop' refers to a sailing vessel with a fore-and-aft rig carried on a single mast. This usually takes the form of a mainsail and a single foresail jib. During the golden age, the term was less clearly defined, and it was used to refer to a variety of vessels with a selection of different rigs. Sloops appeared in naval service from the mid-17th century, one of the first being a prize captured from the privateering port of Dunkirk by the Commonwealth Navy. With a keel length of 40ft (12m) and a beam of just over 12ft (3.7m), she was one of the smallest independent warships in service. This vessel and other naval sloops of the late 17th century carried a minimal armament of four guns. Interestingly, the English also used the term 'sloop' in reference to small, two-mast vessels, with a square-rigged mainsail and topsail. Some naval sloops were three-masted.

The hull plan and lines of a
Bermudan sloop, from
Chapman's *Architectura Navalis
Mercatoria* (1768). Sloops such
as this accounted for the majority
of pirate vessels operating in
the Caribbean during the early
18th century. (Stratford Archive)

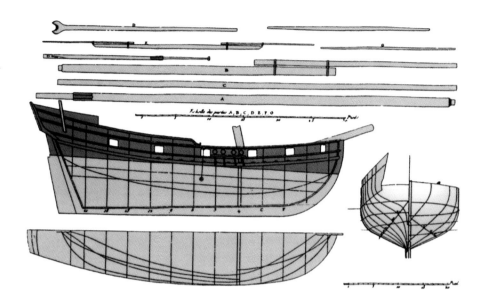

The plans of HMS *Ferret*, a naval sloop of 1711, still survive and serve as an indication of what the larger sloops of this period looked like (Cordingly, 1995). She had a 50ft (15.2m) keel, a 65ft-long (20m) open deck, a beam of just under 21ft (6.4m) and a depth in the hold (draught) of 9ft (2.7m). With a displacement of approximately 115 tons, she was large enough to support an armament of 10–12 guns. In addition, a series of eight oar ports were cut in her hull below the line of her gun ports, enabling her to use oars when she was becalmed. Although it is unclear whether she was fitted with one or two masts, the latter is more likely, as naval sloops built five years later were twin-mast types. While we have a rough idea of what naval sloops looked like, the appearance of pirate sloops is more problematic. Although no plans of merchant sloops of the period have survived, we can try to reconstruct the appearance of these craft from a combination of pictorial evidence and mid-18th century plans, compiled in Frederick Henry Chapman's *Architectura Navalis Mercatoria*. We know that sloops built in Jamaica and Bermuda were particularly prized for their speed during this period. The Jamaican vessel, developed from the fast pinnaces of the previous century, was built of red cedar and was recognizable by its low freeboard and steeply raked mast. Similar fast sloops were built in Bermuda, and Chapman provides plans for a vessel of this type.

The sloop shown by Chapman is 60ft (18.3m) long (with a 45ft keel), and has a beam of 16ft (4.9m), making her smaller and narrower than her naval counterpart. This sloop also carried a single mast, fitted at a rakish angle of approximately

12 degrees from the perpendicular, sloping aft. She is fitted with a long bowsprit, angled upwards at 20 degrees from the horizontal. Judging from the yards depicted, her rig consisted of a gaff-rigged fore-and-aft spanker, a square-rigged topsail, and probably one or two foresail jibs. The upper and lower booms of the driver are almost as long as the sloop itself, meaning that she carried a large amount of sail compared to her size and displacement (which has been estimated at around 95–100 tons). Like the *Ferret*, Chapman's Bermuda sloop was pierced to carry 12 guns. Despite an upwards slope towards the stern, the vessel is flush-decked, with no break for a quarterdeck.

This depiction ties in perfectly with three rare depictions of colonial American sloops of the early 18th century. An engraving showing New York harbour produced by William Burgis in 1717 shows the small sloop *Fancy*, a vessel that served as a private yacht. Like many of the other sloops in the engraving, the *Fancy* is shown with a single mast and a sail plan that follows the one outlined by Chapman in his mid-18th-century study. An interesting touch is her roundhouse, a curved shelter covering the rear of her quarterdeck. An engraving by William Burgis dated 1717 shows a sloop anchored off Boston Lighthouse. Although well

Edward England, wearing a gentleman's coat and smallsword with the battle between his ship the *Fancy* and the East Indiaman *Cassandra* depicted in the background. After a brutal action where the two ships cannonaded each other for hours, the *Cassandra* surrendered. England's leniency towards the enemy crew led to his removal as captain. (Stratford Archive)

A brigantine, identified by her two square-rigged foremast sails, and a gaff-rigged sail on her mainmast. These craft were used by Caribbean pirates during the golden age, but were more commonly associated with the buccaneers of the 17th century, a link that may suggest the origins of her name – as a brigands' vessel. Engraving from Lobat's *Nouveau Voyage* (Paris, 1722). (Stratford Archive)

armed, with seven gun ports per side, she represents a merchant vessel, rather than a warship. This is supported by contemporary accounts referring to the increased sale of small guns to merchant ship owners in the early 18th century, as threats from both privateers and pirates encouraged the increased armament of merchant vessels. A third engraving, of the port of Charleston, South Carolina, shows a range of shipping in the foreground, including several sloops. These are all single-mast, but only one is shown carrying a square-sail yard on her topmast. Although we cannot be certain as to the appearance of pirate sloops, the similarity of these depictions to the Chapman drawings and the *Ferret* plans provides us with a more accurate picture of their appearance than we could reasonably hope for, given the paucity of precise information that has survived.

Brigantines are slightly more straightforward. We have several contemporary descriptions of these vessels, and their rig continued unchanged for a century after the golden age. Again, Chapman provides a series of plans that aid our understanding of what these ships looked like and how they sailed. Whatever the term 'brigantine' had meant before 1690, by the start of the golden age of piracy it had come to mean a square-sailed rig on a foremast, and a fore-and-aft rig and square-sail rig combined on the mainmast. The term was abbreviated to 'brig' by the middle of the 18th century, but by that time this term referred to a vessel with a fore-and-aft-rigged spanker, no square-sail in front of it, and a trapezoid main staysail stretched between the foremast and the mainmast. It is likely that earlier in

The pirate schooner *Panda*, commanded by perhaps the last Caribbean pirate, 'Don' Pedro Gibert. A smuggler who only committed one piratical act – when he captured the American vessel *Mexican* in 1832 – Gibert also became the last man to be executed for piracy in the United States. (Stratford Archive)

the century, the term 'brig' was used when referring to this variant of the standard brigantine rig, in much the same way as the term 'snow' was applied to a square-rigged variant with a secondary vertical mast mounted immediately behind the mainmast. All of these vessels were used in small numbers by pirates, but largely as a matter of necessity rather than choice. The brigantine and its variants lacked the high proportion of sail area to displacement that characterized the sloop, and to a lesser extent the faster square-rigged ships of the period such as slavers.

During the early 18th century, a new type of vessel made its appearance on the Atlantic seaboard. The schooner was a vessel with two masts, a fore-and-aft rig, and sometimes an additional square topsail rigged on her foremast to provide increased momentum. The first mention of a schooner appeared in the *Boston Newsletter* of 1717, and six years later another Boston newspaper wrote an account of a pirate schooner commanded by John Phillips, operating off Newfoundland. In fact, the schooner was a New England vessel, captured by Phillips off the Grand Banks. While schooners were certainly used by some of the later pirates, and while two-mast vessels of this type may have existed in North American waters before 1717, they were never popular, accounting for a mere five per cent of all pirate attacks from 1710 to 1730. Despite this, schooners were popularized by later writers of piratical fiction, as they corresponded closely with the vessels these writers could see in everyday use. The true small pirate vessel par excellence of the golden age remained the sloop.

PIRATE FLAGSHIPS

As we have seen from the statistics given in the preceding text, just over a third of piratical attacks conducted during the golden age were made by cut-throats in large, square-rigged vessels. The ultimate goal of any pirate who wanted to trade up was the acquisition of a powerful vessel, capable of being turned into a formidable warship. A single pirate ship of this kind could devastate trade in its area of operation, as was the case when Blackbeard arrived off Charleston in 1718, and when Bartholomew Roberts cruised off the West African coast three years later.

In order to understand the effectiveness of these ships, we need to examine what kinds of larger vessels were in operation at this time. We are also fortunate in being able to draw on evidence from a number of pirate shipwrecks during this period.

Today, the word 'ship' means any large, seagoing vessel. To the mariners of the 18th century, the term had a far more precise meaning. To them, a ship was a sailing vessel that had three masts and carried square-rigged sails. This included the majority of warships, including ships-of-the-line, the larger merchantmen, East India Company ships and some slave ships (or 'guineamen'). Other substantial sailing vessels such as polaccas (polacres), tartans and fluyts were not strictly considered ships.

A fluyt was the most common type of merchantman of the 17th century. Originally a Dutch design, these high-sided vessels with two or (more commonly) three masts were designed for economy of effort. They were slow and carried a relatively small sail area for their size, but they could be operated by a far smaller crew than other vessels of a comparable size. Although they were of little use as buccaneering or pirate ships, buccaneers during the late 17th century sometimes used them as transports for men, supplies or plunder. By the 18th century, other faster vessels were available to the pirates, and the lumbering fluyts became nothing more than easy prey.

In the waters of the Mediterranean Sea and the Indian Ocean, pirates sometimes adopted the local craft of the area. Of these, the most common were polaccas, feluccas or tartans. Of these, the polacca was found as far west as the Caribbean, and its type of rigging could be found in other three-mast vessels, even ships. Its distinguishing characteristic was that its square-rigged yards could be lowered for ease of setting, and a fore-and-aft-rigged spanker was fitted to her mizzen mast. Although similar to a ship, its form of sail plan gave the vessel type its own identity. A felucca was a narrow, fast vessel of Arabic origin, occasionally used by pirates in the Indian Ocean. It carried lateen sails on its two masts. A smaller version was the tartan, which was distinguished by the pronounced forward rake of her foremast-cum-bowsprit and her ability to operate under oars. Another more common variation on the ship was the bark (or barque). It was essentially a three-mast vessel rigged like a ship, but instead of square-rigged sails on its mizzen mast it carried a fore-and-aft-rigged sail, usually lateen-rigged.

Returning to fully fledged ships, a number of pirates used these vessels as their flagships, armed with up to 40 guns. The French warship that Bartholomew Roberts renamed the *Royal Fortune* and the Royal Africa Company ship *Onslow* were exceptions to this rule, as they were better armed than any other pirate ship. Ships of this size were hard to find. The average size of English (from 1707, British) merchant ships during the golden age of piracy was between 100 and 200 tons, the larger vessels usually being from London, and engaged in trade with the West Indies or the American colonies. Specifically, many of these larger ships

This well-armed fluyt of the late 17th century is pierced for 18 guns, an indication of the threat posed by pirates to maritime trade in the Americas. The shallow draught of these vessels made them well suited for trade with smaller Caribbean ports and ideal as buccaneering transport vessels, capable of carrying 150 well-armed men apiece. (Stratford Archive)

were involved in the 'triangular trade', shipping trade goods to West Africa, slaves to the Caribbean, and rum or sugar back to London. By contrast, the majority of the coastal vessels that plied the waters of the Atlantic seaboard or the Caribbean displaced less than 100 tons.

Even the largest merchant vessels tended to be undermanned, as wages cut into profit. The 180-ton slave ship *Henrietta Marie*, which was wrecked off the coast of Florida in 1700, had a crew of only 20 men and was defended by eight small minions (3–4-pdrs). She was a typical merchantman, meaning that the pirates who attacked such ships heavily outnumbered the majority of merchant crews. Even a small pirate sloop with a crew of 30 men could capture a large merchantman, if the attack was made with enough vigour. Faced with a vessel like the *Queen Anne's Revenge*, the merchantmen had no chance whatsoever. A merchant captain captured by Blackbeard in December 1718 reported what he saw on board the pirate flagship to the colonial authorities: 'the ship … was a French "guinea man" [he heard on board], that she had then thirty six guns mounted, that she was very full of men. He believes three hundred … and that they did not seem to want for provisions.'

Not long after, Blackbeard used this floating fortress to blockade Charleston. Local citizens reported what they saw: 'This company is commanded by one

Bartholomew Roberts ('Black Bart'), at Whydah, on the West African coast, 1722. Behind him his pirate 'flagship', the *Royal Fortune*, is shown entering a roadstead, following the *Great Ranger*. In the background a fleet of anchored slave ships await their fate. (Stratford Archive)

Teach (alias Blackbeard), who has a ship of 40 odd guns under him and 3 sloops tenders besides and are in all above 400 men.'

Fortunately for us, the *Queen Anne's Revenge* grounded in Beaufort Inlet, North Carolina (then called Topsail Inlet) in June 1718, just weeks after raising the blockade of Charleston. Although Blackbeard removed his booty when he abandoned the vessel, her remains provide archaeologists with a useful insight into pirate flagships of the period.

The *Queen Anne's Revenge* probably began life as the *Concorde*, a French 14-gun ship of 200–300 tons. The ship became a well-armed merchantman, and made three slave-trading voyages to the Guinea coast. In November 1717, she was captured off St Vincent by Blackbeard. Blackbeard increased her armament to 40 guns. An archaeological investigation of the wreck that began in 1997 has revealed the physical remains of the *Queen Anne's Revenge*, her armament and her fittings. The wreck lies in 24ft (7.3m) of water, and to date 21 guns have been observed and six recovered, of various sizes and nationalities, although these are predominantly British. The team expect to find more ordnance on the site during the excavation. Musket shot, roundshot and small arms all suggest the vessel was extremely well armed. A bell dated 1705 fits the profile of Blackbeard's flagship, as does the presence of a pewter syringe similar to those that would have been

A view of the harbour and town of Boston in 1723, from an engraving based on an original drawing by William Burgis. It shows a range of vessels, from large three-masted transatlantic merchantmen to New England coastal sloops and fishing vessels. The Royal Naval guard ship in the foreground is shown firing a salute. (Stratford Archive)

included in the chest of medical supplies Blackbeard took on board off Charleston. As both archaeological and archival research are continuing, it is hoped the wreck will provide us with enough information on the vessel to confirm its identity, and to further our understanding of Blackbeard and his flagship.

One of the only pirate flagships to exceed the size and power of the *Queen Anne's Revenge* was the *Royal Fortune*, the flagship of Bartholomew Roberts. A Danish victim of Roberts recalled what the ship looked like:

> The said Roberts' ship is manned with about 180 white men and about 48 French Creole negroes and has mounted 12 eight-pounders; 4 twelve-pounders; 12 six-pounders; 6 [bronze] eight-pounders, and 8 four-pounders; and in [beneath] her main and foremast has 7 guns, two- and three-pounders, and 2 swivel guns upon her mizzen.

This powerful 42-gun ship was originally a French Fifth Rate warship, which had been relegated to service in the Garde de la Coste under the orders of the governor of Martinique. She was captured in the West Indies and sailed to West Africa as the *Royal Fortune*. Her hull was probably too rotten for Roberts' crew to operate her effectively, and she was abandoned in favour of the *Onslow* which, as mentioned previously, was duly re-christened *Royal Fortune*, after the pirates transferred the guns listed above from one ship to the other.

A smaller vessel but still a powerful one was the *Adventure Galley*, commanded by Captain William Kidd. Built in Deptford, London, in 1695, the vessel was a purpose-built privateer, combining the conventional square-rigged sail plan of a ship with a series of oar ports in the lower hull, which enabled her to be rowed during a calm. She displaced 287 tons, carried a crew of 152 men and was armed with 34 guns. Although no illustration of this famous pirate vessel survives, she would have been similar to her sister vessel the *Charles Galley*, built in the same yard some 19 years before for naval service. Her keel was 114ft (34.7m) long, and the galley had a 28 ¹⁄₂ft (8.7m) beam, with a draught of just over 8 ¹⁄₂ft (2.6m). Kidd abandoned the *Adventure Galley* in a bay in north-eastern Madagascar in 1698, as her hull was rotten. Her hulk was then torched and sunk by the pirates. In the summer of 1999, the first of three expeditions led by pirate historian Barry Clifford and archaeologist John de Bry searched the area and uncovered the remains of two ships, some 50ft (15.2m) apart, in shallow water. It is believed that one is the *Adventure Galley* and the other is the wreck of a smaller pirate ship,

The sleek French merchantman shown in this engraving dated 1714 is very similar to the description of *La Concorde*, the Nantes slave ship Blackbeard took as his flagship. He re-named her *Queen Anne's Revenge*, and turned her into a floating fortress armed with upwards of 40 guns. Slave ships were built for speed, and so made excellent pirate ships if they were captured. (Stratford Archive)

known as the *Fiery Dragon* (commanded by Captain Billy One Hands). The burnt remains of English oak timbers and pewter suggest the first find was Kidd's flagship, but more work needs to be undertaken to positively identify the shipwreck. The *Fiery Dragon* was probably a smaller ship, of some 150 tons, and was known to have been filled with plunder when she sank following an accidental fire in 1721, some two decades after the loss of Kidd's vessel.

The *Adventure Galley* was the second pirate ship discovered by Barry Clifford. In 1984, he located the wreck of the *Whydah*, the flagship of the pirate Samuel Bellamy, which was wrecked in a storm off Cape Cod in April 1717. For the past two decades, the *Whydah* has been salvaged by Clifford and his team, revealing a wealth of information on pirate ships of the period. The *Whydah* (named after the West African slave port) was a three-mast ship of some 300 tons, built in London in 1715–16 probably for use as a slave ship. Like the *Adventure Galley*, she was fitted with oar ports and oars (sweeps). She was captured by Bellamy on her maiden voyage in the spring of 1717 as she was returning to London from Jamaica, laden with rum and sugar. Bellamy elected to turn her into his flagship and increased her armament of ten guns to 26 pieces, making her an extremely powerful vessel. Clifford and his team recovered a range of artefacts from the wreck, including ordnance, a ship's bell, small arms, shot, grenades, swivel guns,

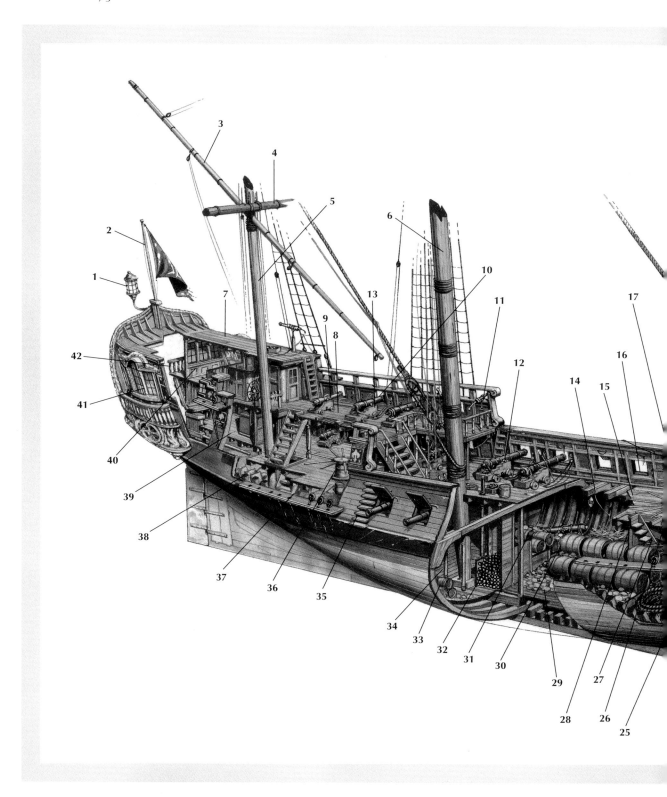

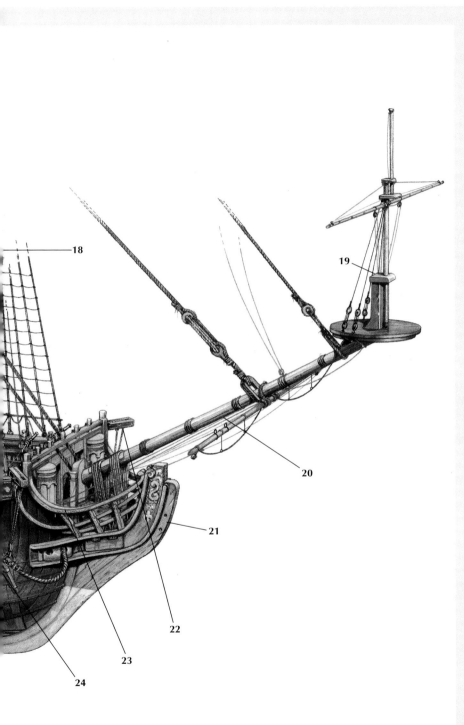

The *Queen Anne's Revenge*, 1718

1 Stern lantern
2 Blackbeard's flag
3 Spanker yard
4 Crosstrees
5 Mizzen mast
6 Mainmast
7 Poop deck
8 Quarterdeck
9 Minion (4-pdr)
10 Converted gun port
11 Swivel gun (1-pdr)
12 (8-pdr) gun
13 Saker (6-pdr)
14 Deck beams
15 Waist
16 Original gun port
17 Cut-down forecastle
18 Foremast
19 Spritsail topmast
20 Bowsprit
21 Position of figurehead (lost in storm before vessel was captured)
22 Cathead
23 Heads
24 Anchor (one of three, with one stowed in the hold)
25 Cable tier
26 Capstan
27 Crew's quarters
28 Hatchway to crew's quarters
29 Ballast (ballast stones and spare ordnance)
30 Water casks
31 Cargo space (hold): gold dust found in this area by archaeologists
32 Shot locker
33 Powder room
34 Ship's pumps
35 Entry way
36 Warping capstan
37 Rum store and armoury
38 Dry provisions store
39 Master's cabin
40 Blackbeard's cabin
41 Stern windows
42 Stern gallery

This gold ring and Spanish eight escudos gold coin (known as a 'doubloon') were recovered from the shipwreck of Bellamy's pirate ship *Whydah*, which was lost in a hurricane off Cape Cod in April 1717. Beneath the gold coin lie irregularly shaped silver eight escudo coins – the 'pieces of eight' of pirate fiction. (Corbis)

timber, iron hull fasteners and other objects that were indispensable to a well-equipped pirate. An analysis of everyday items such as eating utensils, gaming pieces and other personal items might reveal hitherto unknown information about the pirates themselves. A survey of the wreck site reveals that her hull was only 100ft (30.5m) long, making her small, compact, but heavily armed. It is hoped that work on this fascinating site, plus the three other identified pirate wrecks in North Carolina and Madagascar, will provide us with a greater understanding of how these ships were built and operated, although at present only general facts have emerged from the investigations. First, all these ships were very heavily armed, carrying a range of weapons, from pistols and grenades to large guns. Second, apart from *Queen Anne's Revenge*, their hulls betrayed damage by *teredo* worms or poor construction, suggesting the waters of the Caribbean Sea and Indian Ocean were extremely harmful to wooden sailing ships. Finally, all these pirate ships were lost due to accident or carelessness, which underlines the point that the piratical life was an extremely dangerous one. Life expectancy was short, for ships as well as for the pirates themselves.

THE PIRATE SHIP IN ACTION

Large pirate 'flagships' needed large crews. In the Royal Navy during the early 18th century, a Fourth Rate armed with 40–50 guns usually carried a complement of 250 men, as an average of six to eight men were required to crew the guns. Even if only one broadside (or one side of the ship) was crewed at any one time, that still left only a handful of crew to trim the sails and steer the ship. In a large pirate ship, the same numbers were involved, although the tendency would probably be to provide minimal crew of four to six men for each gun and keep the rest of the crew back, in readiness to fight a boarding action. This still meant the ships needed a lot of men, and to fight the *Queen Anne's Revenge*, 60 men were needed just to man one of her broadsides.

As for the guns themselves, archaeological evidence shows that these reflected what one would expect from a cross-section of maritime ordnance of the period. The majority were of British manufacture, cast-iron pieces, predominantly produced in the Wealden region of Sussex. The five guns recovered from the *Queen Anne's Revenge* show a smattering of other nationalities, especially French, and all were cast-iron. By that stage, bronze pieces were both rare and expensive. As the reliability of cast pieces had increased markedly during the later 17th century, bronze guns were limited to use in major warships or East Indiamen, when they were usually mounted near the ship's compass to reduce magnetic distortion. In addition to the main armament of the pirate vessel, evidence from shipwrecks suggests they were extremely well equipped with small arms, shot, powder and grenades.

As discussed previously, for the most part pirates managed to capture their prizes without fighting. Occasionally, though, they encountered a well-armed merchant vessel willing and able to stand its ground. In some cases, this resistance forced the pirates to give up the fight and sail away in search of an easier victim. In other notable cases, the pirates were determined to quash this resistance, and an incredibly bloody fight ensued. The intention here is to look more closely at how they performed during this type of action.

In an account of the engagement between the English East India Company ship *Cassandra* and the pirate Edward England in July 1720, Captain James McRae described how his opponent attacked with two vessels, one of 30 guns and the *Fancy* of 34 guns. The Scottish captain was deserted by the English East Indiaman

Blackbeard's last fight, 1718. This scene depicts the brutal mêlée that ensued when Teach and his crew boarded Maynard's Royal Naval sloop. Teach and Maynard exchange pistol shots, then draw swords and close for their fight to the death. Teach's body was found marked with five bullet wounds and 20 sword cuts. (Angus McBride © Osprey Publishing Ltd)

Greenwich and the Dutch East India Company ship that sailed with her, and she was left alone to face the pirates:

> For though we did not doubt that he [the *Greenwich*] would join us, because when he got about a league from us, he brought his ship to, and look'd on, yet both he and the *Ostender* basely deserted us, and left us engaged with barbarous and inhuman enemies, with their black and bloody flags hanging over us, without the least appearance of escaping being cut to pieces. But God, in his good Providence determined otherwise, for notwithstanding their Superiority, we engaged them both about three hours, during which the biggest received some shot betwixt wind & water, which made them keep off a little to stop their leaks.
>
> The other endeavoured all she could to board us, by rowing with her oars, being with half a ship's length of us above an Hour, but by good Fortune we shot all her oars to pieces, which prevented them, and by consequence, saved our lives.

THE LIFE OF

LAFITTE,

THE FAMOUS PIRATE OF THE GULF OF MEXICO.

Lafitte boarding the Queen East Indiaman.

With a History of the Pirates of Barrataria—and an account of their volunteering for the defence of New Orleans; and their daring intrepidity under General Jackson, during the battle of the 8th of January, 1815. For which important service they were pardoned by President Madison.

Jean Laffite was a French-born smuggler who rose to command a pirate community located outside New Orleans in the first decade of the 19th century. In this account from a 19th-century pirate history, he is confused with Robert Surcouf and credited with capturing an East India Company ship. (Stratford Archive)

OPPOSITE Blackbeard's last fight, 1718. This scene depicts Blackbeard's sloop *Adventure* engaged in battle with Maynard's sloop *Jane*. Maynard hid most of his men below decks, surprising the pirates when they boarded the navy ship. Blackbeard was killed in the bloody mêlée that followed. (Tony Bryan © Osprey Publishing Ltd)

About 4 o'clock, most of the Officers and men posted on the quarterdeck being killed and wounded, the largest ship making up to us with all diligence, being still within a cable's length of us, and often giving us a Broadside, and no hope of Captain Kirby coming to our Assistance, we endeavour'd to run ashore; and tho' we drew four foot of water more than the pyrate, it pleased God that he stuck fast on a higher ground than we happily fell in with; so was dissapoint'd a second time from boarding us.

Here we had a more violent engagement than before. All my Officers, and most of my men behav'd with unexpected Courage, & as we had considerable advantage by having a broadside to his bow, we did him great damage, so that had Captain Kirby come in then, I believe we should have taken both, for we had one of them for sure, but the other pyrate (who was still firing at us) seeing the *Greenwich* did not offer to assist us. He supplied his Consort with three boats full of fresh men. About 5 in the evening, the *Greenwich* stood clear away to Sea, leaving us struggling hard for life in the very jaws of death, which the other pyrate, that was now afloat, seeing this, got a warp out, and was hauling under our Stern, by which time many of my men were killed or wounded, and no hopes left of us from being all murdered by enraged barbarous Conquerors, I order'd all that could, to get into the longboat under the cover of the smoke of our guns, so that with what some did in boats, & others by swimming, most of us that were able reached ashoar by 7 o' clock. When the Pyrates came aboard, they cut three of our wounded men to pieces. I, with a few of my people, made what haste I could to the Kingstown, 25 miles from us, where I arrived next day, almost dead with fatigue and loss of blood, having been sorely wounded in the Head by a musket ball.

The brutality of this hard-fought action is repeated several times in accounts of actions with pirates featuring Henry Every in the Indian Ocean, Stede Bonnet and Blackbeard in the Carolinas, Bartholomew Roberts off West Africa and several others. This was unlike any neatly fought naval action, with the exchange of long-range broadsides. Instead, these engagements more resembled street fighting, with both sides aware that no quarter was expected nor given. Both sides used terrain (shoal water, land or reefs) to best advantage, and combined manoeuvre with point-blank exchanges of ordnance, small arms and grenades. A draw was out of the question. These engagements were bloody fights to the death.

Pirate Codes

The popular image of pirates is one of a lawless group of cut-throats, operating beyond the fringes of society. While elements of this conception are correct, they were also frequently well organized, at least in terms of self-imposed legal codes and charters. Piracy in the early 18th century actually provided an example of experimental democracy in action, long before such notions became popular. In most recorded cases, a pirate vessel was owned and operated by the crew, who conducted themselves according to rules they imposed to control most aspects of their piratical activity. The division of plunder was agreed to and laid out, officers were elected, codes of discipline enforced and punishments defined. Rather than an anarchic body, a pirate crew, although having immense individual freedom, were constrained by a code of conduct, in a way similar to the articles employed on contemporary merchant or naval ships.

Every pirate ship followed its own set of rules (or articles) that were actually written up and agreed to by all parties before the cruise ever started. If the crew of a merchant ship mutinied and turned to piracy, this was often the first action after taking over the ship. The precedent for this had been set in the preceding century. In the late 17th century, buccaneers had used a form of written charter (or *Charte-Partie*), outlining conditions of service, restitution in case of death or injury and the agreed division of any booty. This was considered a legal document and was even used in Jamaican courts to settle disputes. As buccaneering gave way to piracy in the late 17th century, these became more like secret charters than legal documents. A number of different examples have been preserved. Some, such as those drawn up by Bartholomew Roberts and his crew, were quite draconian, but all provide a rare and useful insight into the pirate's life at sea. Whatever form they took, the articles were rigidly adhered to. The pirates had to turn their backs on the law of nations and the near-absolute power granted to captains at sea. To replace them they set about establishing their own egalitarian form of constitution, and surviving examples all follow a similar pattern.

The captain was usually elected into office by the crew, often by a majority show of hands. He could just as easily be voted out if the crew became dissatisfied with his performance. He had complete authority when the ship was in action, much as was the case on naval vessels. He could kill a crew member who refused to follow orders, and made all the decisions without question.

A Selection of Pirate Ship Names

Some ship names were used by more than one pirate, and some pirates, such as Bartholomew Roberts, renamed their ships several times. Also, some pirates were associated with several ships during their careers. Only the most important ones are recorded here. Ships were often renamed with various names, and the names used indiscriminately. Roberts had a ship called the *Fortune* which was renamed the *Good Fortune*, and later *Royal Fortune*. Changing names was also a means of avoiding identification, or was undertaken as a form of camouflage.

Pirate Ship	Associated Captain
Adventure Galley	William Kidd
Fancy	Henry Every, Edward England
Flying Dragon	Edmund Condent
Happy Delivery	George Lowther
Liberty	Thomas Tew
Pearl	Edward England
Queen Anne's Revenge	Edward Teach (Blackbeard)
Ranger	Charles Vane
Revenge	John Gow, Stede Bonnet, John Phillips, Edward Teach
Rising Sun	William Moody
Royal Fortune	Bartholomew Roberts
Whydah	Samuel Bellamy

When the smoke cleared, the quartermaster took over the division of the spoils. The only other elected officer, the quartermaster shared power with the captain and was his second-in-command. His duties included supervising the running of the ship, except when in battle, and he decided what plunder to take, which captured ships to keep and which should be burned. He was in charge of everything of value taken from a captured ship, which he placed in a common fund until it was divided. He then supervised its distribution and resolved any arguments that arose. The majority of pirates had previously served on warships, and the absolute power of a naval captain was an anathema to them. Their solution was this form of power sharing between captain and quartermaster. Like the captain, the quartermaster could be removed from power at any time by a majority vote.

OVERLEAF Entitled *This Lean Straight Rover Looked the Part of a Competent Soldier*, this painting by Frank Schoonover depicts Blackbeard's pirates as they land in Charles Town during the pirate's blockade of the port in 1718. On that occasion the pirates held the port to ransom, and it was spared being put to the flame. (Stratford Archive)

In most cases, the other officers on board a pirate ship were appointed by the captain (or by both captain and quartermaster). The master (or sailing master) was responsible for navigation, and was a valued member of the crew (often being the only literate person on board). The boatswain was in charge of all seamanship tasks, as well as maintaining the ship, the sails, rigging and tackle. The gunner supervised the gun crews and maintained the ship's armament and all communally held small arms. Other posts included the sailmaker and ship's carpenter, and occasionally larger vessels (including many ex-privateers) employed a surgeon of sorts.

The division of plunder was always a possible area of contention among a pirate crew, so the process was recorded in detail. If a number of ships were operating in consort (as was the case with Bartholomew Roberts' fleet in 1722), the plunder was divided equally between all the ships, in proportion to the crew carried. This aimed to reduce the chance of any one ship absconding with all the loot. The booty was normally divided at the end of a voyage. Before it was split, deductions were made to men who had suffered injury, following a pre-arranged rate. Unlike the prize money of naval service, the ships' officers received at most two shares to the average crewman's one. (In the Royal Navy, a captain could keep up to a quarter, depending on circumstance.) Unlike the buccaneering era, where captured goods frequently included hauls of specie, the usual pirate hauls of sugar, cloth, rum or tobacco were harder to divide. The romanticized view of the crew sitting on a beach dividing up chests full of treasure is a fantasy. More commonly, the cargo would be sold to a known 'middle man' in a secluded inlet or small port. The income would then be divided by the quartermaster. If this was impossible, a rough division was made and agreed upon using the raw commodities themselves. Some forms of plunder, especially rum or other liquor, were divided at the time of capture, as it would be almost impossible to avoid pilfering during the voyage.

Many parts of the pirate code were designed to prevent potential sources of conflict among the crew. In fairly strict examples, like those of Roberts' crew (see page 152), these included rules against gambling, womanizing, fighting and drinking, all the elements that are usually associated with pirates. If plundered alcohol was divided, the crew would get drunk, and this inevitably led to conflict. Even Edward Teach recorded problems with keeping the crew happy (and therefore not voting him out of office) when his ship had run out of rum. The codes are an interesting example of man trying to constrain himself against his worst excesses, while being free to indulge in them at will!

Pirate Flags

While the precise origin of the pirate flag remains unknown, its ancestry can be traced with some certainty. The flag was used to intimidate the enemy or victim and was designed to conjure up fear and dread. It was an important part of the pirate armoury and was the pirate's best form of psychological warfare, especially when combined with a preceding reputation of not showing any quarter if opposed. If a pirate could intimidate an enemy to heave-to without offering resistance, then danger to the pirate crew would be eliminated, and the victim's ship could be taken undamaged, thus maintaining its value. Threatening images on the flags were often associated with a known pirate (and hence his reputation), or could conjure up more specific warnings. For example, Bartholomew Roberts bore a grudge against the island colonies of Barbados and Martinique, so in their waters he used a flag showing a pirate figure (presumably Roberts himself) standing on two skulls. Under one were the letters 'ABH' (standing for 'A Barbadian's Head'), and under the other was 'AMH' (for 'A Martiniquan's Head'). The threat was clear, and sailors from these colonies would expect no mercy if they offered any resistance.

Identifying an enemy at sea has always been a difficult task. In the 16th century, royal ships painted their sails with national emblems (e.g. Tudor roses for English vessels, Catholic crosses for Spanish ones), but these ships operated in distinctive naval squadrons, treasure *flotas* or other armada-like forces. For other vessels, no such symbols were used. Instead, national flags or banners were employed, an identification technique first used in the medieval period. By the 17th and 18th centuries, national symbolism had stabilized enough for publishers to be able to produce flag identification charts, listing the flags of all known maritime nations.

At sea, these symbols indicated national identity and whether the vessel was potentially friendly or hostile, although this was not always a reliable indication. Privateers or pirates (as well as national warships) often used foreign flags and banners in order to entice the enemy within range. As long as these flags were replaced with the appropriate national emblem, this was seen as a legitimate *ruse de guerre*. The best policy was usually to assume all shipping was hostile, especially in time of war.

Privateers, approved as such by their national governments, flew their respective national flag (e.g. the cross of St George for England or the Dutch

OPPOSITE Frank Schoonover's painting *Blackbeard in Smoke and Flame* appeared in the *American Boy* magazine in September 1922. The artist captured the bizarre and ferocious appearance of America's most notorious pirate as he would have appeared during his heyday in 1718. (Stratford Archive)

Charter of Bartholomew Roberts' Crew, 1722

Every man shall have an equal vote in affairs of moment. He shall have an equal title to the fresh provisions or strong liquors at any time seized, and shall use them at pleasure unless a scarcity makes it necessary for the common good that a retrenchment may be voted.

Every man shall be called fairly in turn by the list on board of prizes, because over and above their proper share, they are allowed a shift of clothes. But if they defraud the company to the value of even one dollar in plate, jewels or money, they shall be marooned. If any man rob another he shall have his nose and ears slit, and be put ashore where he shall be sure to encounter hardships.

None shall game for money, either with dice or cards.

The lights and candles shall be put out at eight at night, and if any of the crew desire to drink after that hour they shall sit upon the open deck without lights.

Each man shall keep his piece, cutlass and pistols at all times clean and ready for action.

No boy or woman to be allowed amongst them. If any man shall be found seducing one of the latter sex and carrying her to sea in disguise, he shall suffer death.

He that shall desert the ship or his quarters in time of battle shall be punished by death or marooning.

None shall strike another aboard the ship, but every man's quarrel shall be ended on shore by sword or pistol in this manner: at the word of command from the Quartermaster, each man being previously placed back to back, shall turn and fire immediately. If any man do not, the Quartermaster shall knock the piece out of his hand. If both miss their aim, they shall take to their cutlasses, and he that draws first blood shall be declared the victor.

No man shall talk of breaking up their way of living till each has a share of £1,000. Every man who shall become a cripple or lose a limb in the service shall have eight hundred pieces of eight from the common stock, and for lesser hurts proportionately.

The Captain and the Quartermaster shall each receive two shares of a prize, the Master Gunner and Boatswain, one and one half shares, all other officers one and one quarter, and private gentlemen of fortune one share each.

The musicians shall have rest on the Sabbath Day only, by right, on all other days, by favour only.

tricolour for Holland). By the mid-17th century, privateers flew privateering symbols in addition to national flags. Without the national flag, they would have been considered as pirates. Although the nature of these early privateering flags is

The female personification of Colonial America besieged by pirates, the line of bodies hanging from the gallows proving that she emerged victorious from the bloody struggle. The flag pictured here includes a number of piracy-related symbols: the skull and cross-bones, sword, skeleton and hourglass. Such images suggest just how seriously the pirate threat was taken in Colonial America during the early 18th century. An engraving from a contemporary publication. (Stratford Archive)

unrecorded, in 1694 an English Admiralty law made the flying of a red privateering symbol mandatory for English privateers. The red flag is depicted in earlier Dutch maritime paintings, but the meaning was not recorded. The red flag today is associated with warning, and in the context of late 17th-century privateering, it served the same purpose of warning another vessel not to resist. The flag as defined by the Admiralty in 1694 was an all red flag known as 'The Red Jack'. Its description as 'that recognized privateering symbol' indicated that the device was flown earlier in the century. Privateers later referred to 'sailing under the Red Jack'. At around the same time a new symbol appeared. References to a black flag were noted in reports of privateering actions, the first in 1697. This was raised by a privateer if the victim's vessel showed any kind of resistance, and was a symbol that little or no quarter would be given. Yellow flags were also mentioned, although unlike their current association with quarantine, their precise meaning in the late 17th century is unknown. Therefore by 1700, red and black were flag colours associated with privateering. When the outlets for legitimate privateering dried up at the end of the War of the Spanish Succession in 1714, many privateers turned to piracy. They simply retained their old symbols, although black became the favoured colour. Red continued to be associated with privateering until the 19th century. The American 18th-century privateering colour of a red flag overlaid with white horizontal stripes provided the inspiration for part of the existing flag of the USA.

The use of the term 'Jolly Roger' was not a Hollywood myth and is derived from one of a couple of sources. The French name for the privateering red flag was the *Jolie Rouge* (Jolly Red), and this was said to have been converted into 'Jolly Roger'. Another possible derivation comes from the word 'Roger'. In late 17th-century England the word '*rouge*' was used in association with the rouge laws limiting vagrancy in England. 'Roger' sprang from this, and was used as a slang word for vagabond, beggar or vagrant. The privateering association with 'Sea Beggars' goes back to the phrase used by Dutch privateers (and freedom fighters) in the late 16th century. It continued to be used as a romanticized description of privateers operating in the English Channel, particularly those from the port of Dunkirk. The 'Jolly Roger' described the privateering symbol, whether a red or a black flag. It later changed from the description of a privateering symbol to a piratical one.

The first reference to a modified basic 'Jolly Roger' was in 1700, when the French privateer Emmanuelle Wynne flew a black flag embellished with a skull, cross-bones and an hourglass. It was presumably also used before the turn of the century, although there is no surviving evidence. It may also have indicated that the flyer no longer considered himself a privateer, and was a full-blown pirate.

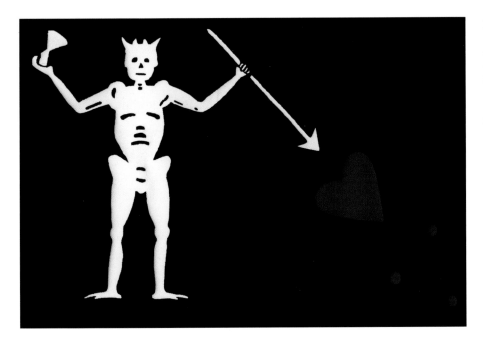

Blackbeard's own version of the 'Jolly Roger' was supposed to depict a skeleton toasting the devil and piercing a heart with a spear. These gruesome images served to underline the fearsome impression cultivated by most pirates. They also suggested that any resistance would result in death. (Stratford Archive)

What is known is that following 1700, additional emblems on the basic red or black flags were increasingly associated with piracy, and different symbols were in turn associated with individual pirate captains.

Of these, the most common symbol was the skull, the symbol of death. It was also frequently depicted in association with cross-bones, another death symbol. Both signs were commonly 'momento mori' on 16th- and 17th-century gravestones all over the British Isles. Other symbols were complete skeletons, spears, swords, hourglasses, initials, hearts, crossed swords, wings and raised glasses. In an era where symbolism in art and everyday life was commonplace, each had a distinct and immediately recognizable meaning. Apart from the death association with bones, skeletons and skulls, dancing skeletons meant dancing a jig with death, a fatalistic reference that suggested the flyer didn't care about his fate. This was also the source of the raised glass symbol ('toasting death'). Weapons were a portent of slaughter to come, while hourglasses and wings indicated that time was running out (or flying away). All these symbols can be found in contemporary allegorical paintings of death or on gravestones.

The symbols were often combined. For instance, Christopher Moody, who operated off the Carolinas in 1717, used a skull and cross-bones, a raised sword and a winged hourglass. Edward Teach flew a flag depicting a skeleton holding an hourglass and a spear, next to a bleeding heart. In addition to his 'ABH/AMH'

The pirate crew of Thomas Anstis holding a mock trial while ashore on Cuba, 1721. Crewmen dressed as judges and bailiffs question a pirate captive with a noose around his neck. Anstis and his crew deserted from Bartholomew Roberts in 1721. After killing Anstis in 1723, most of his crew surrendered to the Dutch authorities on Curaçao. (Stratford Archive)

flag, Bartholomew Roberts also flew one depicting a pirate holding an hourglass, alongside a skeleton clutching a spear. The fatalism in pirate symbolism was evident, and it probably applied to pirates as well as their victims.

National flags were still flown, often in an attempt to show that the pirates still wanted to be seen as privateers who only attacked the ships of other nations. If the countries were at peace, or if the pirate held no privateering commission, this meant little or nothing. In 1718, Charles Vane flew the English flag from one mast and a black pirate flag from another. In 1720, Edward England flew a black flag from his mainmast, a red flag from his foremast and the English flag from his ensign staff.

Pirate Justice

Most pirates during the golden age knew that their run of luck could not go on forever. With the odd exception of the pirate who knew when to retire or accept a pardon and start a new life, almost every pirate met death either in battle or on the gallows. If condemned in England, pirates were taken from a prison in London to Execution Dock at Wapping on the banks of the River Thames, where a wooden gallows was built on the low-water mark. After a brief prayer from a chaplain, the pirate was allowed a few last words, then he would be hung. After three tides had washed over the body, the corpse was usually buried in an unmarked grave.

From 1701, Admiralty Courts, which oversaw all trials involving crime 'below the high-water mark', were established in the American colonies, including English possessions in the Caribbean, and these courts followed the same routines as in England. In the late 17th century, only the captain and leading pirates were hung, but as Admiralty Courts in the Americas cracked down on the pirate scourge during the early years of the 18th century, whole crews were sent to the gallows. This led to a spate of mass trials and hangings, designed to deter others from taking up piracy. In effect, the courts were combating the rise in piratical activities by a propaganda war aimed at potential pirate recruits.

The dates of these executions show that the golden age was really a brief period of ten years, during which the worst pirates and their crews were hunted down, killed in action or executed en masse. The way this business worked is worth examining.

When Captain Ogle captured Bartholomew Roberts' fleet, he netted 264 pirates. This was perhaps the largest pirate band afloat at the time. Of these, 187 were white and 77 were black. Regardless of whether the black prisoners came from West Africa or the Americas, they did not face trial, but instead they were sold into slavery. Captain Ogle, his crew and the admiral of the station shared the profit in the same way they did from the sale of the pirate vessels. The remaining white crew members were brought to trial in Cape Coast Castle in West Africa. Of these prisoners, 52 were hanged, while 77 were acquitted. Of the remainder, 37 were sent to prison; 20 of these were sentenced to seven years of hard labour in the mines on the African Gold Coast (which was effectively a death sentence), and a further 17 were transported to England where they were imprisoned in Marshalsea Prison for various terms. Two prisoners were released

Prominent Admiralty Court Executions

May 1701
William Kidd and eight pirates at Execution Dock, London

May 1701
24 French pirates at Execution Dock, London

June 1704
Captain Quelsh and six pirates at Boston, Massachusetts

Summer 1705
Captain Green and 16 pirates on Leith Sands, Edinburgh

November 1716
Jack Rackam and nine pirates in Kingston, Jamaica

October 1717
Seven pirates from Bellamy's crew in Boston, Massachusetts

March 1718
13 pirates from Blackbeard's crew in Williamsburg, Virginia

October 1718
Stede Bonnet and 30 pirates in Charleston, North Carolina

December 1718
Eight pirates captured by Woodes Rogers in New Providence, Bahamas

November 1719
Charles Vane and one pirate in Kingston, Jamaica

March 1722
52 pirates from Roberts' crew in Cape Coast Castle, West Africa

May 1722
Captain Luke and 40 pirates in Kingston, Jamaica

Summer 1723
Captain Finn and four pirates in St John's, Antigua

July 1723
Captain Harris and 25 pirates in Newport, Rhode Island

March 1724
11 pirates from Captain Lowther's crew in St Kitts

May 1724
Captain Archer and one pirate in Boston, Massachusetts

May 1725
Captain John Gow and seven pirates at Execution Dock, London

July 1726
Captain William Fly and two pirates in Boston, Massachusetts

July 1727
Captain John Prie at Execution Dock, London

on probation; their sentences frozen 'pending the King's pleasure', they were probably press-ganged into naval service. Nineteen men died of wounds or disease before they could be brought to trial.

After a prominent pirate was hanged, the Admiralty Court often wanted to make an example of him, as a warning to others. The body was removed from the gallows and then tied to a post to be washed over three times by the tide, 'as Admiralty law proscribes'. Then the corpse was cut down, tarred, bound in chains and placed inside an iron cage. This was suspended from a gibbet on a prominent headland, often on a busy waterway, or in a similar highly visible location. These gibbets were usually set up at the entrance of ports, like the shore of the Thames estuary near London, at Gallows Point outside Port Royal, or on Hogg Island,

OPPOSITE An early 19th-century depiction of Blackbeard's last fight. The cartoon-like quality of Blackbeard and the 19th-century uniform worn by Lieutenant Maynard are only the most glaring inaccuracies. An even greater error is the presence of the cannon – the fight took place on the deck of Maynard's sloop, but only Blackbeard's vessel carried any ordnance. (Stratford Archive)

The head of Blackbeard hanging from the bowsprit of Lieutenant Maynard's sloop, the *Jane*, as it sailed up the James River to anchor in Jamestown Roads, near Williamsburg, Virginia. (Stratford Archive)

opposite Charleston, North Carolina. The tarred body was left to rot inside its cage, a process that often took up to two years.

This is what happened to the corpse of Captain William Kidd, 'whose body was visible for years after his execution'. The sun, rain and frost rotted the body and seagulls pecked out its eyes, but the cage kept the bones in place, 'as a great terror to all persons from committing ye like crimes'. Pirates later said they would sooner die in battle than 'be hanged up drying, like Kidd'. Due to the cost (and probably the stench), it was usually only the pirate captains and sometimes their lieutenants who were displayed in this way after being hanged. Kidd, Vane, Finn, Archer, Gow, Fly, Prie and Rackam were among those who had their bodies displayed in this manner. Ordinary pirates were simply buried in unmarked graves. The rash of pirate trials around the world in the 1720s and the draconian punishments inflicted proved a great deterrent, and directly led to the end of the major piratical activities which plagued European trade.

Privateers and Pirates 1730–1830

The Development of
Privateering   164

Organization and Recruitment   176

The Privateering Art of War   186

Privateering Vessels   197

Privateer Captains and
Latter-day Pirates   203

Privateering Ports and
Pirate Dens   215

The Anti-piracy Campaign of
the 1820s   223

The French privateering captain Robert Surcouf is shown attacking the English merchant vessel *Hope* in 1798. Surcouf's privateering sloop *Emille* operated with considerable success against British shipping in the Indian Ocean. (Stratford Archive)

The Development of Privateering

COLONIAL ROOTS

Traditionally, conflicts between European powers were reflected by the extension of the war to include their American colonies. War between France and England during the War of the League of Augsburg (1690–97) and the War of the Spanish Succession (1701–14) had few repercussions in North America. The involvement of Spain in both these conflicts laid her open to attacks by the French and then the English. The English colonies (or British from 1707) were too preoccupied with the threat of Indian raids on land and piratical attacks at sea to consider the disruption of their fragile economy or to conduct widespread privateering. Instead, British privateers established bases in the colonies and in the West Indies, and prosecuted their own attacks on the French and Spanish.

Privateering in American waters became established with the War of Jenkins' Ear in 1739 (which preceded Britain's entrance into the War of the Austrian Succession, 1740–48), when colonial privateers were fitted out for attacks against the Spanish. When France entered the conflict in 1744, American privateers began operating in the Gulf of St Lawrence and off the French islands of the West Indies, while French Canadian privateers cruised off New England. Privateers assisted the British Army to transport troops to attack the French fortress of Louisbourg in 1745, and their independent cruises began to demonstrate the effectiveness of privateering. In June 1744, two New York privateers captured a French prize valued at over £11,000, while the following year the 20-gun privateer *Shirley* captured eight French vessels in Canadian waters. In 1746, New York privateers captured several valuable French prizes, and the New York courts record the division of cargoes of indigo (a valuable blue dye), sugar, coffee and cotton, the produce of the French Caribbean provinces. That summer, the privateers *Greyhound* and *Dragon* captured a Spanish privateering vessel, so attacks were not limited to French shipping. One New York paper records a Danish ship being stopped by a New York-based privateer, and Spanish passengers forced to hand over their possessions. As Denmark was neutral, the Danish captain was paid for his trouble and allowed to proceed. Although this clearly overstepped the line between privateering and piracy, the perpetrator, one Captain Troup, was never prosecuted.

Chronology

The War of the Austrian Succession, 1740–48
(Britain versus Spain and France)

1739	War of Jenkins' Ear provokes British conflict with Spain
1744	France allies with Spain
1748	Treaty of Aix-la-Chapelle ends conflict

The Seven Years' War, 1755–63 (Britain versus France)

1755	Undeclared war between Britain and France in the Americas, also known as the French and Indian War
1757	Official declaration of war between France and Britain
1762	Spain allies with France
1763	Treaty of Paris ends conflict

The American Revolutionary War, 1775–83
(Britain versus the American colonies)
(also known as the American War of Independence)

1775	The 13 American colonies rebel against British rule
1778	France allies with America
1779	Spain allies with America
1780	Holland allies with America
1783	Treaty of Versailles ends conflict

The French Revolutionary War, 1793–1802
(Britain versus France)

1793	Louis XVI executed, France declares war on Britain, Spain and Holland
1794	Holland, overrun by France, forms Batavian Republic (French ally)
1795	Treaty of Ildefenso – Spain makes peace, and allies with France
1802	Peace of Amiens ends conflict

The Quasi-War, 1798–1801 (France versus the United States)

1798	'Covert' war between France and United States
1801	President Jefferson ends conflict

The Napoleonic Wars, 1803–15
(France and Spain versus Britain)

1803	Britain declares war with France
1804	Spain allies with France
1808	France invades Spain, Spain at war with France, and allied to Britain
1814	Treaty of Paris ends conflict
1815	Napoleon returns from exile, Britain and Holland declare war on France

Peace following Napoleon's surrender to Royal Navy

The War of 1812, 1812–15 (Britain versus the United States)

1812	United States declares war on Britain
1815	Treaty of Ghent ends conflict

The Latin American Wars of Independence, 1808–30
(Spain versus her colonies)

1808	Spain and Portugal invaded by France.
1809	Insurrection against Spanish rule in most of South America
1811–19	Independence granted to Paraguay (1811), Argentina (1816), Chile (1818) and Colombia (1819)
1822	Ecuador and Brazil (a Portuguese colony) become independent
1823	United provinces (much of Central America) become independent (dissolved in 1839)
1824	Peru and Mexico independent
1825–28	Bolivia (1825), Uruguay (1828) and Venezuela (1830) become independent *(Note: Civil wars and disputes continued throughout South America during this period.)*

The start of the Seven Years' War provided similar opportunities for the American colonists, although French Canadian privateers preyed on New England shipping in retaliation. Although the conquest of New France (Canada) ended privateering activities for a time, fresh opportunities arose when Spain entered the conflict in 1762. For the next two years, ports such as New York, Boston and Charleston all recorded the capture of Spanish prizes.

THE AMERICAN REVOLUTION

The heyday of privateering in the Americas followed the revolt of Britain's American colonies and lasted intermittently until 1814. A few statistics demonstrate the importance of privateering to the American revolutionary cause. Congress commissioned fewer than 50 warships during the revolt, and they were almost exclusively employed as commerce raiders, capturing 196 British vessels. During the war, 792 letters of marque were issued, and these privateers captured in excess of 600 British merchant ships, with an estimated total value of $18 million in contemporary value. Of even greater importance, the privateers captured around 16,000 British seamen, at a time when the Royal Navy was desperately short of men and ships. Losses also included troops, munitions and military equipment vitally needed in the American theatre. Although individually insignificant, losses such as the 240 Hessian troops captured by the privateer *Mars*, or the 100 British soldiers captured by the privateer *Warren*, accrued to form a significant drain on British resources. Post-revolutionary American propaganda claims the capture of over 16,000 military prisoners by the navy and privateers, but modern scholarly assessments place the figure at fewer than 2,000 – still a significant loss when for most of the southern campaign of 1780–81, Cornwallis had a field army of fewer than 2,000 men.

The colonists had no purpose-built privateers when the war started, and no regular navy. Initial attacks were conducted using hastily adapted merchant vessels and small inshore rowing craft known as 'spider catchers', a form of improvised coastal gunboat. The Americans had a number of ports which specialized in building vessels well suited to privateering: small, fast-hulled topsail schooners, which were easily adapted with the addition of guns and crewmen. The first prizes were captured in the summer of 1775, and by the winter of 1775–76, American privateers had become a serious nuisance in the waters of New England and the middle colonies. From November 1775 until April 1776, 31 British or loyalist ships were captured off Boston, and these attacks helped induce the British to

Early Revolutionary War privateers off the coast of Rhode Island, 1775. Depicted here is an early spider vessel – a popular small privateering craft distinguished by its pairs of oars – in the waters of Rhode Island, where attacks between loyalists and rebel colonists occurred throughout the war. (Angus McBride © Osprey Publishing Ltd)

withdraw from the port in March. Similarly, the Royal Navy captured several privateers during the same period, carrying them into Boston as prizes.

With colonial merchant trading virtually at a standstill, many American ports turned to privateering as a means to make a living. As the first wave of converted merchant vessels, whalers and fishing boats were captured by Royal Navy patrols, ship owners began to launch purpose-built privateers, and increasing numbers of letters of marque were signed by Congress or by state authorities. In two years from the summer of 1775, the following privateering licences were granted (listed by state and principal ports):

State	Licences	Port
Massachusetts	53	Boston, Salem, Marblehead, Gloucester, Portland, New Bedford
New Hampshire	7	Portsmouth
Rhode Island	6	Providence
Connecticut	22	Bridgeport, New Haven, New London
New York	7	New York
New Jersey	1	New Brunswick
Pennsylvania	21	Philadelphia
Delaware	0	
Maryland	6	Baltimore, Annapolis
Virginia	0	
North Carolina	3	Wilmington
South Carolina	6	Charleston
Georgia	0	

The British occupation of Rhode Island, New York and parts of New Jersey limited privateering activity in those states, while in the south, a lack of suitable vessels and the proximity of British squadrons made extensive privateering impractical. Loyalists (or Tories) also fitted out privateers, principally based in New York and Newport, Rhode Island.

Privateering continued to provide a popular source of income for these colonial ports, but shipping losses led to a brief decrease in numbers before specially built privateers became active. During 1777, only 73 American privateers were registered, but the numbers increased steadily until 1782, when many vessels were converted to merchant ships:

1778	115 vessels
1779	167 vessels
1780	228 vessels
1781	449 vessels
1782	323 vessels

The biggest difference was not in numbers but in the size of vessel. While the first wave of privateers were converted from small merchant vessels and carried fewer than ten guns, by 1779 large privateers carrying over 20 guns were common, and many were capable of cruising in the mid-Atlantic or in British waters. Vessels such as the *General Washington* or the *General Pickering* were considered the most powerful American ships afloat, given the almost complete demise of the Continental Navy. The Royal Navy would have diverted resources to counter the activities of privateers (as she did so successfully in the War of 1812), but the involvement of France, Spain and Holland stretched the British to the limit. There were simply no ships to spare for a blockade of American ports. The adoption of convoy systems limited but failed to prevent losses to privateers, and by the early 1780s, merchants were lobbying the government to bring an end

One country's privateer or patriot was often seen as little more than a pirate by other nationalities. The Scottish-born Captain John Paul Jones, founder of the US Navy, was accused of piratical attacks around the British Isles. This engraving shows the battle between his *Bonhomme Richard* (44 guns) and HMS *Serapis* (42 guns) off Flamborough Head in September 1779. (Mariners' Museum, Newport News, Virginia)

to the war. By disregarding the threat of privateering until it was too late to control, the British sealed their own fate in the Americas. While the intervention of other European powers on America's behalf turned the course of the rebellion in America's favour, the economic warfare wrought by the privateers made the outcome inevitable.

THE WAR OF 1812

Although an unpopular conflict with many Americans, the War of 1812 initially provided a great opportunity for the ship owners of the United States and to a lesser extent, Canada. British naval power was stretched thin because of the demands of the Napoleonic Wars. A series of trade embargoes and import laws, coupled with a European blockade, had reduced the commercial profits available to many American merchants, so the opportunity of widespread privateering was welcomed as an alternative to commercial trading.

War was declared by President Madison in June, and the small United States Navy scrambled to face a conflict for which it was not prepared. Privateers were seen as a vital part of naval policy, and letters of marque were issued almost immediately. From the onset of the war until its end in January 1815, 517 privateering licences were granted by the president, and over 1,300 prizes were taken, the majority within the first ten months of the conflict.

The effects of such heavy losses were pronounced. British newspapers recounted the damage done to the maritime economy, and in Liverpool, a master of a British merchant ship described how he saw ten American privateers during his voyage over from Nova Scotia. By late 1813, insurance companies refused to insure any vessel bound for Halifax, Nova Scotia, and premiums for other destinations had increased by between 25 and 50 per cent.

The British were not the only nation to suffer. Forty-one privateering licences were issued in New Brunswick and Nova Scotia during the war, and these Canadian privateers preyed on the coastal shipping of New England. To many Canadian ship owners, privateering was a less attractive option than commercial trade, as her merchants still maintained a brisk business with Britain and her colonies in the West Indies, so there was still a less risky alternative. Despite this, Halifax and Liverpool, Nova Scotia, bustled with privateering activity, and one Canadian vessel, the *Liverpool Packet*, captured 50 American prizes alone. From late 1813, British privateers began to operate in American waters, and newspapers printed in the English ports of Liverpool and Plymouth soon reported the sale of

American prizes and their cargo. The waters around Cape Cod became almost too dangerous for American ships to enter by the spring of 1813.

By the end of 1813, the privateering heyday was over. A British naval blockade was established along the American Atlantic seaboard during the winter of 1813–14, and although numerous American privateers continued to operate from ports in France, the Caribbean or South America, the numbers fell sharply, so that by the summer of 1814, insurance rates had almost returned to pre-war levels. Canadian and British privateers were converted back into merchant ships and denied the income from prizes, and American privateering ports such as Salem, Boston, Newport, New York and Baltimore all suffered economic ruin. The blockade effectively halted American trade, and the same ship owners who had welcomed the war as an opportunity to profit from privateering now clamoured for peace. Peace commissioners met in Belgium, and in January 1815 the futile war

Levi Barlow's privateers attacked by loyalists on Nantucket, 1782. Here Barlow and his men are on the jetty, trying to return the loyalists' fire. They are heavily armed, carrying French Charleville muskets converted for sea service and a shortened version of the British India-pattern musket. (Angus McBride © Osprey Publishing Ltd)

A privateering lugger being chased by a British warship in the English Channel, c. 1814, in this copy of a painting by an unknown artist. Bizarrely, the French privateer is shown flying a pirate flag rather than a national tricolour – presumably an artistic way of suggesting it was a pirate ship rather than a legitimate privateer. (Stratford Archive)

was brought to a close. Former privateersmen returned to their peacetime pursuits, and although Latin American countries continued to use privateers in their independence struggles with Spain, privateering ceased to be a legitimate occupation. Apart from an outbreak of piracy in the Caribbean, American vessels were free to trade wherever they wished, and the decades following 1815 saw a boom in American maritime trade. For Americans, privateering was no longer an option, and there was simply too much legitimate activity to make the risks of piracy appealing. Certainly, pirates such as Jean Laffite existed, and a number of former American privateersmen turned to piratical activities in areas outside the reach of the authorities. For the vast majority of mariners and ship owners, however, the trading opportunities presented by a world at peace filled the economic niche once offered by privateering.

One valuable benefit of the privateering experiences of both the American Revolution and the War of 1812 was the development of ships designed from the hull up as large, fast privateers. Vessels such as the *Prince de Neufchâtel* or the

General Armstrong of New York were a new class of 'super privateers', and together with the converted Baltimore schooners, they assisted in the evolutionary process which produced the fast slaving ships or the schooners of the post-war years, and eventually developed into the design known as the clipper ship.

THE LAST PIRATES

Both the Anglo-American War of 1812 and the Napoleonic Wars ended in 1815. Privateering was in its zenith, and although most mariners returned to legitimate employment, several did not. Some sought service as privateers working on behalf of the new Latin American states, while others simply operated outside the law, turning to piracy. For 15 years, a new wave of attacks swept through the American seaboard and the Caribbean. It was the worst outbreak of lawlessness on the high seas for a century.

Although some of these pirates, such as Jean Laffite, were American, the majority came from Latin America. When France invaded Spain in 1808, many Latin Americans took advantage of the Spanish preoccupation with affairs at home and rebelled against their colonial masters. Rebel governments such as those of Venezuela and Colombia handed out hundreds of privateering contracts to anyone willing to attack Spanish shipping. Many of these privateers were unwilling to restrict their attacks to Spanish vessels, and by 1820 vessels of all nationalities entered the waters of the Caribbean at their peril. These piratical attacks were finally ended by aggressive naval action by Britain and the United States.

Victims for these latter-day pirates were easily found. Following the end of the Napoleonic Wars, merchant shipping tried to fulfil the increasing demand for trade goods and raw materials, and booming European and American economies provided ready markets on both sides of the Atlantic. The numbers of merchant vessels in operation doubled over a ten-year period, meaning that the shipping lanes of the world were busier than at any other time in history. The demand for rum, sugar, spices, slaves, timber and other commodities meant that the waters of the Caribbean and the Gulf of Mexico were used by thousands of vessels, and areas such as the Florida Straits, the Bahamas Channel and the Windward Passage became some of the busiest shipping lanes in the Americas.

Many of the pirates who preyed on these ships were opportunists, simply attacking vulnerable ships if the opportunity presented itself. Others were more methodical, preying on certain types of vessels such as slave ships with a view to selling the cargo to fulfil a demand by merchants in league with the pirates.

The *Prince de Neufchâtel* pursued by a British frigate, HMS *Endymion*, 1814. The wind has dropped, allowing the British frigate to close with the American privateer. The French-born Captain Ordronaux is shown anxiously hoping for the wind to pick up before the enemy frigate can close within range. (Angus McBride © Osprey Publishing Ltd)

American shipping was particularly badly hit. Maritime insurance rates soared between 1815 and 1820, and eventually many companies refused to underwrite vessels sailing into Caribbean waters. From 1820, the American and British navies diverted resources to combat piracy in the region, regardless of the political or diplomatic consequences. A combination of aggressive patrolling and attacks on pirate bases eventually forced most surviving pirates to abandon their attacks, and by 1826 this last wave of piracy had been contained.

Although a lot of artistic licence has been used in this 19th-century illustration by Alexandre Debelle for P. Christian's *Histoire des Pirates* (1889), pirates did tend to drink whatever rum they plundered. The figure purports to be Sir Henry Morgan. (Stratford Archive)

A handful of particularly brutal pirates still remained at large into the 1830s, but one by one they were caught and executed, and by 1840 piracy was considered a thing of the past in American or Atlantic waters. These last cut-throats included the Portuguese pirate Benito de Soto (c. 1828–29) and Pedro Gibert (c. 1832–33), and their attacks provided the newspapers with suitably shocking copy. Their capture marked the end of almost 400 years of piracy, buccaneering and privateering in American waters, although it has been argued that the Confederate raiders followed in the footsteps of these earlier cut-throats, and the Northern press during the American Civil War (1861–65) referred to these maritime raiders as pirates.

A Certificate of Membership of the Salem Marine Society, dated December 1815. It shows a general view of Crowinshield Wharf in Salem and the launch of the privateer *Fame* in 1812, one of 40 based in the port during the War of 1812. (Stratford Archive)

conflict, Congress had the administration required to grant privateering licences already in place. This meant that letters of marque were being issued within weeks of the president's declaration. It also bears testimony to the international nature of privateering that although thousands of vessels, both British and American, were captured by privateers during the War of 1812, only a handful of official complaints were made by the victims against their privateering captors. The bonding system and the strict rules governing the distribution of the captured ship and cargo were sufficient to prevent most transgressions of maritime law.

IN CONGRESS

WEDNESDAY, APRIL 3, 1776
INSTRUCTIONS to the COMMANDERS of Private Ships or Vessels of War, which shall have Commissions or Letters of Marque and Reprisal, authorizing them to make Captures of British Vessels and Cargoes.

I.   YOU may, by Force of Arms, attack, subdue, and take all ships and other Vessels belonging to the Inhabitants of Great-Britain, on the High Seas, between high-water and low-water marks, except Ships and Vessels bringing Persons who intend to settle and reside in the United Colonies, or bringing Arms, Ammunition and War-like Stores to the said Colonies, for the use of such Inhabitants thereof that are Friends to the American Cause, which you shall suffer to pass unmolested, the Commanders thereof permitting a peaceable Search, and giving satisfactory Information of the Contents of the Landings, and Destination of the Voyages.

II.   You may, by Force of Arms, attack, subdue, and take all Ships and their Vessels whatsoever carrying Soldiers, Arms, Gun-powder, Ammunition, Provisions, or any other contraband Goods, to any of the British Armies or Ships of War employed against these Colonies.

III.   You shall bring such Ships and Vessels you shall take, with their Guns, Rigging, Tackle, Apparel, Furniture and Landings to some convenient Port or Ports of the United Colonies, that Proceedings may thereupon be had in due Form before the Courts which are or shall be there appointed to hear and determine Causes civil and maritime.

IV.   You or one of your Chief Officers shall bring or send the master and Pilot and one or more principal Person or persons of the Company of every Ship or Vessel by you taken, as soon after the Capture as may be, to the Judge or Judges of such Court aforesaid, to be examined upon Oath, and make Answer to the Interrogatories which may be propounded touching the Interest or property of the Ship or Vessel, and her Lading; and at the same Time you shall deliver or cause to be delivered to the Judge or Judges, all Passes, Sea-Briefs, Charter-Parties, Bills of lading, Dockets, Letters, and other Documents and Writings found on Board, proving the said Papers by the Affidavit of yourself, or some other Person present at the Capture, to be produced as they were received, without Fraud, Addition, Subduction or Embezzlement.

V.   You shall keep and preserve every Ship or Vessel and Cargo by you taken, until they shall by Sentence of a Court properly authorised be adjudged lawful Prize, not selling, spoiling, wasting or diminishing the same, or breaking the Bulk thereof, nor suffering any such Thing to be done.

VI.   If you, or any of your Officers and Crew shall, in cold Blood, kill or maim, or, by Torture or otherwise, cruelly, inhumanely, and contrary to common Usage and the Practice of civilized nations in War, treat any person or persons surprized in the Ship or Vessel you shall take, the Offender shall be severely punished.

VII.   You shall, by all convenient Opportunities, send to Congress written Accounts of the Captures you shall make, with the Number and names of the Captives, Copies of your Journal from Time to Time, and Intelligence of what may occur or be discovered concerning the Designs of the Enemy, and the Destination, Motions and Operations of their Fleets and Armies.

VIII.   One Third, at the least, of your whole Company shall be land-Men.

IX.   You shall not ransome any Prisoners or Captives, but shall dispose of them in such Manner as the Congress, or if that be not fitting in the Colony whither they shall be brought, as the General Assembly, Convention, or Council or Committee of Safety of such Colony shall direct.

X.   You shall observe all such further Instructions as Congress shall hereafter give in the premises, when you shall have Notice thereof.

XI.   If you shall do any Thing contrary to the Instructions, or to others hereafter to be given, or willingly suffer such Thing to be done, you shall not only forfeit your Commission, and be liable to an Action for Breach of the Condition of your Bond, but be responsible to the party grieved for damages sustained by such Mal-versation.

By Order of Congress,
John Hancock PRESIDENT

RECRUITMENT

Before a letter of marque could be issued, the ship owners or investors who backed the venture had to appoint a captain and also at least two of his senior officers – the first lieutenant (or 'master') and his next-in-command (the second lieutenant or 'mate'). These ship's officers would be selected through reputation as sea captains, or occasionally appointed because of family connection or because of their own financial investment in the privateering venture. Few of these men were formally educated, but all shared a similar background of maritime experience. It was not in the owner's interests to appoint captains who did not have the experience needed to undertake the challenging tasks required of them, or to have men who lacked the respect of the crew.

Once a vessel was selected and the captain and officers appointed, the next task was to find a crew. In theory this was a simple process, as most seamen were hired from the home port of the privateering vessel. After a period of warfare, naval recruitment (or the activities of press-gangs) and the sheer number of privateering vessels at sea meant that suitable seamen were hard to find. Most privateering instructions specified the hiring of a certain percentage of 'landsmen' – men with no previous maritime experience – a device used to expand the available pool of labour. The crew were usually recruited for a specific duration or for a single voyage, and paid off when the ship returned to port. Obviously, the more successful the privateering captain and vessel, the easier it would be to find a crew. Advertisements were posted in taverns and in local newspapers, such as this example from the *Boston Gazette* of November 1780:

> An Invitation to all brave Seamen and Marines, who have an inclination to serve their country and make their Fortunes. The grand Privateer Ship DEANE, commanded by Elisha Hinman Esq., and prov'd to be a very capital sailor, will sail on a cruise against the enemies of the United States of America, by the 20th instant. The DEANE mounts thirty carriage guns, and is excellently well calculated for Attacks, Defence and Pursute. This therefore is to invite all those Jolly Fellows who love their Country, and want to make their Fortunes at One Stroke, to repair immediately to the Rendezvous at the Head of His Excellency Governor Hancock's Wharf, where they will be received with a hearty welcome by a number of Brave Fellows there assembled, and treated with what excellent Liquor call'd Grog which is allow'd by all true Seamen to be the Liquor of Life.

GREAT
ENCOURAGEMENT
FOR
SEAMEN.

ALL GENTLEMEN SEAMEN and able-bodied LANDSMEN who have a Mind to diftinguifh themfelves in the GLORIOUS CAUSE of their COUNTRY, and make their Fortunes, an Opportunity now offers on board the Ship RANGER, of Twenty Guns, (for FRANCE) now laying in PORTSMOUTH, in the State of NEW-HAMPSHIRE, commanded by JOHN PAUL JONES Efq; let them repair to the Ship's Rendezvous in PORTSMOUTH, or at the Sign of Commodore MANLEY, in SALEM, where they will be kindly entertained, and receive the greateft Encouragement.----The Ship RANGER, in the Opinion of every Perfon who has feen her is looked upon to be one of the beft Cruizers in AMERICA.----She will be always able to Fight her Guns under a moft excellent Cover; and no Veffel yet built was ever calculated for failing fafter, and making good Weather.

Any GENTLEMEN VOLUNTEERS who have a Mind to take an agreable Voyage in this pleafant Seafon of the Year, may, by entering on board the above Ship RANGER, meet with every Civility they can poffibly expect, and for a further Encouragement depend on the firft Opportunity being embraced to reward each one agreable to his Merit.

All reafonable Travelling Expences will be allowed, and the Advance-Money be paid on their Appearance on Board.

In CONGRESS, MARCH 29, 1777.

RESOLVED,

THAT the MARINE COMMITTEE be authorifed to advance to every able Seaman, that enters into the CONTINENTAL SERVICE, any Sum not exceeding FORTY DOLLARS, and to every ordinary Seaman or Landfman, any Sum not exceeding TWENTY DOLLARS, to be deducted from their future Prize-Money.

By Order of CONGRESS,

JOHN-HANCOCK, PRESIDENT.

DANVERS: Printed by E. RUSSELL, at the Houfe late the Bell-Tavern.

A recruiting poster produced by John Paul Jones in an attempt to recruit sailors and landsmen for his command, the 20-gun corvette USS *Ranger*. Recruiting for the navy was a problem given that privateering was considered far more lucrative. (Stratford Archive)

Once these volunteers arrived, the captain would select the most promising or experienced men, including the required quota of landsmen, or 'landlubbers'. Compared to the navy, privateering offered the opportunity of short voyages, less

The American Revolution became a far more widespread conflict from 1778, and by early 1781, English privateers were licensed to attack French, Spanish and Dutch shipping. Advertisement from the *Exeter Flying Post*, April 1781. (Stratford Archive)

For SALE by the CANDLE,

AT the London Tavern, Foxhole-street, Plymouth, on Wednefday the 9th of May, 1781, at Ten o'Clock in the Forenoon precifely,

The Good Ship TWEE GEBROEDERS, Dutch built, round ftern'd, Burthen 600 Tons, more or lefs, almoft New, and is a real good Ship, well found in Stores, and is fit for the Eaft Country, or Norway Trade, a Dutch Prize, taken on her Paffage from Alicant to Amfterdam, by the Britifh Lion Private Ship of War, Arthur French, Efq. Commander, now lying at Plymouth, and there to be delivered.

Inventories will be timely delivered on Board, at the Place of Sale, or by applying at the Broker's Office, on the New Quay, Plymouth.

PETER SYMONS, Sworn Broker.

severe discipline and far greater financial reward. While the Royal Navy had to resort to the use of 'press-gangs' to crew its ships, privateers had their pick of crew, especially as once on the books, they were largely exempt from the press. The sailors in regular merchant service were not so fortunate, and often service aboard a privateer became the only safe haven if impressment into the navy was to be avoided. The only real drawback was that the privateersmen received no regular wages; they were paid only when they successfully captured a prize.

This reward came in the form of shares, and the method of apportioning them was laid down in the ship's articles, signed by everyone on board when they joined. The articles also stipulated that the captain and his officers abide by the 'Instructions' laid down by the government issuing the letter of marque, and that before the apportion of share money following the legal sale of the prize ship and her contents, the owners and financial backers would get their own return. The standard for this was that the backers divided 50 per cent of the value of each prize between them, leaving the rest of the value to be apportioned between the crew in accordance with the articles. An example of the articles from a Salem privateer of 1780 shows how this worked (opposite).

PRIVATEERING CREWS

It has already been noted that privateers rarely had a problem recruiting crewmen. At least two out of every three sailors were experienced seamen, either from naval or mercantile backgrounds. The principal privateering ports of America, Britain

Rewards and Punishment

1. Any of the company losing an arm or a leg in an engagement, or is otherwise disabled and unable to earn his bread, shall receive £1,000 from the first prize taken.

2. Whoever first discovers a sail that proves to be a prize, shall receive £100 as a reward for his vigilance.

3. Whoever enters an enemy ship after boarding orders are issued, shall receive £300 for his valour.

4. Whoever is guilty of gaming or quarrelling shall suffer such punishment as the Captain and Officers see fit.

5. Any man absent from the ship for 24 hours without leave shall be guilty of disobedience. Whoever is guilty of cowardice, mutiny, theft, pilfering, embezzlement, concealment of goods belonging to the ship or her company, stripping or threatening any man or behaving indecently to a woman shall loose his shares and receive such other punishment as the crime deserves. Such forfeited shares shall be distributed to the remaining ship's company.

6. Seven dead shares shall be set aside by the Captain and Officers among those who behave best, and do most for the interest and service of the cruise. The Captain, Lieutenants, Master, Surgeon and Officer of the Marines shall not be entitled to any part of the dead shares.

7. When a prize is taken and sent into port, the Prize Master and the men aboard are responsible for watching and unloading the prize. If any negligence results in damage, their shares will be held accountable.

8. If the Commander is disabled, the next highest officer will strictly comply with the rules, orders, restrictions and agreements between the owners of the privateer and the commander.

9. If any Officer or any of the company is taken prisoner aboard a captured prize vessel, he shall receive a share in all prizes taken during the remainder of the cruise, as he would if actually aboard. However, he must obtain his liberty before the end of the cruise or make every effort to join the privateer, or else his prize money is forfeited to the owners and the ship's company.

10. The Captain shall have full power to displace any officer who may be found unfit for the post.

11. The Captain and his principal officers shall have full power to appoint an Agent for the ship's company.

12. Shares are to be apportioned as follows:

    Captain: . . . . 8 shares

    First Lieutenant, Second Lieutenant, Master, Surgeon: . . . . 4 shares

    Officer of Marines, Prize Master, Carpenter, Gunner, Boatswain, Master's Mate, Captain's Clerk, Steward: . . . . 2 shares

    Sailmaker, Armourer, Sergeant of Marines, Cook, Gunner's Mate, Boatswain's Mate, Carpenter's Mate, Surgeon's Mate, Cooper: . . . . 1 ½ shares

    Gentlemen Volunteer, Seaman: . . . 1 share

    Boy under 16 years: . . . . ½ share

and France were all bustling maritime centres, and the sailors and fishermen that inhabited them were for the most part well suited for the requirements of the privateer captains. In some cases, as a war progressed, captured seamen volunteered to join the crew of a privateer, and recruitment was not limited to seamen from the nation under whose flag the privateer was operating. An American privateer captured in 1814 by a Royal Navy frigate reportedly included British, French, Canadian, Dutch and Swedish seamen among her American crew.

Another group were landsmen, and most 'Instructions' specified that the crew must contain an agreed percentage of these inexperienced volunteers. For the most part, they were required to learn the skills of their new profession as rapidly as possible, but as privateering cruises were so short and the ships so well manned, they were spared many of the more skilled tasks asked of the professional seamen. These

Privateers depicted by Frank Schoonover for the children's book *Privateers of '76* by Ralph D. Paine, which appeared in *American Boy Magazine*, July 1923. Although a dramatic representation, the figures are dressed appropriately. (Stratford Archive)

landsmen came into their own during a boarding action, and as many were recruited from ex-soldiers or marines, they proved their worth in combat. A further group were the 'gentlemen volunteers', often the offspring of the ship owners or ship's officers. Unlike midshipmen in regular naval service, there was no requirement to train these young men to become officers, although that was certainly a widespread practice. Instead, they often acted as a marine guard, maintaining order within the ship and serving as leaders of boarding parties or sharpshooters when in action. The more experienced gentlemen formed a pool from which 'prize masters' were drawn, although the command of prize ships could equally be given to an experienced mate. Promotion was rare during a cruise, but good performance was rewarded, and skilled mates or gentlemen volunteers were often considered suitable candidates for ships' officers once they had gained enough experience.

Being a sailor was a young man's profession. As with pirate crews, statistical studies have shown that the average privateersman was in his 20s, and few were older than 40. The physical stamina and exertion required of a sailor during the period, combined with the often dangerous and unhealthy conditions, meant that older men were often not up to the task.

The dress of a privateering crew was typical of that of other sailors of the period. No uniforms were worn, but certain adaptations were made to clothes that were usually found on land. Pantaloons or 'petticoat breeches' were common, usually cut from white canvas. These were usually cut to reach above the ankle, and if shoes or stockings were worn, they were clearly visible below the breeches. These trousers developed into the more modern style of bell-bottomed white duck trousers by the early 19th century. Both were held up by leather belts. Plain cotton shirts were common, either with or without a collar, and secured by buttons or a drawstring. From the 1760s, woollen knitted shirts resembling a modern long-sleeved T-shirt were worn, often adorned with horizontal coloured bands. In cold weather, a 'sailor's coat' or 'pea coat' was worn, usually made from blue canvas or wool impregnated with tar. A cloth neckerchief, or 'sweat rag', was also commonly worn according to contemporary illustrations. Headgear included regular cocked or tricorne hats, wide-brimmed round hats, slouch hats made from canvas or knitted woollen caps. Privateering officers often wore coats resembling the uniforms of the regular navy – long blue woollen coats with naval-style buttons and wide lapels. Contemporary paintings show that waistcoats and naval-style white breeches were also common, but certainly practical considerations would have outweighed almost all dress requirements for both officers and men.

The Privateering Art of War

THE PREY

After the first weeks of a war, unarmed enemy merchant ships sailing alone had either been captured or reached the safety of a friendly port. Merchant captains armed their ships before sending them to sea again and clamoured to insure their vessel and cargo. Gunfounding records from the iron industries in the Weald (Sussex and Kent) record a boom in trade at the start of all the conflicts of the 18th and early 19th centuries. Similarly, as shipping losses mounted, insurance companies stipulated the need for increased armament on all ships.

They Rushed into the Moonlight, a painting by Frank Schoonover used to illustrate Ralph D. Paine's book *Privateers of '76*, published in 1923. It shows the preferred boarding weapons of the era – cutlasses and pistols. (Stratford Archive)

Within a few months, most unarmed enemy merchant vessels could only be found in waters they considered safe (usually their own coastal waters), or else they travelled in convoys. Some faster vessels opted to avoid the delays of waiting for a convoy to sail and relied on speed to avoid enemy privateers. Convoys were large, slow-moving affairs, and many ship owners felt that operating independently was worth the increased risk of being attacked by privateers. Often these fast-sailing single ships carried perishable or high-value cargoes, and the worth of the cargo would be affected if the ship waited for the next convoy. These independent vessels were well armed and crewed, and were also more inclined to oppose a privateer who attacked them than a less well-armed vessel in a convoy. Studies have shown that during the American Revolution and the War of 1812, as many as half of the British vessels sailing between the West Indies and Britain opted to sail independently. The captains of these ships knew the risks they faced, risks which were not run by the British alone. The instructions given to the captain of a New England ship from the vessel's owner in 1777 reveal some of the more elementary precautions their crews could take:

The threat by French privateers such as Robert Surcouf forced the English East India Company to group many of their most important ships into convoys during the French Revolutionary and Napoleonic Wars. *A Fleet of East Indiamen at Sea*, oil painting by Nicholas Pocock, c. 1803. (National Maritime Museum, Greenwich, London)

The *General Armstrong* repelling a British attack off the neutral Portuguese port of Fayal, in the Azores, 1814. The height of the British night attack is shown here, with the privateer crew trying to repel the boarding attempt. Privateer Captain Samuel Reid was ultimately forced to land his crew and then scuttle his ship. (Angus McBride © Osprey Publishing Ltd)

Some advice I have to give you. Keep a good lookout from your masthead every half hour for your own safety… if any vessel should give you chase then make from her with all heart. Don't speak with any vessel on your safety if you can help it. Don't trust to no one at the danger times. Don't run after night, as night has no eye.

During the American Revolution and again in the War of 1812, the British instituted a convoy system, where merchant vessels were escorted by Royal Navy warships, often forming convoys of over 100 ships, and sometimes exceeding 200 vessels. One port was designated as the gathering place for ships bound for a particular destination, and on a prescribed day the convoy would sail. In theory, all the vessels in the convoy were under the command of a senior naval officer, whose warship acted as the convoy flagship. In practice, it was almost impossible to instil naval discipline into the merchant crews of the convoy, and the warships spent much of their time acting as shepherds, continually exhorting their charges to keep formation and a steady speed. Most attacks on convoys were made at night, so during the hours of darkness the convoy would reduce sail and the ships would cluster as close together as possible, surrounding the flagship. Smaller warships would patrol the perimeter of the convoy.

Like the U-boats when they attacked the Atlantic convoys during World War II, privateers found that their chances improved if several vessels attacked a convoy as a group. Although most privateers preferred to operate independently, the introduction of convoys during the American Revolution forced them to rethink their method of operation. It became common for two or three privateers to combine for an attack on an enemy convoy, and on rare occasions as many as seven or eight privateers might operate as a unit. While some lured the guarding warships away from the convoy, others would close with it, board and capture some of the merchant ships, then escape with their prizes. Darkness or the cover of bad weather or fog helped during the approach, and the same conditions also made it harder for the convoy to maintain a tight defensive formation. If a convoy became strung out during rough weather, it became particularly vulnerable to attack.

THE CHASE

A look-out in the mast of a typical privateering schooner of the period could expect to see about 15 miles in good visibility, placing him in the centre of a 30-mile circle of visible sea. Look-outs were encouraged to maintain a sharp watch by financial reward, typically a £100 bonus in British ships. Once a prey was sighted, the privateer would give chase.

By sailing on a parallel course to the prey, the privateer could determine quite quickly if he was faster than the other vessel. If the privateer was to windward (i.e. upwind) of the merchantman, and was a faster ship, it could afford to make a series of tacks towards the enemy, getting progressively closer each time. If the enemy was to leeward (i.e. downwind), it could sail away more easily, meaning a longer chase, but the faster ship would eventually overhaul the slower one. The need for speed in a privateering vessel is evident. A privateer usually had a larger crew than a merchantman, so if there was little or no wind, one option was to 'man the sweeps'. This meant fixing oars through oar ports in the side of the privateer's hull. Not many vessels were equipped in this style, but those that were had an advantage over any opponent in light airs. Another option was to tow the privateer after the enemy vessel. The privateer would lower its boats and rig towing ropes between them and the ship; the sailors would row, thereby towing the ship. As privateers invariably had more men on board than their prey, they would have an advantage over the adversary.

In most cases the privateer was a faster and more manoeuvrable ship than the merchant ship it was chasing, and was able to sail closer to the wind and carry

In this romanticized engraving by August-François Biard, early 19th-century pirates are shown using subterfuge to close the gap between them and an American merchant ship without raising the alarm. Tricks of this kind were commonplace during the age of pirates and privateers. (Stratford Archive)

more sail. By manoeuvring onto the windward side of the enemy, the privateer gained an advantage, being able to react more readily to any change of course made by his opponent. In a strong breeze, it also meant that both ships would heel over, with the leeward ship exposing more of its hull to the enemy than its rival.

The best circumstances for an attack were during darkness or restricted visibility, when the enemy would be sighted at close quarters. Privateers also preferred to operate in areas where they could surprise an enemy, lurking behind a land mass or an island. Another method was to pretend to be a friendly ship. A sensible merchant captain in hostile waters would run from any approaching sail, but often the prey could be fooled to delay fleeing until it was too late. A privateering captain would often go to great lengths to disguise his ship by hanging strips of painted canvas over his sides to cover the gun ports, carrying old and patched sails to make his ship seem less threatening, or even towing barrels to make his ship seem slower than it really was. Once an enemy was lured to within gun range of a privateer, the guns would be run out, and a shot fired over the bows of the merchant vessel. In most cases, the victim realized that resistance would only lead to an unnecessary loss of life, and they surrendered. Sometimes, fake guns (called 'quakers') were used, fashioned from logs shaped to represent guns. Faced with overwhelming firepower, an enemy ship would be extremely likely to surrender rather than fight. If they still offered resistance, the privateer would try to board the enemy.

BOARDING

When a privateer was left with no option but to attack the enemy vessel, the captain had to decide whether to use gunfire or try to board the enemy. As discussed previously, the advantage of boarding was that there was less risk that the enemy ship or its cargo would be damaged in the fighting, therefore maintaining its value. Privateering was a matter of profit or loss, and if the enemy looked too powerful, the privateering captain would leave him alone. He weighed up the risks involved and made his decision according to the chance of making a profit by attacking the enemy. Methods of boarding had changed very little over the previous 200 years. Before they attacked, the privateers would have already taken their assigned battle stations. The crew were divided into two halves or 'watches' (port and star-board watches). One would man the guns, while the other prepared to board the enemy. Sand was scattered on the deck to provide a firmer grip for bare feet. The boarders would be formed into small boarding parties of perhaps a dozen men, each group led by a mate, gentleman volunteer or ship's officer. Part of each watch were assigned as 'topmen', standing by to trim the sails or to tack the ship. Some of the boarders would act as marksmen, arming themselves with muskets, hunting rifles and even swivel guns, ready to sweep the enemy decks with musketry.

The captain would try to draw alongside the enemy ship on the windward side. He would then order the wheel to be put over and the two ships would converge until they locked together. Grappling hooks would be thrown to bind the two hulls together. At that point both sides would loose a volley of musketry, trying to cut down as many of the enemy as possible. The privateer's boarding parties would then clamber over the side and onto the enemy ship, supported by gunfire from the marksmen. Before they boarded, the watch manning the guns would abandon their firearms and arm themselves with boarding weapons. There was usually a financial incentive to take part in the boarding of an enemy ship, so nobody wanted to be left behind.

Boarding weapons included the cutlass, boarding pike and boarding axe, but the seamen would also use whatever else lay to hand, such as belaying pins, gun tools, boat hooks and capstan bars. Privateers were usually well provided with boarding weapons and firearms, the weaponry being supplied by the vessel's owners. The *Liverpool Packet*, a small Canadian privateer of 1812, carried a crew of 40 men, armed with 40 cutlasses and 25 muskets. Pistols were also popular, together with blunderbusses, volley guns, muskets, carbines – anything that could fire. Both British and American gunsmiths provided boarding pistols – hand firearms that included a small bayonet for use in hand-to-hand fighting. Hand grenades and even 'stink pots' were also used, the latter being a simple form of chemical weapon, which when lit emitted a sulphurous smoke and vile stench. It was useful in discouraging resistance below deck when thrown through a hatch or gun port.

Accounts of boarding actions involving privateers are rare, the most common being the reports of defenders who either drove off their attackers or surrendered after a particularly brutal fight. These were unusual, and in most cases the defender only put up a token resistance, if they resisted at all. Action between privateers or against warships was rare, and usually only attempted if it was thought that the prize was especially valuable. They usually resorted to gunnery duels from the onset, as both vessels had a substantial crew, making boarding a risky venture. A boarding engagement could last up to ten or 15 minutes, and surrender was signalled when the officers laid down their arms, or their crew were simply overpowered by numbers. A typical example was the capture of the British ship *Pelham* by the Charleston privateer *Saucy Jack* in May 1814. The *Pelham* surrendered after a ten-minute boarding action that left 14 of her 30 crew dead or wounded, including her captain. The privateer had a crew of 50 men, giving them a substantial superiority of numbers. Often, the initial volley from the privateer would cause sufficient casualties for the recipient to surrender as soon as the privateers tried to board. Sometimes, when boarding followed a gunnery engagement using the ship's broadside, the defending ship was so disrupted by cannon fire that the defenders were too disorganized or dazed to put up much of a fight.

GUNNERY

If it was unavoidable, privateers were prepared to capture an enemy ship by gunnery. A typical privateer of the American Revolutionary War was armed with 4- or 6-pdr guns although, at least in the case of British ships, carronades were sometimes carried. Changes in gunfounding technology meant that larger-calibre guns were carried towards the end of the period, so that during the War of 1812, 9-pdrs and even 12-pdrs were not uncommon. They were all smooth-bored, cast-iron, muzzle-loading pieces, with all but carronades mounted on conventional four-wheeled truck carriages. Convention in British privateers and merchant ships was to paint carriages grey, while the Americans favoured red carriages. Yellow or red were both popular with the French and Spanish, although outside the regular navies of these maritime powers, no standard colour scheme existed. Carronades were mounted on slide carriages specially designed for the weapon. The following gun sizes and weights were common to all privateers during the late 18th century.

Captain William Rogers Capturing the Jeune Richard, 1 October 1807, a painting by Samuel Drummond. This illustrates the use of boarding weapons in close-quarter combat. Muskets and pistols were often used as clubs. (National Maritime Museum, Greenwich, London)

Robert Surcouf and French privateers are in the act of boarding the East India Company ship *Triton* in 1796. East Indiamen were well defended and carried their own marines, making them a tough opponent. (Angus McBride © Osprey Publishing Ltd)

Calibre	Length	Weight
3-pdr	4 ½ ft	7 hundredweight
4-pdr	6 ft	12 ½ hundredweight
6-pdr	7 ft	17 hundredweight
9-pdr	8 ½ ft	23 ½ hundredweight
12-pdr	9 ft	32 ¾ hundredweight

From: George Smith, *An Universal Military Dictionary* (London, 1779)

Note: A British hundredweight (cwt.) contains 112 pounds

Ranges were difficult to gauge given the need to smash through ship timbers, but in the early 19th century the effective penetrating range for a 6-pdr was estimated as being 280 yards (256m). The piece had a maximum range of almost a mile (1,610 yards at 6 degrees of elevation). This was for roundshot. Shot designed to cut enemy rigging (such as chain shot or bar shot) had a shorter effective range. In order to fire grape or canister shot, the same gun needed to be within 80 yards (73m) of the enemy ship. A 12-pdr carronade had an effective range of 200 yards (183m). By comparison, the 18-pdr long guns carried on many naval frigates during the War of 1812 could penetrate the hull of another frigate at around 500 yards (457m). When ships were close enough to fire canister at each other, swivel guns mounted on the ship's rail were used to fire langrage, or 'diced shot', at the enemy crew. This anti-personnel weapon was particularly popular with privateers, as the fire of several of these little pieces could severely disrupt an enemy vessel immediately prior to boarding it.

In most gunnery engagements with relatively equal odds, tactics and skill rather than weaponry proved decisive. In 1782, the British privateer *General Monk* (formerly the American privateer *General Washington*) met the American privateer *Hyder Ali*, carrying 16 6-pdrs. The American crossed the bow of the British ship and the two ships were locked together. While marksmen and swivel gunners kept the British privateersmen at bay, the American captain repeatedly fired his guns into the hull of the British vessel, forcing her to strike her colours.

Later that year the captured privateer (renamed the *General Washington*) was fitted with 9-pdrs, and in an engagement with a British merchantman off the Turks and Caicos Islands, six of her guns burst, killing or wounding some of her crew. The British ship raked the American, splitting her mainmast. The *General Washington* was saved by nightfall, and she escaped in the dark. The inferior quality of some home-produced American naval guns during the American Revolution was so marked that some privateering captains preferred to use captured British pieces.

Another example, from the War of 1812, saw the American privateer *Grand Turk* ranged against a British brig called the *Acorn*, armed with 14 12-pdrs. The American vessel carried 18 pieces of the same calibre, and her crew had been operating together for almost two years. The American captain ranged alongside the British ship and forced her to strike in ten minutes, devastated by the faster American rate of fire. Ironically, the fight took place in March 1815, two months after the end of the war.

Gunnery was a last resort for the privateersmen, but if forced into a sea battle, the skill and speed of the crews were vital. Experienced privateering captains

In May 1814, the American privateer *Grand Turk* attacked the HM Packet *Hinchinbrook* in the mid-Atlantic as she was heading home to Britain from the West Indies. The heavily armed privateer badly damaged the British packet, which put up a spirited resistance, but eventually the *Hinchinbrook* managed to drive off her attacker. (Corbis)

exercised their gun crews regularly and encouraged their men to practise using boarding weapons. The best weapons of a privateer (or an early 19th-century pirate) were speed and deception – luring a victim within range before he could escape. In the event that the victim would try to fight back, privateers also had to be thoroughly versed in using their armament to its best advantage, as a quick surrender saved lives and prevented excessive damage to the prize. They also needed to know when to avoid risking a fight they had little chance of winning, such as one against a superior enemy warship. American privateering was effectively ended towards the end of the War of 1812 because they were unable to risk fighting their way through the Royal Naval blockade that sealed off the American Atlantic ports. The few privateers still at large (such as the *Grand Turk*) were also unable to return home, as no privateer was a match for a blockading British frigate or a ship-of-the-line.

Privateering Vessels

A privateer was almost always a privately owned vessel fitted out and armed at the owner's expense, with a specially selected crew. Its object was to capture enemy merchant shipping in time of war, not to fight enemy privateers or warships. The prime prerequisite for a privateering vessel was that she should be fast, able to catch her prey and to escape pursuers. At the beginning of any of the 18th-century or early 19th-century maritime conflicts involving America, Britain and France, purpose-built privateering vessels were a rarity, as they served no legitimate function during the long intermediate periods of peace. At the start of a conflict, it was customary to fit out merchant vessels of all types as privateers, although speedy vessels were the preference. A particularly popular vessel type was the slaver, built to transfer her human cargo across the Atlantic Ocean as fast as possible. Smuggling craft were also ideal as small privateers, and these vessels were especially common along both the British and French coasts of the English Channel. In the Americas, schooners proved ideal craft and were usually capable of overhauling most of the other types of merchant vessels in common use. These makeshift privateers enjoyed an initial period of success until the enemy state began to arm its merchant fleet and send small warships to sea to intercept the

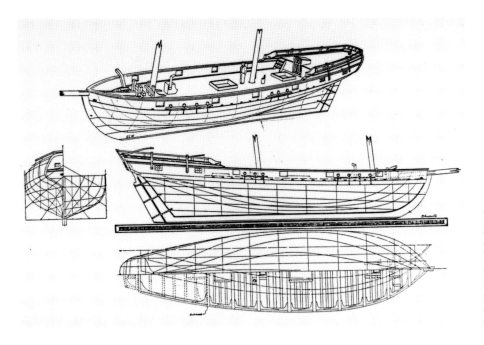

Profile, plan and isometric view of a former privateering schooner captured and purchased into the Royal Navy in 1780, when she was renamed the armed schooner *Bernice*. Although her original name and port are unknown, she was almost certainly an American vessel. (Stratford Archive)

privateers. The number of privateers at sea was gradually reduced as smaller and weaker vessels found their prey too well armed, and slower vessels were captured by the enemy navy. After the end of the first year of the maritime conflict, the numbers of privateers started to rise again as specially built vessels were launched, designed from the keel up as privateering vessels. This pattern was noticeable during the Seven Years' War and the Napoleonic Wars, although it was even more clearly defined during the American Revolutionary conflict and the War of 1812.

What characteristics did ship owners look for when they commissioned a purpose-built privateer? As already noted, speed was vital, but this was a difficult attribute to guarantee when a ship was being designed. Ship designers recognized the basic correlation between a sleek hull design and a suitable spread of sail, but at least until the late 18th century they tended to copy existing fast designs rather than produce their own evolutionary craft. A privateer had to be seaworthy, capable of cruising the enemy sea lanes regardless of the weather conditions. Crucially, she must be capable of handling well in strong breezes with more sail than was commonly carried, and able to sail as close to the wind as possible. Armament was less important, although a privateer had to have sufficient firepower to overawe any merchant ship it came across. The idea was not to fight enemy warships or well-defended merchantmen in a conventional sea battle, but to capture the enemy ship by intimidation, preferably without damaging her hull

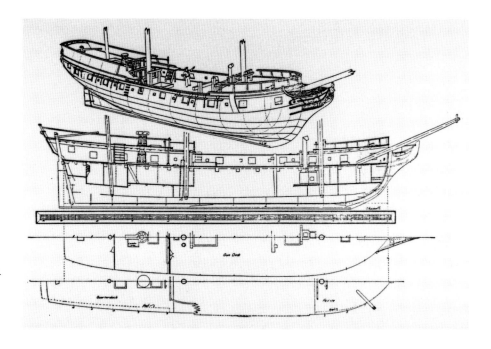

Profile, deck plan and isometric reconstruction of the 20-gun American privateer *Rattlesnake*, launched in June 1781 at Salem, Massachusetts, and captured by the Royal Navy in the same year. She was one of the largest privateering vessels built during the American Revolutionary War. (Stratford Archive)

or cargo. As most privateers had a comparatively large crew compared with their mercantile opponents, boarding was the favoured recourse if the enemy chose not to surrender on demand. This large crew was required to man prize vessels as well as to ensure victory in a boarding action. Another vital feature was hull strength. The need for a slim and sleek hull which ensured speed had to be balanced with the requirement to make the frames of the ship heavy enough to withstand the pressures imposed by a larger spread of sail than would normally be carried in a similarly sized merchant vessel. As only a small broadside of ordnance was usually carried, the stresses imposed on the hull by gunfire were less than those when under a full press of sail, and the hull had to be designed accordingly, with special attention given to the strength of the masts. As it was rare for privateers to stay at sea for extended periods, there was little requirement for extensive hold space for stores and provisions, or to house the cargoes taken from an enemy vessel. The custom was to send the captured vessel back to the privateer's home port with a prize crew, so only money and particularly valuable cargoes were transferred to the privateer herself.

As for the vessels themselves, while the first wave of privateers were small converted fishing vessels or merchantmen, many smaller vessels were retained as privateers. The French, Dutch and British all favoured small cutters, luggers and ketches in European waters. These 'corvettes' were ideally suited to coastal waters but were unable to venture far into the Atlantic Ocean. In his *Architectura Navalis Mercatoria* of 1768, the Swedish naval architect Frederick Chapman included plans for a privateering frigate, designed as a deep-water commerce-raider. Chapman's privateer was 160ft (49m) long, with a beam of 47ft (14.3m) and displaced 950 tons. She was armed with 40 guns (6- and 28-pdrs in two decks), and carried a crew of 400 men. As most privateers of the day were less than 85ft (26m) long, with a displacement of 120 tons, this was a significant departure from the privateers of the period. Although never as large as Chapman's frigate, some French privateers of the French Revolutionary War exceeded 500 tons, and during the War of 1812 American shipyards produced a range of 'super-privateers'. The ground for these specialist vessels had been laid even earlier. Several large and specially built privateers were captured by the Royal Navy during the American Revolution, and brought into service. The process involved completing a detailed survey of the ship, and plans were made of the vessel. These provide a useful insight into American privateering design during the late 18th century.

Gunners on board the American Revolutionary era privateer *Pickering* are shown attacking a vessel of the English East India Company in this spirited and fairly accurate illustration by Frank Schoonover painted in 1921. (Stratford Archive)

In 1778, the British captured the privateer *American Tartar*. She was 115ft (35m) long and carried 20 guns. This was a revelation, as the privateer was larger than anything the Royal Navy had encountered before. In 1781, the American privateer *Rattlesnake* was captured and used by the Royal Navy. She was a miniature version of the ship designed by Chapman. It appears she was built in Salem and carried 20 guns and a crew of 85 men. She was probably built by John Peck of Boston, who reputedly had never heard of Chapman. The *Rattlesnake* was therefore a pure American design, intended to fill the perceived need of an ideal privateering vessel. A smaller privateer for which plans exist was the *Bernice*, used by the Royal Navy as an armed schooner. It was clearly capable of great speed and is similar in its lines to later Baltimore and Chesapeake schooners.

During the War of 1812, American designers built even larger privateers, such as the *Prince de Neufchâtel*. She was built in New York but followed the designs of contemporary French privateers. At about 130ft (40m) long, she carried 18 guns, mostly carronades, with long 18-pdrs as bow chasers. This 'super-privateer' had a spectacular career, capturing numerous British prizes and fighting off a British boarding attempt before finally being captured in December 1814. American maritime historians have described the vessel as the pinnacle of privateering design, combining power, speed and superb handling qualities. In fact, she was distinctly smaller than many of the large French privateers that operated in the West Indies and Atlantic, and she was matched in size by privateering schooners from Baltimore, Salem and Boston such as the *Herald*, *America* or *Boxer*, all considered examples of 'super-privateers', or at least specialist privateering ships. The American schooners of the War of 1812 were perfectly designed for their privateering role, and their list of prizes betrays their efficiency at hunting and capturing enemy shipping. Compared with earlier vessels, they were spectacularly successful, with a combination of expert crews and ideal vessels.

American privateers during the American Revolution were painted almost exclusively using the earth-pigment paints available in the American colonies at the time. Particularly common was a brick-red colour produced from iron oxide. Similarly, a yellow ochre was also readily available, as was a mid-brown Sienna and a mid-grey lead-based paint. Of these, the three former colours appear to have been the most popular for vessels. Black, or 'lamp black', was also available but became more common as a privateering and merchant ship colour during the early 19th century. White was rarely used, although it was popular as a land-based paint. It was relatively expensive, and at sea the colour tended to yellow and fade rapidly. Other colours, such as blues, reds and greens, were used sparingly, as the paint had to be imported from Europe and was consequently expensive. Certain combinations appear to have been common: an ochre or sienna hull with black stripes was popular, as was a black hull with red oxide or ochre stripes. Gun ports were never chequered on privateers as they were on warships during the early 19th century. These colour schemes reflected merchant practice and allowed the privateering vessel to disguise herself as a merchantman if desired. By the War of 1812, many British and American privateers favoured black hulls with a horizontal ochre stripe down the side. Paintings depicting French privateers during the period show black hulls with white stripes or, more commonly, all black hulls.

Benito de Soto and his crew of the *Black Joke* sailing away from their prey, the British barque *Morning Star*, in February 1832. The pirates locked the barque's crew below decks and scuttled the ship before abandoning her. (Stratford Archive)

Privateer Captains and Latter-day Pirates

Of the hundreds of privateering captains of the period, the following form a representative sample, although they include some of the more successful commanders. The list also includes a naval officer and a selection of the last Caribbean pirates active during the early 19th century.

JONATHAN HARADEN

Period of operation: 1776–82

Jonathan Haraden was born in Gloucester, Massachusetts, in 1745, but moved to Salem as a child. He served his apprenticeship at sea, and when the American colonies revolted in 1775 he was a natural choice as a privateer. In 1776, he was appointed first lieutenant on the privateering schooner *Tyrannicide*, commanded by Captain Fiske of Salem. During that summer, the *Tyrannicide* captured a Royal Naval cutter, a packet schooner and several merchant ships, and repeated her successes on several other cruises reaching as far afield as Bermuda. In August 1779, she was burned on the Penobscot River to avoid letting her fall into enemy hands. Haraden returned to Salem.

In the spring of 1780, he sailed as the captain of the new Salem privateer *General Pickering*, a 180-ton schooner armed with 14 6-pdrs and carrying a crew of 45 men. Haraden planned to make the Spanish port of Bilbao his base and sailed with a cargo of West Indies sugar to help pay for supplies in Europe. During the voyage, he was attacked by a British cutter, which he fought off, and in the Bay of Biscay he came upon the British privateering brig *Golden Eagle*. It was night, and both vessels were taken by surprise and could hardly see each other. Haraden called on the British captain to surrender, claiming he was 'a United States frigate of the heaviest class'. The British privateers surrendered, only to find that the *General Pickering* was no more powerful than their own ship.

When he was approaching Bilbao with his prize on 4 June, Haraden was attacked by the large British privateer *Achilles*, of 40 guns. The British recaptured Haraden's prize, and as spectators watched from the shore the two privateers fought for three hours, before the *Achilles* gave up the contest and sailed away with the *Golden Eagle* as a consolation prize. Haraden's ship limped into Bilbao. Haraden returned to Salem in the autumn and continued his activities, capturing dozens of

British vessels off the New York coast. Haraden won a reputation for deception and bluff, and by the end of the war had amassed a hard-won fortune in prize money.

SILAS TALBOT

Period of operation: 1775–81

Born into a poor family in Dighton, Massachusetts, Silas Talbot went to sea as a boy, and by 1772 appears as a house owner and sea captain in Providence, Rhode Island. In 1775, he joined a Rhode Island infantry regiment as a captain, and served in the operations around Boston which culminated in the British withdrawal from the city in March 1776. In New London, he met Captain Esek Hopkins and offered to help guide his Continental Navy ships to a secure haven in Providence. He then rejoined the Continental Army outside New York. The British captured the city in a brilliantly fought campaign and forced Washington to retreat up the Hudson River. A plan was laid to attack the British fleet anchored off the city, and Talbot offered to help. The fireship attack was a failure, and Talbot was badly injured. He returned to Providence to recuperate, and then in 1778 the newly promoted Colonel Talbot assisted in another failure, a French attack on Newport, Rhode Island.

OPPOSITE A portrayal of the probably fictitious incident where John Paul Jones shot a sailor under his command when the man wanted to surrender during the battle between the *Bonhomme Richard* and the *Serapis*, September 1779. (Mariners' Museum, Newport News, Virginia)

Captain Silas Talbot was a distinguished Rhode Island privateering captain who led his men in attacks on British warships on the Hudson River in 1776, then operated off New England against Tory shipping until he was captured in 1780. (Stratford Archive)

Turning his back on regular service, Talbot fitted out a small privateering schooner called the *Hawk* with two guns and 60 crew. He captured the British blockading vessel *Pigot*, then set out in search of larger prey. He captured several British merchantmen during 1779, as well as two loyalist privateers, including the powerful Newport brig *King George*. While still officially serving in Washington's army, Colonel Talbot had become a successful privateer.

His privateering sloop *Argo* of 100 tons carried a respectable 12 6-pdrs and a crew of 60 men, all 'ex-army' seamen, and in 1779 he began a fresh cruise, operating off Long Island, Nantucket and Cape Cod. He sent scores of prizes into New Bedford, Massachusetts, including two more privateers, the *Dragon* of 14 guns and the *Hannah*, also of 14 guns, including 12-pdrs. For his achievements, he was made a captain in the Continental Navy. In 1780, he took command of the privateer *General Washington*, carrying 20 6-pdrs and a crew of 120 men. After a few successes, he ran into a British fleet and was captured. He was released from prison in Britain in 1781 and eventually returned to Providence. After the war, he continued in naval service and even commanded the frigate USS *Constitution* during the Quasi-War with France.

JOHN PAUL JONES

Period of operation: 1775–81

Born John Paul in south-west Scotland in 1747, he sailed to Virginia in 1760 to join his elder brother. He became a seaman and within seven years had become the captain of a West Indies merchantman. Some unrecorded incident prompted him to change his identity, adding Jones to his name. In 1775, John Paul Jones was commissioned as a lieutenant in the Continental Navy and commanded a number of ships. In early 1778 he sailed for Brest, with orders to use the French port as a base for commerce raiding.

By April 1778, he was attacking shipping in the Irish Sea, then landed at Whitehaven, where he destroyed a small fort and burned the ships in port. Slipping away, he made his next appearance on the Scottish coast near Kirkcudbright, where he tried to kidnap the Earl of Selkirk from his home. The earl was away, so Jones took the family silver instead. This was considered an act of piracy by the British public, and he was demonized in the British newspapers. He then captured the 20-gun British brig *Drake* before returning to Brest.

Jones was rewarded with a new command, a converted French Indiaman renamed *Bonhomme Richard*. In August, he put to sea in company with French privateers and captured three British ships off Ireland. By September, he was in the

North Sea but became separated from all but one of the French vessels. Bad weather forced him to abandon a raid on Leith near Edinburgh, and he continued to cruise down the coast. On 23 September 1779, he encountered a British convoy off Flamborough Head. Jones attacked the escort, the 50-gun *Serapis*, while his consort engaged a British sloop. Jones resolved to fight the British ship at close quarters, and the ships exchanged broadsides at point-blank range. When asked to surrender, he replied with the now famous line, 'I have not yet begun to fight.' American musket fire swept the British decks, and Jones eventually boarded the enemy, forcing it to strike. Both ships were severely damaged, and the *Bonhomme Richard* eventually sank, leaving Jones to limp away in his prize.

In France Jones was regarded as a hero, and he went on to serve in the Russian Navy before dying in 1792. Today he is regarded as the father of the United States Navy.

John Paul Jones raiding the Earl of Selkirk's house, 1778. Jones is shown here inside the earl's mansion, wearing the uniform of an officer in the Continental Navy. As his looting suggests, Jones occasionally skirted the boundaries between legal and illegal behaviour. (Angus McBride © Osprey Publishing Ltd)

ROBERT SURCOUF

Period of operation: 1794–1810

The French Revolutionary War began in 1793, and while the French fleet found itself blockaded in the ports of Brest and Toulon, other harbours became centres of privateering activity. As the Royal Navy also maintained a powerful presence in the West Indies, larger French privateers opted to cruise in the less heavily defended waters of the Indian Ocean. The most successful of these privateer captains was Robert Surcouf, who originated in the privateering port of St Malo, in Brittany.

He began his career at 13, when he ran away to sea. He worked through the ranks, and when the French Revolution began he was the captain of a French slave ship, operating between the colony of the Île de France (Mauritius) and the East African coast. When the French revolutionaries outlawed the slave trade in 1795, Surcouf looked elsewhere for employment. His ship was ideally suited for

The *Emille*, a French privateer commanded by Robert Surcouf, attacking the English merchant vessel *Hope* in the Indian Ocean, c. 1798. Surcouf continued his success after the French Revolution and was created a baron by Napoleon Bonaparte. (Stratford Archive)

privateering, and Mauritius lay astride the British sea lane from India to Europe via the Cape of Good Hope. The governor of the island denied him a letter of marque, probably because he was unable to raise enough of a bond. Undeterred, Surcouf re-armed his small slaving brig *Emille* and went in search of prey.

One of his first successes was the capture in the Bay of Bengal of the *Triton*, a British East Indiaman returning to London with a rich cargo. He captured several other ships, only to have them confiscated by the governor of Mauritius. Surcouf promptly sailed for France, acquired a letter of marque and returned to Mauritius to claim his prizes. He continued to harass British shipping throughout the war, and captured another valuable East Indiaman, the *Kent*, with two small privateers, the *Confiance* and the *Clarisse*.

During the Peace of Amiens he returned to France, and when war broke out again refused a commission in the regular navy and operated his privateering squadron from St Malo. In 1807, he sailed for the West Indies in the 'super-privateer' *Revenant*, and then retired after two successful cruises. Feted as a hero by the French and awarded with a barony by Napoleon, Surcouf continued to invest in privateering ventures until the end of the Napoleonic Wars.

THOMAS BOYLE

Period of operation: 1812–15

Thomas Boyle remains one of the few privateer captains who captured a regular enemy warship. His roots are obscure, but by the start of the War of 1812 he was considered one of Baltimore's most distinguished seamen. In July 1812, he was given command of the privateering schooner *Comet*, a converted merchantman armed with 16 guns. He captured a well-armed British merchantman carrying sugar and cotton from Surinam, which surrendered after a bitter gunnery duel. The *Comet* went on to take two more sugar carriers before returning to Baltimore in November. A British squadron moved up the Chesapeake while the *Comet* was in port, but Boyle ran through the blockade in late December and escaped with only minor damage.

By January, Boyle was off Pernambuco in Brazil, and by pretending to be a Portuguese vessel he approached a small convoy of three British ships and a Portuguese escort. The Portuguese brig tried to defend the convoy, but after a lengthy fight the *Comet* captured one of the merchantmen and escaped. The Americans captured a British ship, only to be chased from the area by the frigate HMS *Surprise*. Boyle evaded the British warship and set course for the West

Indies. In February 1813, he captured a merchantman off St Johns which turned out to be a straggler from a convoy. The *Comet* gave chase and captured two more stragglers before being chased off by the escorts. Boyle returned to Baltimore and was given command of the 'super-privateer' *Chasseur*. His first cruise was off the British coast, where he captured 18 ships, before returning to New York in October 1814.

In February 1815, the *Chasseur* was cruising in the Florida Straits when she encountered the Royal Naval schooner *St Lawrence*. The two ships were well matched, with 12 guns each, but the American privateer was better handled. After exchanging several broadsides, the privateers eventually boarded the British warship and captured her. The *Chasseur* took her important prize back to Baltimore, only to find the war had ended.

JEAN LAFFITE

Period of operation: 1810–20

The details of Jean Laffite's early life are vague, but he was probably born in France around 1780. By 1809, he and his brother Pierre ran a blacksmith's shop in New Orleans, which also provided a cover for a smuggling operation. From 1810 Laffite became the leader of a band of pirates and smugglers based in Barataria Bay, south of the city. For four years his men attacked Spanish shipping in the Gulf of Mexico, selling plunder and slaves to Louisiana merchants and slave traders in a series of secret auctions. In 1812, the governor of Louisiana arrested the Laffites on charges of piracy, but the brothers escaped on bail, and their activities continued largely unhindered. In 1814, a British fleet had blockaded the mouth of the Mississippi Delta. Laffite impressed the British with his ability to evade the blockade, so they decided to use the pirates to help them. In September 1814, British officers met Laffite, offering him a reward if he would help them attack New Orleans. Instead, Laffite warned the Louisiana authorities, an action that resulted in state warships locating his base and destroying it. By then, a British attack was considered imminent, and General Andrew Jackson proposed a truce with the pirates if they would help defend the city. In January 1815, a British force landed, and in the resulting battle of New Orleans the invaders were repulsed with heavy losses. Laffite and his pirates were rewarded by an official pardon from President Madison, and while many gave up piracy, the Laffite brothers ignored the offer, stole a ship and sailed to Galveston in Texas. Laffite's piracy continued until 1820, when he made the mistake of attacking American ships. The US Navy sent a force

that destroyed Galveston and its pirate fleet. Laffite escaped, but it is considered likely that he died in Mexico a year later.

BENITO DE SOTO

Period of operation: 1827–33

Benito de Soto was a Portuguese sailor who led a mutiny on an Argentinian slave ship in 1827. The loyal crewmen were cast adrift off the Angolan coast, and de Soto was elected leader of the mutineers, who chose to turn pirate. De Soto renamed the vessel the *Black Joke* and sailed for the Caribbean, where he sold the cargo of slaves before commencing his attacks. He concentrated on Spanish ships, killing the crews and sinking every vessel he came across. The old pirate adage 'dead men tell no tales' was evidently taken to heart. By early 1830, the pirates were operating off the coast of Brazil, occasionally sailing into the mid-Atlantic to

Jean Laffite at the battle of New Orleans, 1815. Laffite and his men are manning a ship's cast-iron carronade behind the American earthworks. The American fire shredded the attacking British ranks, and General Jackson thanked Laffite for his part in the victory, earning the pirates a pardon. (Angus McBride © Osprey Publishing Ltd)

cruise the busy trade route between Europe and the Cape of Good Hope. His prey were ships returning from India and the Orient, laden with spices, opium or tea. On 21 February 1832, de Soto captured the barque *Morning Star*, on passage from Ceylon to England. The pirates fired into the merchantman at point-blank range, forcing the survivors to heave to. Ordering the British captain aboard the *Black Joke*, he cut him down with a cutlass, then sent his men on board the defenceless prize. After killing and raping at will, they locked the survivors below decks and the ship was scuttled. The pirates then sailed off in search of fresh prey. The prisoners escaped and kept the vessel afloat using her pumps until they were rescued by another ship early the next morning.

De Soto headed for the coast of Spain, where he sold his plunder. There his luck ran out. The *Black Joke* struck a reef near Cadiz and sank. The surviving pirates walked to Gibraltar, where they hoped to steal another ship. Instead, they were recognized by one of their former victims, arrested and sent to Cadiz to stand trial. De Soto and his crew were subsequently hanged in 1833.

PEDRO GIBERT

Period of operation: 1832–33

In 1830, the former privateer Pedro Gibert commanded a trading schooner called the *Panda*. He decided that smuggling and illegal slave trading would prove more profitable, so from 1830 until 1832 he operated a smuggling business between Florida and Cuba, with a base on Florida's St Lucie Inlet. On 20 September 1832, he sighted the American brigantine *Mexican* in the Florida Straits. The American vessel was chased and captured in what may have been an impromptu act of piracy. Before his vessel was boarded, the captain of the *Mexican* hid his ship's paychest containing $20,000 in coins.

The pirates boarded the prize, locked up the crew, then ransacked the ship. Gibert tortured the captain, forcing him to reveal the location of the chest, before returning to the *Panda* with the plunder. When asked what to do with the prisoners, Gibert told his men, 'Dead cats don't mew. You know what to do.' The pirates locked the crew below decks and set fire to the *Mexican* before sailing away. Somehow, one of the crewmen escaped and freed his companions. The crew put out the fire and limped north to New York.

The *Panda* remained in Florida waters until January 1833, when it sailed for Africa. By March, Gibert was off the West African coast hoping to find slaves, even though the trade was illegal in the area. A British warship came across the *Panda*,

OPPOSITE Benito de Soto in Gibraltar, 1832. Here Benito is discovered on the streets of Gibraltar by a wounded soldier, who was a passenger on the British *Morning Star* – a ship captured and scuttled by de Soto. De Soto was subsequently arrested and hanged, along with his crew. (Angus McBride © Osprey Publishing Ltd)

'Don' Pedro Gibert and the Mexican, 1832. Gibert is depicted returning to his ship, Panda, after setting the Mexican on fire. Once the pirates had gone, one of the crewman escaped, released the others and put out the fire. (Angus McBride © Osprey Publishing Ltd)

the schooner was boarded, and Gibert and his crew were arrested as illegal slavers. Despite an attempted escape, the pirates were transported to England, where their true identity was discovered. Gibert and 11 other pirates were extradited to the United States to stand trial for piracy, and in a Boston courtroom they were identified by the crew of the Mexican. Pedro Gibert and three pirates were sentenced to death, the rest getting lesser sentences, and the condemned men were hanged in 1835, the last pirates to be executed in the United States of America.

Privateering Ports and Pirate Dens

PRIVATEERING PORTS

Privateers operated under strict rules, one of which was the requirement to bring prizes back to a home port. There a marine court would decide if they were taken legally and then put the vessels and cargo up for sale. Finally, the profits would be divided between owners and crew. Most privateers recruited their crew from their home port, the base where the vessels were built. Local ship owners and investors backed the privateering venture, and the prizes were sold there. The result was that in these centres, privateering provided a major economic boom, and the successes and failures of the privateering war had a direct influence on the economy of the port and its hinterland.

In Britain, France, Canada and the United States, certain ports developed into privateering centres during the period. Although this study concentrates on privateering in American waters, the British and French privateering structure provides a useful counterpoint to an examination of American privateering. Each country approached privateering in a different way and achieved a range of results from its privateering expeditions. In some cases, ship owners took to privateering on an opportunistic basis, or were faced with little alternative if the war prevented their merchant shipping from freely engaging in trade. As such, it provided the only alternative to the economic ruin of the port. Failure in an individual

The American colonists made extensive use of privateers to counter Britain's naval supremacy in American waters. It was only following the French naval success at the battle of the Chesapeake in March 1781 that the British naval stranglehold of the colonies was lifted. (Mariners' Museum, Newport News, Virginia)

Map showing the principal American privateering ports during the American Revolution and the War of 1812. (Author)

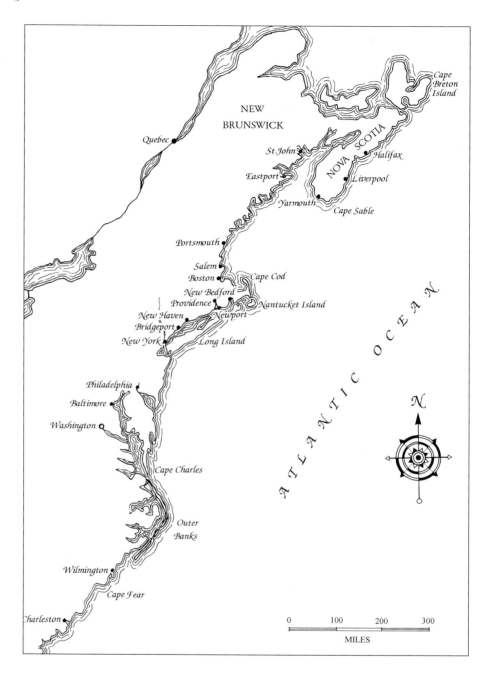

privateering venture might also bring private ruin, but failure to succeed in the privateering war could ruin the fabric of the port's economy. This was the situation faced by most American ports during the War of 1812; initial successes were reversed by a crippling blockade of her ports and consequently their near-ruin.

America

During the American Revolution, a number of ports became established as privateering bases, principally in New England: Boston, Salem, New Haven and Bridgeport were the best examples, although Philadelphia was also prominent until its capture by the British in October 1777. In the War of 1812, Baltimore replaced Philadelphia as the largest privateering centre south of New York. New York itself served as a base for loyalist privateers during the Revolution, and in 1812 it was ranked alongside Baltimore as the major privateering port on the Atlantic seaboard. The majority of these ships were tiny, mounting fewer than four guns, but as most of the Canadian and British shipping within reach was unarmed, that seemed unimportant.

Privateering became an American obsession, and a Boston observer recorded in late 1776 that 'the spirit of privateering is got to the highest pitch of enthusiasm: almost every vessel from 20 tons to 400 is fitting out here'. The target of these New England privateers was initially the British and Canadian fishermen operating off the Grand Banks. As the war developed, larger vessels were able to range as far as the West Indies, or even reach British waters, from French or Spanish bases. The same level of activity was repeated during the War of 1812. In July 1812, the *Boston Globe* reported that 'the people of the Eastern States are labouring almost night and day to fit out privateers. Two have already sailed from Salem, and ten others are getting ready for sea.'

Taking Salem as an example, the small Massachusetts port provided a base for over 158 privateers of various sizes throughout the Revolutionary War, although it seems no more than 40 were operating at any one time. Many of these were prizes captured by Salem privateers and bought by local ship owners, who turned them into privateers. During the War of 1812, Salem shipbuilders began constructing purpose-built privateers as soon as war was declared. The *America* was one of the first of these, capturing 40 prizes during four cruises. Her owner, George Crowninshield of Salem, made a profit of around $600,000, a fortune for the time. While American privateering ports underwent a boom during the American Revolution, the reverse was true during the War of 1812, especially after the full impact of the British blockade was felt. Initial success was replaced by a complete blockade of the privateering ports and a steady loss of privateering vessels. A widespread reliance on privateering in any community imposed a strain on available local manpower and natural resources. Ships were being built, timber brought to the shipyards, and seamen and carpenters recruited to serve in the privateering venture. This was all undertaken when the country was at war, and resources were needed elsewhere. During the American Revolution, hard currency was at a premium, and the fledgling United States had no national reserves. Consequently, the economy was volatile and inflation was rampant. Probably the only places where currency was brought into the country were the privateering ports. By providing a rare source of imported commodities, these ports were vital to American material and economic survival. It can even be argued that despite the blatantly profiteering nature of the enterprise, the privateers from Salem, Boston and New Haven did as much to secure America's independence from Britain as any soldier in George Washington's army. By waging an economic war, the American privateers kept their own economy alive and subjected the British economy to pressures that made the continuance of the war unpalatable.

Britain and Canada

Canadian ports were used to harbour privateers during both wars, and Halifax, Liverpool and Yarmouth in Nova Scotia, and Eastport in New Brunswick maintained active privateering communities. In Britain, naval bases such as Portsmouth and Plymouth were often avoided, at least until after 1805, so preferred privateering ports included the Channel Islands, London, Bristol or Liverpool. American vessels were a secondary privateering target, with French shipping providing the traditional staple for British privateers. Britain was never blockaded, so both her privateers and her merchant fleet were free to operate throughout the period. Despite shipping losses through enemy privateering, British maritime commercial activity was so widespread that privateer attacks had little overall effect on the island's economy. The British privateering peak came in the last years of the American Revolutionary War, when Dutch and French prizes proved easy targets for the British. Over 800 British privateering licences were issued during the American Revolution, compared with only 175 during the War of 1812. Unlike their American opponents, most British privateers were coastal vessels, designed to capture shipping in the English Channel, not in the middle of the Atlantic.

France

The principal French privateering ports were La Rochelle, Nantes, Bayonne, St Malo and Dunkirk; privateering crews largely avoided Brest and Toulon because of the strong naval presence there. During the American Revolution, French, Spanish and Dutch ports provided bases from which American privateers could raid British territorial waters. They also provided sources for French guns and munitions. Prize

Privateering ports in northern
Europe during the American
Revolutionary, French
Revolutionary and Napoleonic
Wars. (Author)

agents were established in ports such as La Rochelle and Nantes, and American privateers even cruised in company with their French colleagues. During the French Revolutionary and Napoleonic Wars, privateers (or 'corsairs' to the French) thrived in ports where a British blockade was incomplete or difficult to maintain due to wind and tidal conditions. Ports such as Nantes and Bayonne on the Bay of Biscay became corsair havens, supported by capital from cities where the blockade was more strictly enforced. A tight blockade of the Channel ports effectively quashed privateering in Dunkirk and St Malo after the heady period of Robert Surcouf's privateering raids into the Indian Ocean. As the Napoleonic Wars progressed, economic decline within France and the increased risk of capture made privateering an enterprise that was too risky to undertake for most ship owners.

THE LAST PIRATE DENS

The wave of piracy that was unleashed on the Caribbean in the decade after 1815 was a direct result of the end of legitimate wartime privateering. This new wave of pirates thrived on the political instability of the Caribbean basin, and flourished in areas where government authority was lax or non-existent, or where they were able to bribe local officials. Pirates needed access to markets for the sale of their plunder, and as slaves constituted one of the most common forms of plunder, regions that supported a slave economy were particularly popular. Although the export of slaves from Africa was illegal, cities such as New Orleans provided a ready market for slavers and pirates. Pirate bases had to be remote from areas of authority, but they also needed to provide access to these marketplaces. The following three areas provided for the special needs of these last pirates.

Barataria

Barataria Bay was an inlet to the west of the Mississippi Delta, linked to the river by a network of small rivers, bayous and lagoons. It is perhaps most famous as being the base used by Jean Laffite from 1812 to 1815, but there is evidence it was used even earlier by both smugglers and pirates. Laffite used the island of Grand Terre as a base, and a nearby island contained slave pens (barracoons). Many of the pirates came from the local Cajun population, a community expert in navigating the hidden bayous of coastal Louisiana. The maze of waterways made it difficult to find the pirate base, while the same waterways provided easy access to the markets of New Orleans. Merchants and slave owners were brought to hidden meeting places, where slaves and stolen goods were auctioned by Laffite's men, and the local Cajun population and informants within the city provided warning of any government attack on the pirate base. In 1814, a concerted effort by the US Navy led to the discovery of Barataria, and although the pirates escaped capture, their base was no longer considered a safe haven. After the establishment

The Mississippi Delta and its surrounding hinterland of bayous. Barataria, the secret island base used by Jean Laffite and his pirates, lay to the west of the main river channel and river entrance to New Orleans. (Stratford Archive)

of military authority following the battle of New Orleans in 1815, many pirates looked elsewhere for a secure base of operations.

Galveston

Laffite and his men moved along the Gulf of Mexico to Galveston in Texas, a small settlement which for a few years became a new safe haven for pirates. Texas was a frontier region operating in a section of disputed territory beyond the authority of Texas, Mexico, the United States or Spain. Piracy thrived along the Texan coast for five years from 1815, and both Mexican and Texan traders saw Galveston as a lucrative source of contraband, including slaves, guns and more conventional cargoes. Other pirate settlements were established on Matagorda Bay and on the Sabine estuary, although Galveston became the premier pirate base in the region from 1817. All three boasted easy access to the sea, combined with safe inland escape routes through the bays, rivers and coastal waters of the Texan coast. Mexican shipping was particularly susceptible to pirate attacks, but the authorities were too concerned with the threat of a Texan rebellion to launch a punitive

During its anti-piracy operations, the US Navy employed a flotilla of small 'mosquito boats' which were capable of seeking out pirates in the coastal waters of Cuba. This scene depicts an attack by these craft against Cuban-based pirates in 1823. (Stratford Archive)

expedition. As American shipping losses mounted, in 1820 an American naval force was sent to Galveston to deal with the pirates. The base was destroyed and the vessels either burned or captured, but pirate attacks continued. It was only in the late 1820s when a concerted anti-pirate campaign was conducted by American and British naval forces that pirate operations ended along the Texan coast. Many former pirates settled in Texas, and a number turned to privateering on behalf of the fledgling state of Texas when it rebelled against Mexico in 1836.

Cuba

From 1820, the ports and inlets along the northern coast of Cuba provided a new base for pirates. Spanish colonial officials turned a blind eye to pirate attacks, and pirates such as Charles Gibbs purchased political protection at the cost of giving local authorities a share of their plunder. Particularly popular bases were the ports of Matanzas and Caibarien, as they lay astride the busy shipping lane through the Florida Straits.

From 1823, American naval forces patrolled the coast, and a diplomatic drive spearheaded by President Monroe forced the Spanish authorities to crack down on corruption and piracy. By 1824, the threat was past, and with their vessels destroyed, many pirates turned to banditry on Cuba itself.

The Anti-piracy Campaign of the 1820s

The 1820s saw a resumption of piracy which had not been experienced in American waters since the days of Blackbeard and Bartholomew Roberts a century earlier. The end of the War of 1812 (in 1815) and the Latin American Wars of Independence (1810–25) meant that the waters of the Caribbean were full of privateers, not all of whom wanted to return to peaceful commerce. American shipping was particularly badly hit, and in 1823 a Baltimore newspaper estimated that there had been over 3,000 attacks on American vessels during the previous decade. Insurance companies raised their premiums to levels that surpassed those charged at the height of the British blockade in 1815, and ship

The armed brig USS *Enterprise* sailing into action against pirates off the coast of Cuba, c. 1821. The vessel went on to clear pirates from the coastal ports of Texas later that same year. (Stratford Archive)

223

Commodore Porter and the
'Mosquito Fleet'. Porter is shown
embarking on a launch in Key
West harbour to conduct a
Sunday inspection of his ships at
anchor. He wears the full dress
uniform of a United States Naval
commodore. (Angus McBride
© Osprey Publishing Ltd)

owners, the press and the public all demanded action. The Royal Navy stepped up
its patrols, making Jamaica a centre for its anti-piracy patrols, while Barbados
served as a base for operations in the West Indies and off the coast of South
America. A small American squadron was already operating in the Gulf of Mexico,
and in October 1821 the USS *Enterprise* caught four pirate ships at anchor off the
coast of Cuba. The schooners were the fleet of Charles Gibbs, an American

privateer-turned-pirate. The pirates were either killed, captured or forced to flee ashore, although Gibbs would remain at large for a further ten years. The United States government was impressed by the action, and President Monroe ordered the establishment of an anti-piracy squadron to be based in Key West, off the southern tip of Florida.

This US Naval force was known as the 'Mosquito Fleet' due to the small, shallow-draughted vessels used by the anti-piracy squadron. The phrase had extra meaning for the American sailors, as in the summer, malaria-carrying mosquitoes plagued the island base. The fleet consisted of 16 vessels including well-armed brigs, fast Baltimore schooners, an early paddle steamer and even a decoy merchant ship armed with hidden guns. The fleet commander was Commodore David Porter, a veteran of America's attack on the Barbary pirates in 1801 and the War of 1812. Porter's orders were to suppress piracy and the slave trade, protect the commerce and citizens of the United States, and transport American specie when required. The orders given to the various commanders of the Royal Naval West Indies or Jamaica Squadrons were similar, and all three formations faced a daunting task.

The 'Mosquito Fleet' was operational by the late summer of 1822, and Porter commenced cruises off the coast of Cuba and in the Gulf of Mexico. He immediately ran into diplomatic problems, as Cuba was one of the main pirate havens but fell under the control of the Spanish crown. The pirates proved elusive, and often their attacks were little more than crimes of opportunity, with seemingly innocent merchant vessels and fishing craft attacking passing shipping, then fleeing into Cuban ports or into the backcountry of the Florida Keys to escape retribution. Pirate attacks on shipping in Florida waters and the threat of Indian attacks on settlements forced Porter to divert precious resources to safeguard Florida's citizens, but by 1825 the Keys were protected by troops, and Porter turned his attention to Cuba. The Spanish authorities resented American or British interference, and many local officials were prepared to turn a blind eye to piracy, particularly if they were suitably rewarded. Porter called for a condemnation of piracy by the Spanish authorities and cut out pirate vessels in Cuba's smaller harbours and inlets, bringing a barrage of official complaints by the Cuban administrators. Eventually, Spanish ship owners saw the benefits of Porter's actions and lobbied the Cuban authorities to support Porter's activities. In April 1823, he defeated the infamous Cuban pirate known only as Diabolito ('Little Devil'). The pirate and his band were cornered off the northern coast of Cuba and forced to abandon their ships and flee inland. The Royal Navy had

Commodore David Porter, commander of the American West Indies Squadron based in Key West during the late 1820s. His success ensured that the threat of piracy was removed from the Caribbean once and for all. (Stratford Archive)

similar successes off the coast of South and Central America, and by 1824 both the British and American navies turned their attention to the Gulf of Mexico, where dozens of pirates had sought refuge in what is now Texas and northern Mexico. By 1825, hundreds of pirates had been captured, killed or forced to accept the lesson that piracy no longer paid. Piracy had virtually ceased to exist in American and Caribbean waters by the end of the year, and although a handful of rogue pirates continued to operate in the Atlantic or the Caribbean as late as the 1830s, they could be counted singly, and not in their hundreds.

GLOSSARY

Abaft	A nautical term meaning 'to the rear of'.
Barca longa	A Spanish vessel that carried a single square sail.
Barquentine	Also known as 'barque' or 'bark'; a sailing ship with three to five masts of which only the foremast is square rigged, the others being fore-and-aft rigged.
Blunderbuss	A muzzle-loading firearm with a flared, trumpet-like barrel.
Bowsprit	A spar extending forward from a ship's bow, to which the forestays are fastened.
Brig	A two-mast vessel, with square-rigged masts, and a fore-and-aft sail abaft the mainmast.
Brigantine	A two-mast vessel, with a square-rigged foremast and a fore-and-aft-rigged mainmast, with a square-rigged topsail.
Buccaneer	The name given to backwoodsmen on modern Haiti in the mid-17th century, which came to be used when speaking of the mainly English and French raiders of the Spanish Main; from *boucannier*.
Careen	The process of beaching a sailing ship, heeling her over, then cleaning weed and barnacles off her underside.
Carronade	A short smoothbore, cast-iron cannon designed as a short-range naval weapon with a low muzzle velocity.
Castellano	A Spanish-held fort.
Chain shot	Cannon balls linked with chain.
Felucca	A narrow, fast vessel of Arabic origin occasionally used by pirates in the Indian Ocean.
Flibotes	A term that refers to the small 'fly boats' used by French buccaneers.
Fluyt	A merchant vessel of Dutch design, with a shallow draught and a narrow, rounded stern. By the 18th century the term had changed, and the same vessel was known as a 'pink', which could carry anything from one to three masts, although traditionally a fluyt had three masts, fitted with square sails.
Fly boats	See *flibotes*.
Fore-and-aft rigged	A vessel with sails set in line with the hull, not at right angles as is the case with square-sails.
Gaff-rigged	A vessel with a fore-and-aft-rigged sail, mounted on a fore-and-aft yard extending from a vertical mast. It could be used in conjunction with a corresponding lower yard at the

	base of the sail. Most gaff-rigged sails during this period were referred to as 'spankers'.
Galleon	A large, three-masted square-rigged ship, used chiefly by the Spanish as an armed transport for treasure being taken from the New World to Spain.
Grapeshot	A cluster of iron balls shot out of a cannon.
Guineaman	A slave ship.
Interloper	A non-Spanish settler in Central and South America.
Jib	A triangular staysail set ahead of the foremost mast.
Lateen-rigged	A vessel with triangular sails on a long yard at an angle of 45 degrees to the mast.
Lateen yard	A triangular sail set on a long yard mounted at an angle on the mast, and running in a fore-and-aft direction.
Letter of marque	A government-issued contract granting privateers official permission to attack enemy ships during wartime under the condition that the sponsoring government got a share of the profits.
Mizzen mast	The mast aft of the mainmast.
Pink	See *fluyt*.
Pinnace	A term that refers to the oared longboat of a larger ship, with a single mast, of less than 60 tons' burden. It also refers to larger vessels, of 40–80 tons, which were independent vessels in their own right.
Piragua	A dugout canoe used in and around the Caribbean. While most were fairly small, some were larger, fitted with sails for open-water journeys. By the early 18th century the term had also come to be associated with a two-masted flat-bottomed coastal vessel found in the Caribbean that shared many characteristics of these larger dugouts.
Pirate	One who robs at sea or plunders the land from the sea, regardless of nationality and without commission from a sovereign nation.
Polacca	Also known as 'polacre'; a 17th-century sailing craft commonly found in the Mediterranean and distinguished by its square-rigged yards, which could be lowered, and a fore-and-aft-rigged spanker fitted to her mizzen mast.
Privateer	A privately owned warship whose captain held a privateering commission (known as a letter of marque), permitting him to attack the merchant vessels of an enemy nation in time of war. This term also refers to the man who held the commission.

Quoin and stool bed	A system of elevating guns on a ship which involved a quoin, or wedge manipulated at the breech end of a cannon.
Schooner	A two-mast vessel with fore-and-aft-rigged sails on both masts. Some larger schooners could carry one or more square-rigged topsails.
Shallop	A large vessel with one or more masts and carrying fore-and-aft or lug sails.
Ship	A vessel with three masts, fitted with square-rigged sails. More recently, the term has come to refer to any large vessel, but in the 18th century, only vessels fitting this definition were referred to as ships.
Slaver	A fast, square-rigged ship used to transport slaves.
Sloop	A vessel with a single mast, with a fore-and-aft-rigged mainsail, and a single fore-and-aft-rigged jib foresail. By the mid-18th century the term had also come to refer to armed warships fitted with more than one mast.
Snow	A vessel fitted with two masts, outwardly resembling a brig or brigantine, with a square-rigged mainsail, foresail and topsails. In addition the fore-and-aft sail abaft her mainmast was set on a separate mast pole (a 'trysail mast') attached immediately behind the mainmast.
Spanish Main	The name given to the Caribbean coast of the Spanish empire, which included the northern coast of South America and the entire Caribbean basin.
Spanker	See *gaff-rigged*.
Square-rigged	A vessel whose sails are set on horizontal yards mounted at right-angles to the ship.
Staysail	A triangular fore-and-aft sail extended on a stay.
Swashbuckler	A term derived from 'sword and buckler', a preferred Spanish weapon combination in the 16th century, when 'swashbuckler' referred to a weapon-armed thug or brigand, the name coming from the sound of a sword striking a buckler.
Tartan	A smaller version of the felucca, which was distinguished by the pronounced forward rake of her foremast-cum-bowsprit and her ability to operate under oars.
Topsail	A sail set on the upper portion of a mast (the 'topmast').
Trysail mast	A separate mast pole attached immediately behind the mainmast.
Windward Passage	The body of water that lay between the westernmost part of Hispaniola and the eastern part of Cuba.

FURTHER READING

Apestegui, Cruz, *Pirates of the Caribbean: Buccaneers, Freebooters and Filibusters, 1493–1720*, Conway Maritime Press (London, 2002)

Botting, Douglas (ed.), *The Pirates* (Time-Life Seafaring series), Time-Life Books (Amsterdam, 1978)

Burg, B. R., *Sodomy and the Pirate Tradition: English Sea Rovers in the 17th Century Caribbean*, NYU Press (New York, 1983)

Chapelle, Howard I., *The History of American Sailing Ships*, Konecky & Konecky (New York, 1982, first published 1935)

Chapelle, Howard I., *American Small Sailing Craft*, Norton Inc. Publishing (New York, 1951)

Clifford, Barry, *The Pirate Prince: Discovering the Priceless Treasures of the Sunken Ship Whydah*, Simon & Schuster (New York, 1993)

Clifford, Barry, *The Black Ship: The Quest to Recover an English Pirate Ship and Its Lost Treasure*, Headline Press (London, 1999)

Cordingly, David, *Under the Black Flag: The Romance and Reality of Life among the Pirates*, Random House (London, 1995)

Cordingly, David (ed.), *Pirates: Terror on the High Seas from the Caribbean to the South China Sea*, Turner Publishing (London, 1996)

Cordingly, David and John Falconer, *Pirates: Fact and Fiction*, National Maritime Museum, Greenwich (London, 1992)

Dudley, W. S. (ed.), *The Naval War of 1812: A Documentary History* Naval Historical Center (Washington, DC, 1985, 2 volumes)

Earle, Peter, *The Sack of Panama*, Viking (New York, 1981)

Exquemelin, Alexandre Olivier, *The Buccaneers of America, 1689* (Reprinted by Rio Grande Press, Glorieta, New Mexico, 1992)

Gardiner, Robert (ed.), *Cogs, Caravels and Galleons: The Development of the Three-Masted Full-Rigged Ship* (Conway History of the Ship series), Conway Maritime Press (London, 1992)

Gardiner, Robert (ed.), *Form Line of Battle: The Sailing Warship 1650–1840* (Conway History of the Ship series), Conway Maritime Press (London, 1992)

Gardiner, Robert (ed.), *The Heyday of Sail: Merchant Shipping before the Coming of Steam* (Conway History of the Ship series), Conway Maritime Press (London, 1992)

Garittee, Jerome R., *The Republic's Private Navy: The American Privateering Business as Practiced by Baltimore during the War of 1812*, Wesleyan University Press (Middletown, CT, 1977)

Gosse, Philip, *The Pirate's Who's Who, 1924* (Reprinted by Rio Grande Press, Glorieta, New Mexico, 1988)

Gosse, Philip, *The History of Piracy: Famous Adventures and Daring Deeds of Certain Notorious Freebooters of the Spanish Main* (New York, 1932, reprinted New Mexico, 1988)

Haring, C. H., *The Buccaneers in the West Indies in the XVII Century* (London, 1910)

Hutchinson, W. A., *A Treatise on Practical Seamanship*, Scholar Press (London, 1979, first published in 1777)

Johnson, Charles, *A General History of the Robberies and Murders of the Most Notorious Pirates*, 2nd edition (1724)

Konstam, Angus, *The History of Pirates*, Lyons Press (New York, 1999)

Konstam, Angus, *Pirates: Terror on the High Seas*, Osprey Publishing (Oxford, 2001)

Konstam, Angus, *Blackbeard: America's Most Notorious Pirate*, Wiley (Hoboken, NJ, 2006)

Lee, Robert E., *Blackbeard the Pirate: A Reappraisal of His Life and Times*, John F. Blair Publishing (Winston-Salem, NC, 1974)

Lydon, James J., *Pirates, Privateers, Profits*, Gregg Press (Upper Saddle River, NY, 1970)

Marley, David F., *Sack of Veracruz: The Great Pirate Raid of 1683*, Netherlandic Press (Ontario, 1993)

Marley, David F., *Pirates: Adventurers of the High Seas*, Arms & Armour Press (London, 1995)

Marx, Jennifer, *Pirates and Privateers of the Caribbean*, Krieger Publishing Company (Malabar, Florida, 1992)

Morris, Roger, *Atlantic Seafaring: Ten Centuries of Exploration and Trade in the North Atlantic*, International Marine Publishing (Auckland, NZ, 1992)

Palmer, Michael, *Stoddert's War: Naval Operations during the Quasi-War with France, 1798–1801* (Columbia, SC, 1987)

Pawson, Michael and David Buisseret, *Port Royal, Jamaica*, Clarendon Press (Oxford, 1975)

Pope, Dudley, *Harry Morgan's Way: A Biography of Sir Henry Morgan*, Secker and Warburg (London, 1977)

Pringle, Patrick, *Jolly Roger: The Story of the Great Age of Piracy*, WW Norton (London, 1953)

Rankin, Hugh F., *The Pirates of North Carolina*, NC Department of Cultural Resources (Raleigh, NC, 1960)

Rediker, Marcus, *Between the Devil and the Deep-Blue Sea: Merchant Seamen, Pirates and the Anglo-American Maritime World, 1700–1750*, Cambridge University Press (Cambridge, 1987)

Ritchie, Robert C., *Captain Kidd and the War against the Pirates*, Harvard University Press (New York, 1996)

Rogozinski, Jan, *Pirates! An A–Z Encyclopaedia*, Da Capo Press (New York, 1995)

Stanley, Jo (ed.), *Bold in her Breeches*, Pandora (London, 1995)

Starkey, David J., *British Privateering Enterprise in the Eighteenth Century*, University of Exeter Press (Exeter, 1990)

Starkey, David J., *Pirates and Privateers: New Perspectives on the War on Trade in the Eighteenth and Nineteenth Centuries*, University of Exeter Press (Exeter, 1997)

Swanson, Carl E., *Predators and Prizes: American Privateering and Imperial Warfare, 1739–1748*, University of South Carolina Press (Columbia, SC, 1991)

Verrill, Hyatt, *The Real History of the Pirate, 1923* (Reprinted by Rio Grande Press, Glorieta, New Mexico, 1989)

Wood, Peter, *The Spanish Main* (Time-Life Seafarers series), Time-Life Books (New York, 1979)

The following are works that are either out of print or contain specialized material. All are available through the inter-library loan service, or in specialist maritime libraries or bookshops.

Allen, Gardner W., *A Naval History of the American Revolution* (Boston, MA, 1913, reprinted 1970, 2 volumes)

Allen, Gardner W., *Massachusetts Privateers during the American Revolution* (Cambridge, MA, 1927)

Chapin, H. M., *Privateering in King George's War, 1739–48* (Providence, RI, 1928)

Clark, W. B., *Ben Franklin's Privateers* (Baton Rouge, LA, 1956)

Crowhurst, P., *The French War on Trade: Privateering 1793–1815* (Aldershot, 1989)

Grummond, J. L., *The Baratarians and the Battle for New Orleans* (Baton Rouge, LA, 1961)

Jameson, J. F. (ed.), *Privateering and Piracy in the Colonial Period: Illustrative Documents* (New York, 1923)

Maclay, E. S., *A History of American Privateering* (New York, 1923)

Toth, Charles W. (ed.), *The American Revolution and the West Indies* (Port Washington, NY, 1975)

INDEX

References to illustrations are shown in **bold**.

Achilles 203
Acorn 195
Admiralty Courts 157–61
Adventure 91, **145**
Adventure Galley 100, **101**, 103, 136–7
Adventure Prize 103
Africa *see* East Africa; Madagascar; West Africa
agriculture 27
Aix-la-Chapelle, Treaty of (1748) 165
America 201, 217
American colonies
    Admiralty Courts 157–61
    and piracy 9, 80, 153
American Revolutionary War (1775–83) 10, 165, 166–70, 187–9, 203–7, **215**, 217–19
American Tartar 201
Amiens, Peace of (1802) 165
Anstis, Thomas 115, 156
Antigua 159
Antilles 20–5, 61–2
Arawaks **22**
Archer, Captain 159
Architectura Navalis Mercatoria (Chapman) 128–9, **128**, 130, 199
Argentina 165
Argo 206
Armada de Barlavento 20
armament
    buccaneers/pirates 81, 113, 122, **133**, 141
        Queen Anne's Revenge 134, **138–9**, 141
        Whydah 137
    privateers 192–6
articles 146
Avery, Henry *see* Every, Henry

Bahamas
    map **79**
    and pirates 79–80, 84–5
    see also New Providence
Bahamas Channel 173
Baltimore 171, 209, 210, 217
banyans (beach parties) **26**
Barataria Bay 210, 220–1, **221**
Barbados 61, 151, 224
Barlow, Levi **171**
Barnet, Captain 93
bases *see* ports and bases
battles
    buccaneers 42–7
    see also sea fights

beach parties **26**
Bellamont, Richard, Earl of 100, 103
Bellamy, Samuel 83, 137–40, 159
Bernice 197, 201
Biard, August-François: engravings by **190**
Bilbao 203
Billy One Hands 137
Black Bart *see* Roberts, Bartholomew
Black Joke **202**, 211–13
black pirates 27–8, 75–6, 157
Blackbeard *see* Teach, Edward
boarding 82–3, **82**, 191–2, **193–4**
boatswains 149
Bolivia 165
Bonhomme Richard **169**, **204**, 206–7
Bonnet, Stede 89, 96, 99–100, **99**, 123, 159
Bonny, Anne 91–4, **92**, **94**
Boston **135**, 159, 166, **167**, 171, 205
Boxer 201
Boyle, Thomas 209–10
Bradley, Joseph 47
Brasiliano, Rok 33
Brazil 104, 165, 209, 211–13
brethren of the coast: origin of phrase 24, 25–7
Britain
    and privateering
        letters of marque 176
        ports 218, **219**
        as privateer 10–11, 165, 170–1, **188**, 195, 203
        as target 166–73, 195, **196**, **202**, 203–10
    Royal Navy anti-piracy campaign 224–6
    wars 164, 165
    see also England
Bry, John de 136
buccaneers
    battles 42–7
    commanders 49–60
    composition of bands 27–9
    dress **22**, **25**, 29–31, **49**
    etymology and definition 6, 21
    organization and allegiance 31–5
    plunder **9**, 66–7
    ports 61–6
    rise 20–5
    sea fights 47–8
    ships 24, 47–8, 68–70
    tactics 40–2
    weapons 36–40
The Buccaneers of America (Exquemelin) 12

Index

Buck 115
Burgis, William: engravings by **119**, 129–30, **135**

Caesar, Julius 6
Cagway *see* Port Royal
Caibarien, Cuba 222
Calico Jack *see* Rackam, Jack
Campeche
    de Grammont's occupation (1685) 43, 59, 60, 71
    L'Olonnais at 54
    Myngs' attack (1663) 50–1
Canada (New France), and privateering 164, 166, 170, 171, 176, 218
Cape Coast Castle, West Africa 157, 159
Cape Cod 171, 206
Cape Fear River 101
Cape Lopez 106
captains and commanders
    buccaneers/pirates 49–60, 88–106, 210–14
    leadership contests **72–3**, 97, 103, 146–7
    privateers 180, 185, 203–10
Caracas 58
careening 110, **122**
Carolinas 85–6, **85**
Cartagena, Venezuela **19**
    siege and sack (1697) 33, 34–5, **35**, 41, 66
    and treasure fleets 19, 20
Cassandra 129, 141–4
Castellano San Lorenzo, attack on (1671) 47, 52
Cayenne, Tortuga **23**, 24, 62
Centurion 50
Chapman, Frederick Henry: books by 128–9, **128**, 130
Charles 97, 114–15
Charles II, king of England, Scotland and Ireland 50
Charles Galley 136
Charleston (formerly Charles Town) 89, 100, **110**, **148**, 159, 166
charters 146, 152
Chasseur 210
Chesapeake, battle of the (1781) **215**
Chile 165
Clarisse 209
Clifford, Barry 136–40
coins and coinage *see* money
clothing *see* dress
Colombia 165
Comet 209–10
commanders *see* captains and commanders
Concorde see Queen Anne's Revenge
Condent, Christopher 86
Condent, Edmund 147
Confiance 209
convoys 187–9, **187**
    see also treasure fleets
Cooke, Edmond 71
Cordingly, David 27, 74, 116
Coro, Venezuela 50

La Coruña, Spain 114
Coxton, John 71
Cromwell, Oliver 16
Crowninshield, George 217
Cuba
    Anglo-French raid (1668) 34, 52
    anti-piracy campaign 225
    L'Olonnais' raids 54
    pirate bases 222, **222**
    Spanish government 19
    and treasure fleets 20
Curaçao 56
Cussy, Pierre-Paul Tarin de 65–6

Dampier, William 26
Davis, Howell 103, **104**
Deane 180
Debelle, Alexandre: illustrations by **28**, **93**, **175**
Delaware River 117
Delivery (formerly *Gambia Castle*) 115–16, 120
Denmark 164
Diabolito ('Little Devil') 225
doubloons **140**
Dragon 164, 206
Drake 206
Drake, Sir Francis 16, 48
dress
    buccaneers **22**, **25**, 29–31, **49**
    pirates **77**, **78**, **105**
    privateers **184**, **185**
Ducasse, Jean-Baptiste 44, 66
Dunkirk 127, 220
Dutch East India Company 142

East Africa 208
East India Company 103, 141–4, 209
    ships **187**, **194**, **200**
Ecuador 165
Eden, Governor 89
Edinburgh 159
Emille **162–3**, **208**, 209
Endymion, HMS **174**
England
    16th century 16
    capture of Jamaica (1655) 6, 16, 24–5, **25**, 63
    Caribbean colonies and bases 16, 61–2
    English buccaneer groups 21, 25, 26, 35, 63–5, 71
    invasion of Hispaniola (1655) 63
    wars 164
    see also Britain
England, Edward 86, 120, **129**, 141–4, 156
Enterprise **223**, 224–5
Estrées, Comte d' 56
Every, Henry (Avery; 'Long Ben') **82**, 97–8, **98**, 114–15
Execution Dock, Wapping 157, 159

executions 157–61
Exquemelin, Alexandre
    on buccaneer recruitment 32
    illustrations from book 34, **42–3**
    on L'Olonnais' death 56
    on Morgan's buccaneers 40
    overview 12

Fame **178**
Fancy (England's ship) **129**, 141–4
Fancy (Every's ship) **82**, 97–8, **98**, 115
Fancy (small sloop) **119**, 129
Fateh Mohammed 97
Fayal, Azores **188**
Ferret, HMS 128
Fiery Dragon 137
filibusters: etymology and definition 6
Finn, Captain 159
Fiske, Captain 203
flags **105**, 151–6, **153**, **155**
Flamborough Head **169**, 207
Florida
    anti-piracy campaign 225
    destruction of French settlement (1565) 16
    destruction of treasure fleet off (1715) 95, 108
    and Gibert 213
Florida Straits 75, 173, 210, 222
Fly **11**
Fly, Captain William 159
Flying Dragon 147
Fortune (formerly *Ranger*) 60, 119
    see also Royal Fortune
France
    and American Revolutionary War 205, **215**
    Caribbean colonies and bases 16–17, 61–2
    Florida settlement 16
    French buccaneer groups 21, 25, **33**, 34–5, 62–3, 65–6, 71
    French buccaneer invasion of Jamaica (1694) 44
    and Hispaniola 62–3
    and privateering
        letters of marque 176
        ports 218–20, **219**
        as privateer 10, 11, 164, **172**, **194**, 208–9
    relations with Spain 61–3, 71
    siege of Cartagena (1697) **33**, 34–5, **35**, 41, 66
    Spanish invasions of Saint Domingue 44
    wars 164, 165
Francesca 59
freebooters: definition 6
French and Indian War *see* Seven Years' War
French Revolutionary War (1793–1802) 11, 165, 208–9, 219–20
Frey, Oliver: paintings by **8**

Galveston, Texas 210–11, 221–2
Gambia Castle see Delivery

Gang-i-sawai **82**, 91–2, 97–8, **98**
Gardiner's Island 102
General Armstrong 173, **188**
General Monk (formerly and later *General Washington*) 195
General Pickering 203
General Washington 195, 206
gentleman volunteers 185
Ghent, Treaty of (1815) 165
Gibbs, Charles 222, 224–5
Gibert, 'Don' Pedro 131, 175, 213–14, **214**
Gibraltar, Venezuela 54, 57–8
Golden Eagle 203
Good Fortune **119**
    see also Royal Fortune
Gow, John 147, 159
Graaf, Laurens Cornelis Boudewijn de 59–60, 67, 69
Grammont, Michel de ('Le Chevalier') 40, 43, 56–9, **57**, 60, 69
Grand Turk 195, 196, **196**
Grant, George 117
Great Ranger **134**
Green, Captain 159
Greenwich 142–4
Grenada, Nicaragua 52
Greyhound 164
La Guaira 58
Guayabal 45
Gulf of Mexico 210, 221–2, 225, 226
Gulf of St Lawrence 164
gunners 149
gunnery *see* armament

Halifax, Nova Scotia 170
Hampolol, battle of (1685) 43–4
Hannah 206
Happy Delivery **122**
Haraden, Jonathan 203–5
Harris, Captain 159
Havana, Cuba 20, 52
Hawk 206
Henrietta Marie 134
Herald 177, 201
Hinchinbrook, HM Packet **196**
Hispaniola **21**, **23**
    and buccaneers 21–5, **22**, 59
    English invasion (1655) 63
    French-Spanish relations 61–3
    see also Saint Domingue
A History of Pirates (Johnson) 12–13, **13**
Holland
    attacks on Spanish 61
    buccaneers 62–3
    Dutch East India Company 142
    and privateering 24
Holman, Francis: paintings by **11**
Honduras 54–5, **56**

Index

Hoorn, Nikolaas van 59–60
Hope 162–3, 208
Hopkins, Esek 205
Hornigold, Benjamin 84–5, 88
Hudson River 110, 205
Hunter, Governor 110
hurricanes 107–8, **108**, **118**
Hyder Ali 195

Ildefenso, Treaty of (1795) 165
India
    Great Moghul's treasure ship 82, 91–2, 97–8, **98**
    see also East India Company
Indian Ocean 91–2, 97–8, 103, **107**, 108, 162–3
insurance 186, 223
Ireland 206
Isla de Pinos 60

Jackson, General Andrew 210
Jamaica
    anti-piracy laws 71
    anti-piracy patrols 224
    and buccaneers 25, 63–5
    English capture (1655) 6, 16, 24–5, **25**, 63
    French buccaneer invasion (1694) 44
    income from buccaneers 67
    Myngs' defence 49–50
    pirate executions 159
    Spanish invasion (1658) 43, 50
    see also Port Royal
Jane 91, **145**, **158**, **160**
Jennings, Henry 84, 95, 108
Jeune Richard **193**
Johnson, Captain Charles: books by
    on Bonnet 99
    on Every 114
    on Low 117
    overview 12–13, **13**
    on pirate ships 111, 120
    on Roberts 123
    on Teach 88, **90**
    on women pirates 93–4
    on Worley 117
Jolly Rogers 154–5, **155**
Jones, John Paul 169, 181, **204**, 206–7, **207**
justice, pirate 157–61

Kent 209
Kidd, Captain William 77, 100–3, **101–2**, 159, 160
    ships 136–7
King George 206
Kingston, Jamaica 159
Kirby, Captain 144

Laccadive Islands 103

Laffite, Jean 143, 172, 173, 210–11, **211**, 220–1
Lake Maracaibo *see* Maracaibo
landsmen 184–5
Latin American Wars of Independence (1808–30) 165, 172, 173
League of Augsburg, War of the (1690–97) 165
Leith: Jones' raid (1779) 207
letters of marque 9, 10, 24, 176–9, **177**
Liberty 147
Little Devil *see* Diabolito
Liverpool, Nova Scotia 170
Liverpool Packet 170, **192**
Long Ben *see* Every, Henry
Long Island 110, 206
Louisburg, attack on (1745) 164
Louisiana 60, 210
Low, Edward 117, **118**
Lowther, George 116, 120, **122**, 159
Luke, Captain 159
Lyme, HMS 90

McRae, Captain James 141–4
Madagascar 80, **85**, 86, 103
Madrid, Treaty of (1670) 71
manning the sweeps 189
Maracaibo 42, 54, **55**, 56–8, 67, 71
Maracaibo Bar
    battle off (1669) **44**, 52
    shipping off **116**
Margarita **29**
Mars 166
Marston Moor 49, 50
Martien, David 64
Martinique 97, 105–6, 151
Massey, John 116
masters 149
Matagorda Bay, Texas 221
Matanzas, Cuba 222
Mauritius 208–9
Maynard, Lieutenant 83, 88, 90–1, **142**, **145**, **158**
Mexican 131, 213, **214**
Mexico
    independence 165
    pirate attacks 221
    silver from 67
    Texan rebellion (1836) 222
Mississippi Delta 210, 220–1, **221**
Modyford, Sir Thomas 51, 52, 53, 64, 71
money
    denominations and values 67
    doubloons **140**
    pieces of eight **140**
    shortage of coinage 87
Moody, Christopher 155
Moody, William 147
Morgan, Henry 51, **175**

end of buccaneering 53, 71
at Maracaibo Bar (1669) 44, 52
overview 51–3
Panama campaign (1670–71) 35, **42–3**, 43, 44–7, 52–3, **53**, 67
and Port Royal 64
Porto Bello campaign (1668) 43, 46, 47, 52, 67
as privateer 116
ships 68
Morning Star **202**, 213
Morris, John 64
Morris, Colonel Lewis **119**
Mosquito Fleet **224**, 225–6
mutinies 114–16
Myngs, Christopher 28, 31, 34, 43, 49–51

Nantucket 206
Napoleonic Wars (1803–15) 165, 209, 219–20
Nassau 84
Nau, Jean David ('L'Olonnais') 54–6, **55–6**, 69–70
Neptune 60
Nevis 21
New Bedford 206
New France *see* Canada
New Granada: extent and government 18
New Orleans 220
New Orleans, battle of (1815) 210, **211**
New Providence, Bahamas **79**, 84–5, 96, 159
New Spain: extent and government 18
New York **101**, **119**
American Revolutionary War 205
Dutch map **74**
and privateers 100, 110, 164, 166, 171, 217
Newcastle, Delaware 117
Newfoundland 104
Newfoundland Banks 80
Newport, Rhode Island 159, 171, 205
Nicaragua 55–6

Ocracoke Island and Inlet 85, **85**, 88–9, **89**, 96
officers 146–9, 180, 185
see also captains and commanders
Ogeron, Bertrand d' 63
Ogle, Captain 106, 157
L'Olonnais *see* Nau, Jean David
Onslow 106, 119, 120, 122, 133, 136
Ordronaux, Captain **174**
Ostender 142
Oxford, HMS 52
Oyley, Governor d' 63

Pacific coast settlements **70**, 71
Paine, Ralph D.: books by **184**, **186**
Panama
17th-century map **34**
fortifications 20

main square **45**
Morgan's campaign (1670–71) 35, **42–3**, 43, 44–7, 52–3, **53**, 67
and treasure fleets 19, 20
Panda **131**, 213–14, **214**
Paraguay 165
Paris, Treaty of (1763) 165
Paris, Treaty of (1814) 165
Payton, Richard: paintings by **14–15**
Pearl see Royal James
Peck, John 201
Pelham 192
Pérez de Guzmán, Juan 45–7
Pernambuco, Brazil 209
Peru
buccaneer attacks 71
independence 165
silver from 18, 20, 67
Petit Goâve 63, 65–6
Philadelphia 217
Phillips, John 131
Pickering **200**
pieces of eight **140**
Pierre le Grand 24, 47
Pigot 206
pirates
bases 84–6, 220–2
captains and characters 88–106
codes and rules 146–9
crews 74–8, 144
dress 77, 78, **105**
flags **105**, 151–6, **153**, **155**
justice 157–61
last of the 173–5, 210–14, 220–6
leadership contests **72–3**, 97, 103, 146–7
motivation 76–8
plunder 87, 117
ships 8–9, 80, 107–44
converting prizes 120–3
cutaway **138–9**
design of ideal 107–13
flagships 132–41
in action 141–4
list with associated captains 147
maintenance 110, **122**
origins 113–20
rig 123
small 124–31
speed 111–13
warfare 79–83, 141–4
weapons 82–3
plunder
division 149
prizes 182, 183, 215
treasure, buried 77, 86, 102
types **9**, 66–7, 87, 117

Index

Pocock, Nicholas: paintings by **187**
Port Royal (formerly Cagway), Jamaica **14–15**
  as anti-piracy base 84
  anti-piracy laws 71
  and buccaneers 40, 43, 63–5, **64**
  earthquake (1692) 65
  English capture (1655) 63
Porter, Commodore David **224**, 225, **226**
Portobelo (formerly Porto Bello), Panama
  Morgan's raid (1668) 43, **46**, 47, 52, 67
  and treasure fleets 19–20, **66**
ports and bases
  buccaneer 61–6
  pirates 84–6, 220–2
  privateers 171, 215–20
Portugal
  Atlantic monopolies 16
  French invasion (1808) 165
  pirate attacks 103, 104
  privateer attacks 209
Portugues, Bartolomeo el **32**, 33
Potosi silver mine 67
Pouançay, Jacques 59, 65
Prie, Captain John 159
Prince de Neufchâtel 172–3, **174**, 201
Principe Island 104
Prins, Laurens 45
privateers and privateering
  boarding 191–2, **193–4**
  buccaneers and 24, 60
  captains 180, 185, 203–10
  the chase 189–91
  crews 182–5
  definition 9
  development 164–75
  discipline 183
  dress **184**, 185
  flags 151–4
  officers 180, 185
  overview 9–10
  pirates and 100, 116
  ports 171, 215–20
  prizes 182, 183, 215
  recruitment 180–2
  ships 166, 172–3, 197–202
    colours 201–2
    plans 197–8
  warfare 186–96
  weapons 186, 191–2, **193**
prizes 182, 183, 215
Providence, Rhode Island 115, 168
Puerto Caballos 55
Puerto Principe, Cuba 52
Pyle, Howard: paintings by **9, 17, 30, 72–3, 101–2, 109**

quartermasters 147
Quasi-War (1798–1801) 11, 165
Queddah Merchant 103
Queen Anne's Revenge (formerly *Concorde*) 8, 88, 89, 119–20, 134–6, **138–9**
Quelch, Captain 159

Rackam, Jack ('Calico Jack') 84, 91–4, **94**, 97, **115**, 159
Ranger (pirate ship; later *Fortune*) 118–19
Ranger, USS 181
Rattlesnake **198**, 201
Reade, Mary 92–4, **93–4**
recruitment
  buccaneers 32–4
  pirates 74–6
  privateers 180–2
Red Jacks 154
Rediker, Marcus 116
Reid, Captain Samuel 188
Revenant 209
Revenge 89, 99
Rhett, William 100, 123
Rhode Island 115, 159, **167**, 168, 171
rings, gold **140**
Riohacha 42
Rising Sun 147
Roberts, Bartholomew ('Black Bart') **105**, 134
  and Anstis 156
  attacks 80, 104–6, 123
  crew charters 146, 152
  crews 75, 157–9
  dress 78, **105**
  flags 151, 155–6
  length of voyages 109
  operating methods 149
  overview 103–6
  ships 81, 106, 118–19, 120, 122, 126–7, 133, **134**, 136
Rogers, Captain William **193**
Rogers, Woodes 84–5, 91, 95–6, 159
Royal Africa Company 106, 115–16
Royal Fortune (various Roberts ships) **134**
  armament 81, 122, 133
  distinctions between 104, 106, 119
  (formerly *Fortune*; *Good Fortune*) 119
  (formerly French warship) 119, 133, 136
  (formerly *Onslow*) 106, 119, 120, 122, 133, 136
Royal James (formerly *Pearl*) 90, 100, 120, **123**
Ryswick, Peace of (1697) 71

Sabane de Limonade, battle of (1691) 44, 60
Sabine estuary, Texas 221
sailing masters 149
sailors: daily life 76
Saint Domingue
  and buccaneers 17, 63, 65–6, 71

Spanish attacks (1690s) 20, 41, 44, 60, 66
see also Hispaniola
St Johns 210
St Kitts (Christopher) 21, 24, 105, 159
St Lawrence 210
St Malo, Brittany 208, 209, 220
St Martin 24
Salem 171, **178**, 203, 217
Samana Bay, Hispaniola 59
Samuel 80, 123
San Francisco 60
San Lorenzo *see* Castellano San Lorenzo
San Pedro 55
Santa Marta 42
Santiago de Cuba, Myngs' assault on (1662) 31, 43, **49**, 50
Santo Domingo **48**, 63
Saucy Jack 192
Scarborough, HMS 88
Schoonover, Frank: illustrations by **26**, **148**, **150**, **184**, **186**, **200**
sea fights 47–8, 141–4, 192–6
see also boarding
Selkirk, Earl of 206, 207
Serapis, HMS **169**, 204, 207
Seven Years' War (1755–63) 165, 166
Seville, and treasure fleets 19–20
Sharpe, Bartholomew 70
ships and vessels
    balandras 125
    barca longa 125, **126**
    barks (barques) 133, **202**
    brigantines 111, **116**, 126, 130–1, **130**
    brigs 123, 126, 130–1
    buccaneer/pirate 8–9, 24, 47–8, 68–70, 80, 107–44
        converting prizes 120–3
        cutaway **138–9**
        design of ideal 107–13
        flagships 132–41
        in action 141–44
        list with associated captains 147
        maintenance 110, **122**
        origins 113–20
        rig 123
        small 124–31
        speed 111–13
    corvettes 199
    feluccas 132
    fireships **112**
    fluyts 132, **133**
    fly-boats 125
    galleons **114**
    guard ships **135**
    longboats 68–9
    merchantmen 133–4, **135**, **137**
    mosquito boats 222
    pingues 125

pinnaces 68–9, **74**, 124–5
piraguas 68, **124**
polaccas 132
privateer 166, 172–3, 197–202
    colours 201–2
    plans **197–8**
schooners 111, 131, **131**, **197**
shallops 125
slave ships 134, **134**, **137**
sloops **74**, 111–12, **119**, 125–30, **128**, **135**
snows 123, 126, **127**, 131
spider catchers 166
tartans 132–3
yachts, two-mast **116**
see also individual ships by name
Shirley 164
Silsbee, Captain Nathaniel 177
silver 18, 20, 67
slaves and slavery
    pirate attacks on slave ships 85
    runaways as buccaneers/pirates 27–8, 75–6
    slave ships 134, **134**, **137**
    trade outlawed by France 208
Soto, Benito de 175, **202**, 211–13, **212**
Spain
    17th-century vulnerability 16
    battles against buccaneers 42–7
    and Hispaniola 62–3
    invasion of Jamaica (1658) 43, 50
    invasions of Saint Domingue (1690s) 20, 41, 44, 60
    as privateer target 164, 166
    relations with France 61–3, 71
    troop capabilities 40–1
    wars 164, 165
Spanish Main
    charts and maps **7**, **18**
    extent and government 16, 18–19
Spotswood, Alexander 90, 96
storms 107–8, **108**, 118
Surcouf, Robert 143, **162–3**, **194**, 208–9
Surprise, HMS 209
Swallow, HMS 105, 106
Swan, Captain 26
swashbucklers 7–8

tactics
    buccaneers 40–2
    pirates 79–83, 141–4
    privateers 189–96
Talbot, Silas 205–6, **205**
Teach, Edward ('Blackbeard') 8, **89–90**, **150**
    bases 84, **85**, 88–9
    and Bonnet 99–100
    and Charleston 89, 110, 134–5, **148**
    crew **96**, 149, 159

Index

death 83, 90–1, 142, 145, 158, 160
flags 155, 155
operating methods 127
overview 88–91
ships 8, 88, 89, 119–20, 134–6, 138–9, 145
and Vane 89–90, 96
weapons 83, 88, 90
teredo worms 110, 140
Tetre, Abbé Jean Baptiste Du 29
Tew, Thomas 147
Texas 210–11, 221–2
Thirty Years' War (1618–48) 40
Tigre 59
Tihosuco 60
topmen 191
Tordesillas, Treaty of (1497) 16
Tortuga 23–5, 23, 62–3, 62, 68
torture 17, 41, 42, 55–6
treasure *see* plunder
treasure fleets
anchorages 66
buccaneer attacks 66–7
destruction by hurricane (1715) 95, 108
routes 19–20
and Windward Passage 23–4
Treasure Island (Stevenson) 87
Triton 194, 209
tropical cyclones 108
Troup, Captain 164
Trujillo 58
typhoons 108
Tyrannicide 203

United States
anti-piracy campaign (1820s) 223–6
pirate attacks 174
and privateering
captains 203–7, 209–10
letters of marque 176–9, 177
ports 171, 217–18
as privateer 165–73, 167, 174, 195, 196, 200
ships 197–8, 216, 199–202
as target 170–1
wars 165
see also American colonies; American Revolutionary War
Uruguay 165

Valladolid, Yucatan 60
Vane, Charles 95
crew 96
death 97, 159
flags 156
overview 95–7
and Rackam 91
and Teach 89–90, 96
ships 113, 118

Vasseur, Jean le 63
Venezuela 56–8, 165
Venta de Cruces, battle of (1670) 43, 45
Vera Cruz, Mexico
de Grammont's attack (1683) 40, 59, 60, 69
fortifications 20
and treasure fleets 19, 20
Versailles, Treaty of (1783) 165
Villahermosa 52, 68
Virgin Islands 99–100
voyages: length 108–9

Walden, John 106
War of 1812 (1812–15) 11, 165, 170–3, 187–8, 209–11, 217
War of Jenkins' Ear (1739) 164, 165
War of the Austrian Succession (1740–48) 10, 164, 165
War of the Spanish Succession (1701–14) 71, 164
Warren 166
Washington, George 205
weapons
bayonets 39
blunderbusses 28, 83
buccaneers 36–40
grenades 38, 83
muskets
British India-pattern 171
Charleville 171
matchlock 36–7, 37
pikes 39
pistols 37–8, 83, 90, 186, 193
privateers 186, 191–2, 193
swords 38–9
cutlasses 83, 186
hangers 39
rapiers 39
see also armament
West Africa
Cape Coast Castle 157, 159
and pirates 80, 106, 107, 115–16, 118
weather 107
Whydah 134
Whitehaven: Jones' raid (1778) 206
Whydah, West Africa 134
Whydah 83, 137–40
artefacts from 140
William 92–3
Williamsburg, Virginia 159
wind compasses/charts 111
Windsor, Lord 50, 63–4
Windward Passage 23–4, 80, 97
women pirates 91–4, 92–4
Worley, Captain 117
Wynne, Emmanuelle 154

Yucatan Peninsula 43–4, 51, 59, 60